UNDAUNTED

An Autobiography

UNDAUNTED

An Autobiography

ETHNÉE HOLMES À COURT
WITH LIZ VAN DEN NIEUWENHOF

Sun
Pan Macmillan Australia

First published 1998 in Macmillan by Pan Macmillan Australia Pty Limited
First published 1999 in Sun by Pan Macmillan Australia Pty Limited
St Martins Tower, 31 Market Street, Sydney

Reprinted 1999

National Library of Australia
cataloguing-in-publication data:

Holmes à Court, Ethnée.
Undaunted.
ISBN 0 7251 0762 6.
1. Holmes à Court, Ethnée. 2. Holmes à Court, Robert - Family.
3. Holmes à Court family. I. Title.

920.72

Typeset in 12/16 pt Weiss by Post Pre-press Group, Brisbane
Printed in Australia by McPherson's Printing Group

Editor's note: Due to the time period spanned in this work, and for consistency of
terminology, all South African geographic references pre-date independence and units
of measure are imperial.

I dedicate this book to the memory of my two sons: Robert, entrepreneur
of international repute who always reached for the stars
and Simon, sculptor and lover of African wildlife who always
dreamed of far horizons and sailed the oceans of the
world in his yacht Maggie May II.

ACKNOWLEDGMENTS

It is difficult to know where to start my list of thankyous, and the names I mention are in no particular order.

The first person who springs to mind, however, is my 'ghost', Liz van den Nieuwenhof, a South African born Australian. Liz has been of invaluable assistance in helping me write this book and, from our very first conversation over the phone, I knew we would hit it off. Liz stayed with us at Heytesbury, armed with a tape recorder and many leading questions and we talked solidly for hours on end. We laughed a lot and often broke into South African phrases, or Afrikaans sayings for which there are simply no English equivalents. We soon made headway and I am most grateful to Liz for all the help she gave me in such a limited time. I could not have wished for a better ghost writer.

I have to thank my agent, Hickson Associates, for finding Liz. I have had much correspondence and many conversations with Jill Hickson and Sophie Lance who have both been most helpful.

Four months into the writing process I travelled to Sydney – armed with about a hundred photos and a list of possible titles for this book – where I met my publisher, Amanda Hemmings, my editor, Alexandra Mohan and all the helpful staff at Pan Macmillan. Liz and I were delighted by Amanda's charming speech introducing us, and also relieved to discover that Alex wasn't a man as we had previously thought! I am indebted to Alex who has been a very patient editor – thankfully I've been guided!

Thank you also to my life-long friend, Mary, who not only wrote the foreword to my book and has been encouraging me to write it for years, but who also thought of the title! Mary and I share so many memories they could easily fill another book of our own.

I would like to thank my good friend Stan Fildes who introduced me to the publishing world. Stan was the go-between when I ventured into the writing world in an article for *African Safari* magazine, autumn 1995 entitled 'My Chobe Days'. Stan encouraged me to pen my memoirs which became the basis for *Undaunted*.

I have Mike Finn, my 'computer tutor', to thank for all his help. He is still teaching me to master my bigger and better computer and the internet and email, which are a part of my life now. I can't imagine writing a book without this technology. The electronic typewriter is a thing of the past!

I want to thank Patrick Bromfield, a very old friend, and my Simon's ex-boss from the Game Department in Bechuanaland Protectorate. Patrick helped me remember some of the happenings in the Chobe Game Park – and we discovered there is sufficient material there for yet another book!

Simon's crew on yacht *Maggie May II* have added anecdotes to my story: Milton Skinner, ex Australian Navy, was full of admiration for Simon and lent me his detailed diary; Gregg Lott also provided some very colourful descriptions; Ron Wink sailed with Simon for about two years and I thank him for his anecdotes and continued friendship.

Special thanks to Bodo Muche, Simon's close friend who now lives in Queensland. Bodo and Simon used to sculpt together and Bodo has now made a name for himself with life size horses in bronze and a special request for a ewe and lamb and a miniature for the Queen which he presented in person. I thank him for his 'stories' and for his wonderful friendship to my Simon.

Last of all, Ronnie, who tried to make me promise not to

mention him! I want to thank him so much for encouraging me to complete *Undaunted* and for his unlimited patience in coping with irregular meals, and perhaps my irregular temperament!

And to everyone else who I have run out of space to mention – I haven't forgotten all my helpful friends. Thank you all.

If you can fill the unforgiving minute
With sixty seconds' worth of distance run,
Yours is the Earth and everything that's in it . . .

RUDYARD KIPLING

Foreword

A foreword is not a foregone conclusion; it is an introduction, and this book stands on its own merits as an opening of a treasure chest. This reveals gems which give us a glimpse into a life which sparkles with action through joy, adventure, wonder and tragedy.

I have known Ethnée, a loyal friend, for close on eighty years as an irrepressible character, horse lover and pioneer, whose record will touch some chord in your own lives, until – in the words of William Cowper – 'Your heart replies'.

The undaunted efforts and courage of this woman, who left no stone unturned to achieve her ambitions, offer us a challenge that could enable us to leave the world a better and happier place if we could see it through eyes other than our own.

Read her story and travel through the realms of gold.

MARY MOODIE
JOHANNESBURG, SOUTH AFRICA

CONTENTS

PROLOGUE

Heytesbury Stud, Western Australia, 2 September 1990. The morning began like no other, for it was still dark and bitterly cold when the telephone pierced a deep and dreamless sleep. With each persistent ring willing me to mental alertness I began to panic, and suddenly a feeling that it was going to be terrible news set my heart pounding.

It was Janet, my daughter-in-law. 'Robert has had a heart attack,' she said, her voice raw with emotion. I don't recall if anything else was said, only that Robert had been rushed to the nearby Armadale–Kelmscott Memorial Hospital.

Our stud manager rushed me there in record time but on my arrival I couldn't find anyone. Stifling the temptation to scream I kept running along the labyrinth of corridors, hoping someone would come to my rescue and lead me to my son.

I was too late. When I finally reached his ward his lifeless body lay stretched out on a hospital trolley and Janet, her face contorted with grief, looked to me and cried out, 'It's not fair. You've lost both your sons.'

I was numb with shock but her lament amplified the greatest tragedy that could befall a mother. And nothing, absolutely nothing, could have prepared me for this cruel twist of fate that would see me outlive both my beloved sons. First Simon, my youngest, died in mysterious circumstances in the wilds of Southern Africa and now my Robert, gone too, without a last goodbye.

We all stood there in that cold, dismal ward, with grief holding us as fast as quicksand. The fact that Robert, who always pursued life with such relentless vigour, was no longer with us seemed too unreal to grasp.

Janet rushed off to make calls after pleading with me not to remove Robert's body. My grandchildren remained by Robert's side, absolutely beside themselves with grief. When a well-meaning nurse asked us if we would like some tea, Catherine broke down completely and through strangled sobs cried out, 'I don't want tea, I just want my father back.'

It seemed as if we were there forever, that we would never be released from this terrible nightmare. Outside, meanwhile, the Darling Ranges had been set aflame by a spectacular sunrise, tendrils of gold light spreading toward the eucalypt-lined perimeters of Robert's magnificent Heytesbury Stud farm. It was Father's Day, a day he had intended to spend on his property, his Arcadian sanctuary and the one acquisition he prized above all else.

From a most uninspiring tract of land he had carved this splendid nursery of thoroughbreds and it had become the most treasured link between my son and myself. It was home to me and my Robert's favoured rural retreat. This was where he had come to relax and unwind and where we had often gone riding together, across the paddocks and up on the hills, reminiscing about times and countries past.

Ours had been an eventful and often tumultuous journey, one that began in Africa, saw us handed terrible tragedies and then become reunited in Australia. Who could have thought I would live out the remaining chapters without my sons, so many miles from where I originally embarked on a voyage like no other?

Chapter One

AN AFRICAN DAWN

While battles raged on the fields of Flanders and in the trenches of Gallipoli I was born of the earth of Africa and into a world of intrigue and adult misadventure. It was 15 October 1915. My mother named me after the heroine of a novel that was very much in vogue at the time but her personal situation, I am afraid to say, came nowhere close to matching its romantic tenor. Yet my mother, Florence – a beautiful albeit headstrong woman – took to adding a dramatic dimension when she absconded from an unhappy marriage with me firmly tucked under one arm and a suitcase in the other. I was, I think, about two years old at the time. I was never apprised of the more piquant details of her marriage breakdown but later, as a young woman, I came to believe that her husband's indiscretions were instrumental in her taking such dramatic flight.

For his sins I never knew my father. Indeed, to this day I'd be hard-pressed to find a single clue as to his identity or what later became of him. Someone once mentioned that he had worked in a bank but I never established the veracity of this snippet of information. To me it was as if he had never existed. This was not entirely surprising given that in those days divorce was anathema and my mother, the daughter of an upstanding and much-respected clergyman in a small country town, was mindful not to set tongues wagging.

As a young girl, though, I somehow sensed that something

really terrible must have happened in my mother's marriage for she was not a woman given to taking extraordinary or impulsive actions without good cause. Nevertheless, with a baby in her arms, she retreated to her parental home, reverted to her maiden name of Oates and never, ever referred to her ill-fated marriage or to her errant husband. And it was always made abundantly clear to me that in my grandparents' household it was a forbidden subject and the one, solitary skeleton that would forever remain hidden in the family closet. Even later, having survived so many taunts at school about not having a father, it never even occurred to me to try and find out more about him.

Sometimes I wonder why I never made an attempt to track him down but then, looking back, there was simply no reason to rake over past unhappiness, for my childhood, set against the backdrop of colonial South Africa, proceeded to be such a blissful and idyllic one. And as an only child surrounded by doting adults I was left wanting for nothing.

At the head of the household was my grandfather, Reverend William Oates, a retiring and thoughtful man whose father came out to South Africa with the 1820 British Settlers. After completing his schooling he assisted my great-grandfather on his farm near Grahamstown, a town in the Cape Province renowned for its many beautiful church spires and sedate elegance, until he became ordained as a minister.

At about that time he met my grandmother, then Miss Celia Amanda Hill, the granddaughter of the famous Dr Croft, manufacturer of Croft's Tincture of Life (a foul-tasting, coffee-coloured powder hailed as a cure for a host of maladies) and inventor of the first snakebite serum. They married shortly after my grandfather's ordination and in about 1879 moved to Somerset East, a picturesque and tranquil little town nestled in the Golden

Valley in the Eastern Cape, to take charge of the Congregational Church. It was here, in the Manse, that my mother was born, the seventh child of the seventh child – an auspicious coincidence of birth said to have bestowed on her a certain feyness of character. And it was to the Manse she duly returned in 1917, clutching me and a deep desire for a new and happier life.

She got that and much more at the Manse, a stately old house that was always filled with prayer and beautiful music as both my mother and her sister, my beloved Auntie May, were extremely gifted musicians. Auntie May was my mother's eldest sister and totally devoted to caring for my grandparents. She had never married but she once, many years later, confided in me that there had been a man and a great romance. I suspect nothing became of it because my dear, prim Auntie May was somewhat put off by the thought of sex. I don't think she much cared for it. I utterly adored her and in many ways she became my primary guardian because my mother had to spend long spells away from home during the course of her studying and training to become a maternity nurse.

Auntie May was a music teacher and a very delicate, feminine woman. She wore her grey hair tightly woven, the work of numerous curling pins she took to wearing at night, covered by a dainty little boudoir cap. Her music room was at the end of the house and you could hear her pupils playing the same tunes over and over again. She composed her own music and every year arranged an annual concert for all her pupils at the local town hall. Naturally I insisted on taking part in all her productions, usually as a fairy or gnome because neither required an aptitude for music.

My mother had also studied music and was as talented as Auntie May. In fact, she could play almost any instrument and was possessed of the most exquisite soprano voice. She could even imitate a boy's voice and sound just like a choir boy.

I suspect it was always a source of some bemusement to my mother that I had not inherited so much as a scrap of her talent for music. Before my birth she apparently spent many hours at the piano hoping it would instil in me an early appreciation of music but, alas, her labours proved in vain. I have yet to master playing a single musical instrument and to add insult to injury I also seem incapable of holding a note. I am almost tone deaf and as a child the only tune I recognised was 'God Save the King' simply because everyone stood up when it was played.

Musical merriment aside, life at the Manse was strictly regimented, as my grandmother was a stickler for tradition and would not countenance anyone straying from her time-honoured rituals. Once a week we would have morning prayers in the dining room and all the domestic servants joined us, sitting on hard wooden benches at one end of the room. My grandmother, a rather regal woman who wore high-waisted dresses and a long plait neatly wound round her head, read a prayer and there would be one hymn which the servants loved. Then my grandfather would give a short sermon or talk.

Grace was always said before and after a meal and each evening Auntie May would take me to say goodnight to everyone in the house, including my grandfather who would have adjourned to his study.

He loved spending the little free time he had contemplating and reflecting in his book-lined study. The room had a lovely thick carpet and on cold nights a coal fire always burned in the grate. What I remember most vividly was my grandfather's enormous desk with its many drawers, cubbyholes and a special section for storing secret documents. It was at this desk that we would normally find him reading, preparing a sermon or writing his poetry.

He was a wonderful, gentle man with a snow-white beard that he always kept immaculately trimmed and he had the clearest of grey eyes, which I have supposedly inherited from him. He also had a penchant for drinking a large glass of warm milk laced with brandy, which my Auntie May dutifully brought him on our customary evening rounds.

And, of course, going to church was obligatory on Sunday mornings. Fortunately our little church was adjacent to the Manse for I was deemed to be a delicate child and Auntie May, fearing I would catch cold, had me wearing two pairs of bloomers, two pairs of socks and layer upon layer of clothes. I was literally swaddled up to my ears and must have cut the most pitiful sight sitting there all rugged up in the front pew.

Because of my supposed fragility I was not sent to school but my Auntie May had arranged for me and my friend Mary Stegmann to be taught by a governess. Mary's father was the family's solicitor and my mother had brought her younger brother into the world.

Mary was a year older than me and deaf but we became inseparable. Ours has been a friendship that survived a war and many of life's ups and downs and we correspond to this day. I still remember my first meeting with my oldest friend. I had been given a big white teddy bear some years before by some neighbours. I was hugging Teddy when we met and he helped to break the ice between two shy little girls. As it turned out, Teddy would come to play just as constant a role in my life as did Mary.

Dear, sweet Mary was persuaded to join me in playing the most wicked pranks on our hapless governess. We called her 'Doff', which I think was our abbreviation for Dorothy. If truth be told, I didn't much care for her or her tedious lessons. Mary, on the other hand, was a lot more studious but I always managed to inveigle her into doing ghastly things like putting frogs and snails in Doff's desk drawers.

I think poor old Doff took an intense dislike to us and all our silly capers, which no doubt stemmed from my chronic aversion to the three R's. Although Mary was deaf she was marvellous at lip-reading, so we were able to communicate without making a sound. This further infuriated dear Doff.

I was happiest playing with Mary or my animals. As a child I do not ever recall being without pets and in those days I had Winkie my cat and several tortoises. As an only child, though, there were times when I felt terribly lonely and I'd take to playing with my imaginary friend, Peter, which, as fate would have it, was to be the name of my first true love.

Eventually Mary and I were sent off to different schools, she to the girls' high school and I to a nearby Catholic convent, where my mother hoped rigorous competition with other girls would ignite a desire to learn.

Once again I failed her abysmally. It seemed I was just not academically minded, despite all the encouragement I received from those long-suffering nuns. All I enjoyed was drawing, as evidenced from my end of year report which read: 'Could do better and shows little interest in subjects except drawing which is excellent, she shows real talent'.

No doubt acting would have come a close second had it been on the school curriculum for I became an expert malingerer. Whenever I was overcome by a desire to stay home from school, which happened frequently, I'd have one of my 'giddy spells'. Dear Auntie May, of course, wouldn't hear of me going to school in so 'delicate a state' and I was promptly bundled into bed, with all my pets and my teddy for company.

I could not have been happier. Naturally I gained a reputation for being a spoilt little brat as I was indulged and cosseted by everyone at the Manse, including all our devoted servants.

Indeed, my childhood years glided by at an unruffled and genteel pace. I knew nothing but contentment but then I guess my mother, Auntie May and my grandparents were intent on compensating for the absence of a father in my life. I certainly never felt deprived in any way. I had Mary, my favourite big white teddy and all my animals as beloved companions and an entire household bent on keeping me happy.

There was, I felt then, absolutely nothing that could intrude on so magical an upbringing. I was not to know that my enchanted childhood, that wondrous, carefree interlude, was about to draw to a very abrupt close. The pampered and delicate granddaughter of a clergyman was about to be plucked from her secure sanctum and banished to a faraway place and a life that would prove to be in stark contrast to all that had gone before. And what made it especially bewildering was that it was all my mother's doing.

Chapter Two

THE OLD MAN

My snug and silken world began to unravel when my mother left for Southern Rhodesia to visit her married sister, Constance, who was the housekeeper of a wealthy landowner.

Since her return to Somerset East my mother had been determined to make a new life for us. For eight years she dedicated herself totally to her work as a maternity nurse, something considered rather out of the ordinary for a woman in those days. Unfortunately it meant we spent a lot of time apart, for maternity nurses were often called upon to stay on farms for extended periods to assist farmers' wives before and after their babies were delivered.

Once I was able to accompany her and our first trip together was to Bloemfontein, a flat and sun-bleached town in the Orange Free State, where my mother underwent training at the nurses' college. I remember a great fuss being made of me at the hospital for they were apparently not accustomed to having a young child among the student nurses.

After that there were occasional trips to farms but my mother preferred to leave me in Auntie May's expert and devoted care. However, the instant she returned, the house would come alive and resound with laughter and music.

My mother was an extremely attractive and a very outgoing woman and she loved to entertain at home, where it became customary for guests to gather around the piano and join her in song. People clearly adored her but for all her admirers my mother remained single and unattached. That was until she left for Rhodesia on her holiday and encountered Harry Robert Cumming (or 'The Old Man' as he was known to many, a term of endearment). He was Aunt Constance's employer.

Harry Cumming was a celebrated and much-revered figure on the settler-tamed landscape. He came to Rhodesia in 1893 from South Africa, fell in love with the land and immediately set to work exploring and pegging farm rights for various companies. Later he served in the war against the Matabele tribe under Captain Kirton and became known among Africans in the region as Machelobe, 'the man who rises in the middle of the night'. This honorific dated back to an incident that became the stuff of folklore and today still stands recorded as Cumming's Ride, one of the most courageous horse-rides of Rhodesia's early history.

It happened back in 1896 when, on a hot, humid afternoon an African herdsman, N'Daza, warned Cumming that the Matabele impis were massing to attack his farm and they planned to burn and loot the farm store and drive his cattle away. Cumming, then only twenty-six years old, had been farming his 13,000 acres of Altyre Ranch near Fort Rixon for two years. It was the first warning of the Matabele rebellion.

The farm store stood on the road to Belingwe and Cumming passed on N'Daza's warning to his neighbours and to travellers calling in at the store. At first many disbelieved N'Daza's story and ignored the warning. But by the end of the fourth day twenty white people were camping in and around the store as the fires of the Matabele impis could be seen at night glowing on the distant hills.

On the evening of the fifth day, sensing an attack, Harry Cumming set out on horseback to ride to Bulawayo for help. The distance was over a hundred miles. All he carried was a shotgun and three cartridges. He rode through the night, following the tracks that he knew. Sometimes, as the distant fires of a Matabele camp seemed to stand in his way, he made a detour, picking his way carefully through the bush in a wide loop.

Dawn the next day found him dropping down through thick bush to a valley where he knew he'd find the water he badly needed for his horse. He hurried a little, the bush suddenly cleared and Cumming pulled up hard. Facing him fifty yards away was a wakening camp of Matabele impi. Three hundred surprised black faces turned to look at the lone white rider.

For a few seconds the scene was frozen. Then Cumming caught up his shotgun, spurred his exhausted horse to a gallop, fired a single shot into the air and, shouting 'Come on, boys!' to an imaginary patrol behind him, galloped straight through the camp. In less than half a minute he reached the obscurity of the bush on the far side of the camp.

It took him twenty hours to reach Bulawayo. He was utterly exhausted but, to his consternation, found in Bulawayo much confusion following the rumours of a Matabele uprising. Cumming was able to confirm that a rebellion had actually started and the only way he could raise assistance in the town, which had hurriedly formed a laager or encampment, was to harangue the crowd from the vantage point of a wagon wheel. Four hours later a twenty-strong patrol, under Captain Southey and Sergeant-Major O'Leary, left for Cumming's store.

Within days the farm store was successfully defended and Harry Cumming, the great Machelobe, was garlanded a hero. And true to the style of a courageous hero he swept my mother off her dainty little feet, in an orchard of all places.

Initially my mother's stay with her sister on the property called Christmas Gift Farm was taken up with much socialising and dancing in the nearby town of Gwelo, and the first anyone knew of

Cumming's romantic intentions was when someone spotted two sets of telltale footprints – one large and one very small – in the orchard. This surreptitious tryst among the orange trees marked the beginning of my mother's whirlwind courtship.

But the first inkling I had that something was amiss and that there could be a potential rival for my mother's affections was when, on her return home, she drew me aside and said somewhat enigmatically, 'Ethnée, you're going to meet a friend of mine and you have to call him Uncle Harry.'

Well, 'Uncle Harry' duly arrived to meet the family and, needless to say, I took an instant dislike to him. I didn't care for what was going on. I think I was made to recite to him one night, albeit reluctantly and with a face like thunder. I had a real fit of the sulks which was awful for my mother as she had doubtless hoped I would make a good impression. And then the bombshell!

My mother cheerfully announced she was going to marry this man, twenty-two years her senior, and that we were going to leave Somerset East and live on his farm in Rhodesia. I was absolutely devastated. I couldn't believe that my normally kind, gentle mother could be so uncaring as to cast my life – and Mary's – into such disarray and emotional turmoil.

My mother, however, seemed impervious to my pain and confusion for it was as clear as a cloudless African dawn that she was in seventh heaven. Finally, after having had to bear the stigma of a failed marriage and about eight years of hard work, a comfortable new world beckoned. Unfortunately her excitement did nothing but underscore my abject misery. I cried myself to sleep night after night until the dreaded wedding day became an inescapable reality.

And so it was that on a cold June morning my mother was married. My grandfather officiated at the ceremony, which was held in my uncle Dr Tennyson Oates' house in Port Elizabeth, and attended by numerous relatives. Predictably, I was the only one at the wedding who felt no cause for celebration and cried shamelessly throughout the ceremony. Everyone else, though, seemed genuinely delighted for my mother, who stood resplendent and radiant beside a beaming Harry Cumming, the interloper I had now been instructed to call Daddy.

Nonetheless, they gave me six months to get used to the very novel idea of having a father in my life while my mother, the new Mrs Harry Cumming, was taken abroad on a long and very romantic honeymoon.

I don't think anyone fully understood just how anxious I was about leaving the security of my childhood home for the wilds of Southern Rhodesia. I was about ten years old and had, up until then, been cocooned in a pleasurable world where I was fussed over by a coterie of kindly women and the prospect of losing all that was too horrendous to contemplate. However, dear Auntie May, herself in deep despair at the thought of us being separated, stoically set about emotionally preparing me for the big move ahead and this included a grand farewell party with all my friends.

I printed the invitation cards while my aunt, in her artistic way, rearranged our large dining room to make it look like a café with small tables, each with a checked tablecloth and matching table napkins. She had also placed a number of beautiful flower arrangements around the room and there was a gramophone playing records.

There were also numerous games, including digging in a tub of sawdust for little gifts and a much-anticipated treasure hunt in the garden. Auntie May, who no doubt looked on me as the child she never had, had gone to endless trouble to ensure that it would be a day I'd never forget. Certainly it made for a fitting dénouement to a cherished childhood and I remember glumly feeling that nothing, absolutely nothing on Christmas Gift Farm could possibly match anything quite so perfect.

The day my mother returned to Africa from her honeymoon abroad was the day I felt my enchanted life had all but ended. She and The Old Man had gone directly to Christmas Gift Farm, where her wedding present, a gleaming new Morris car, stood awaiting her arrival. They had arranged for me to be accompanied by my grandparents and Auntie May on the great trek north, something most kids would have excitedly regarded as the ultimate adventure but which I disconsolately dismissed as a procession of misery.

Mary and I promised to write and exchange photographs and our maid Minnie, who was utterly heartbroken, called out, 'Miss Effnie, I miss you already, come and visit us one day. I'll look after Winkie and all your pets but take Teddy. May the good Lord keep you safe.' With that I set off with my grandparents and Auntie May for Southern Rhodesia. It was December 1926 and in those days the train trip to Bulawayo took three or four days.

The route north wended its way up through South Africa, Bechuanaland and across the vast, sun-blistered plains of Southern Rhodesia. It was a journey that steam train aficionados would now find impossible to recapture for it took us through some of the most spectacular and unspoilt parts of southern Africa, where the horizons were as yet unmarred by the marauding urban sprawl and shanty towns that would come later.

What I enjoyed most during our long trip was the hubbub that met us at almost every stop. As soon as our train pulled into a station the railway platform would be instantly transformed into a colourful, noisy African bazaar as local traders tried to sell us their wares. They had baskets containing tortoises, poekies (little night apes), beads, necklaces and all sorts of curiosities and delicacies, which, to my grave disappointment, I wasn't even allowed to touch because Auntie May deemed them 'too dirty'.

I recall our eventual arrival in Bulawayo quite distinctly. My mother and The Old Man stood side-by-side waiting for us on the platform and I thought it rather odd that he was wearing a pith helmet. I had not seen anyone wear one of those before but was soon to discover that in Southern Rhodesia most men took to sporting them. My mother, boasting a new and fashionably short haircut, looked stunning and radiantly happy. She had arranged for me to travel in the yellow Overland car with her and The Old Man while my Auntie May and grandparents continued the remainder of the journey to Gwelo by train.

To my utter amazement it was my mother who slipped behind the wheel of the large, yellow vehicle. The Old Man, it seemed, was more than happy for a woman to be in the driver's seat even if she could barely see over the steering wheel. So with my mother at the wheel we set off along dusty and bone-rattling tracks on a trip that would take all day. I began to feel just the faintest stirrings of excitement as a whole new world began to unfold before me.

Along the road I spotted duiker which would leap nervously into the bush as we neared, a stately secretary bird that appeared unfazed by our noisy intrusion and flocks of guineafowl scampering for cover in the tall grass. I began mentally composing my first letter to Mary, regaling her with all the details of my grand adventure into the very heart of Africa.

Before leaving for Christmas Gift Farm we took a day trip to the Matopos, some miles out of Bulawayo and climbed the granite hill to see the grave of Cecil John Rhodes, whom The Old Man had known very well. Rhodes had formed the British South Africa Company in 1889 which occupied Mashonaland and Matabeleland, thus forming Rhodesia.

From his memorial we were treated to a magnificent vista of biscuit-brown plains dotted with the distinctive masasa trees that left us awestruck and that Rhodes was inspired to call World's View. It had about it a timeless tranquillity that would, in the years to come, prove the most wonderful and peaceful haven to me during periods of immense sadness and upheaval. And thanks to The Old Man it marked the starting point of my initiation to a new life where, I would rapidly discover, little girls never feigned giddy spells.

In fact, from the outset The Old Man took it upon himself to lick me into shape and where better than on the wide and glorious expanse of Christmas Gift Farm, which, needless to say, cast a bewitching spell on me the instant I began to explore the wild countryside. The old rambling homestead was typical of those days, with its large mosquito-netted verandah and a long, cool passage that led to numerous bedrooms, one of which I was given all to myself.

My grandparents and Auntie May were to stay with us for the duration of the Christmas holidays and in the evenings we would sit before a lovely log fire and exchange fabulous bush stories. Although it was summer we had rainy days and the nights were quite cold. They were pleasurable and entertaining evenings, for The Old Man was a very good storyteller and he seemed to hold a fascination for ESP. I sat mesmerised, listening to his extraordinary accounts of how his dog always knew when he was due back from a hunt or how his horse seemed to read his thoughts.

He also told us of how a small round table in the house was supposedly haunted. One night soon after, I distinctly heard a thump, thump, thump and then silence. The next morning I was anxious when The Old Man remarked that the table was not in its usual place. That night, having prepared for bed and on my usual ritual of bidding everyone goodnight, in my haste to get down the long, dark passage my dressing gown sash caught in my bedroom door and pulled me back. My anguished scream brought my mother rushing to my room where she found me deathly pale and glued to the spot.

It didn't take The Old Man long, though, to exorcise all those childish fears and my pampered ways. After my grandparents and Auntie May bade me a sad farewell and returned to Somerset East, he announced that I would be given a year to run wild on the farm and get strong. So instead of trudging off to school like most young girls my age, The Old Man set about turning me from a spoilt brat into a tough little creature who would soon begin to revel in a newfound freedom and independence.

He would make me run a mile every morning, following me in the car to time me, and each week there had to be an improvement. Within months I became a rather fast and strong runner which later stood me in good stead, as I went on to win all the 100 yard events at school. He also taught me to swim and dive, offering me a shilling as soon as I could swim the length of the swimming pool and half a crown when I could dive from the top board. Then he taught me to shoot and gave me a .410 with which to shoot all the birds that attacked the fruit in the orchard. I got a penny for each bird I shot. So with my swimming, shooting and diving I soon began amassing a small fortune by way of pocket money.

Within months the wan little girl from Somerset East was no more. Under The Old Man's relentless tutelage I was inducted to the rough-and-ready ways of an African farm and graduated a full-fledged tomboy. My refined, gentle Auntie May would have been dismayed. But I was clearly thriving on all the robust activity and invigorating farm air. I took to riding a boy's bicycle, discarded dresses in preference for shorts and, at that stage, would have given anything to be a boy.

There were car driving lessons, which required sitting on a number of cushions so I could see over the steering wheel. I also proved a dab hand at carpentry and made a cart for our dog to pull – with all our other pets as passengers. I almost convinced myself that it would be possible to invent an engine and call it the Cumming Wonder.

All these little triumphs marked a coming of age and with The Old Man's guidance I emerged from the chrysalis of a cosseted childhood to become an independent, strong and spirited young girl. Indeed, I had, to The Old Man's obvious delight, proved more than equal to the task of being toughened up. Yet the greatest reward for my tenacity and staying power in this baptism of fire was that I forged a closer relationship with the man I once vowed never to call Father.

And with time I grew to love and admire him deeply. In fact, it didn't take me all that long to realise that behind the flinty-faced façade in which blue eyes blazed like gas flames there beat a very big heart. He absolutely doted on my mother and although he had three grown-up children from his first wife he willingly adopted me as his daughter.

Thus, as a family, we settled down to a very comfortable and prosperous life on Christmas Gift Farm where we were denied nothing and had all our domestic needs and chores attended to by a battalion of servants. I think they were all quite excited to have a little girl on the property because The Old Man had been on his own for such a long time.

My mother brought two of her domestic workers with her to Rhodesia. Sarah had been her personal maid for some time and was determined to follow her mistress to pastures unknown. Rose was the junior and had not long been in our employ but she was equally as keen to make the move. Unfortunately Rose soon met a boyfriend, fell pregnant and then requested to return to her family in South Africa. Sarah, however, remained with us for the rest of her life. She eventually married a very respectable African gentleman and they were given a cottage on the farm where she raised a family of her own.

Then there was Jack, who worked in the laundry and took superb care of The Old Man's khaki suits which always boasted crisply pressed seams. From Monday to Friday Jack busied himself in the laundry where a wood stove kept the irons heated on top. But come the weekends he was nowhere to be found. I soon discovered that Jack had a certain penchant for locally brewed beer that would take him to neighbouring farms. Permits had to be issued by the owners of the various farms for a certain quantity of beer to be brewed and Jack always seemed to know exactly where he would be sure to find some.

Come Monday mornings you would find Jack hunkered over the ironing looking a little the worse for wear. But, surprisingly, he never failed to turn up for work for fear of displeasing Sarah, who had been entrusted to supervise all domestic staff.

Indeed, it was Sarah who was charged with 'vetting' all prospective staff for my mother, although the two of them encountered some difficulty in finding a really good cook. After much searching, they found a man who impressed them a great deal and he was duly employed. The procedure was that my mother and Sarah would plan the menus each morning, then Sarah would instruct the cook and leave him to his own devices.

One evening we had guests for dinner and roast guineafowl was on the menu. They had been superbly cooked, wrapped in bacon and served with slices of bread underneath, the roast potatoes were crisp, the green vegetables done to perfection. However, when the gravy dish appeared the tray was loaded with every imaginable sauce – bread sauce, mint sauce, cranberry sauce, mustard sauce and a cheese sauce. My mother was terribly embarrassed and told the waiter to place all the sauces on the side table and to pass only the bread sauce around. After the guests departed the cook was summoned to explain the reason for such culinary overkill. 'Madam, in my last job I cooked the guineafowlies, but I couldn't remember which sauce it needed so I sent them all for Madam to choose,' came the quaint reply.

Christmas Gift Farm featured prominently on the social calling list and guests often came to stay. The Old Man was rather well connected and was considered one of the country's most affluent and successful entrepreneurs. He made his fortune back in the pioneering days shortly after he befriended Tom Meikle, a prominent businessman who then owned several stores and later ran a number of hotels, including the famous Meikles Hotel. Apparently they entered a wager of sorts, with Meikle promising The Old Man a partnership if he could make £300 within a given time frame. We never ascertained exactly how The Old Man made the £300 but he did become a partner in the Meikle's empire.

The Old Man also had several mining interests and one of his small goldmines, the Lucky Seven, was quite successful and he sold it very well. One claim he had pegged remained idle for a while and he was about to start work there when he was offered a substantial price. He accepted and walked away with a good deal of cash. It later became the biggest mine and the richest in Rhodesia.

The Old Man's enterprising streak also extended to farming and like so many of the pioneers of southern Africa he had acquired a ranch shortly after his arrival in Rhodesia. He named it Altyre, after the Gordon Cumming family of Altyre in Scotland. Later The Old Man bought thousands of acres of farmland over a hundred miles from Altyre, then sold half for about half a crown per acre and paid for his land on Christmas Day. That is how the farm got its name of Christmas Gift. He then became the first landowner to experiment with cotton and tobacco crops and had very successful citrus orchards that were renowned for his Black Cat oranges exported overseas.

My mother brought to Christmas Gift Farm a *joie de vivre* and swiftly mended The Old Man's bachelor ways. He had long lived alone after his first wife returned to England with their children, vowing never to return to Africa, a continent she had clearly grown to detest. I could never understand what it was that she would have found so disagreeable, for the Africa I appreciated and loved during my year of liberty was a place of infinite magic.

Even though a large proportion of the farm was taken up with crop farming and The Old Man's much-prized orchards, there were still areas that had lots of wildlife. And as soon as dawn broke with all the triumphant glory of high theatre over the veldt I'd ride off into the high, dew-beaded African grass seeking new delights. I was never disappointed for the place teemed with all kinds of antelope, and snakes.

They once caught a fifteen-foot python and I was instructed to hold one end of it while The Old Man took a photograph of it. He took the skin somewhere to be treated and had a pair of snakeskin shoes made for my mother, as well as snakeskin ties and belts for himself and the family.

Our first holiday as a family was to Johannesburg in the old yellow Overland car. It was a fascinating ten-day journey. We followed narrow dirt roads and my mother kept telling The Old Man to reduce his speed of thirty-five miles an hour. We saw a lot of game and when we set up camp each night our African 'boy' kept a fire going whilst I slept in the car and my parents had a tent, and sure enough there were lion footprints in the vicinity. When we left that area we came into open country and The Old Man decided to take a short cut over the granite hills about 100 miles from the Matopos. These short cuts always ended in long cuts. There was no road, but worn footpaths over the granite outcrops which the Africans used. The Old Man told us of many adventures he had experienced in 'the old days' and they had done a fair amount of hunting in that area, so he felt confident about his short cut. I seem to recollect retracing our footsteps several times but eventually we found a road, or rather a track.

In those days there was no bridge over the Limpopo River as the Beit Bridge was built many years later. We slept on the banks as it was becoming too dark to cross. Africans arrived at dawn with a team of oxen and donkeys to take cars across the Limpopo River. This was a major operation and their main source of income. The Old Man greased parts in the engine, and the luggage was placed in a rowing boat. The river was low at this time of the year, and there were many sand banks where crocodiles were able to sun themselves. My mother, myself and my white teddy settled ourselves in another rowing boat and we set off for the far bank to South Africa. As we watched the yellow Overland plunge into the water the team of oxen and donkeys took charge. It was a slow operation, but we arrived safely and were drier than the yellow Overland! We made little headway that day and set up camp as soon as we found a suitable spot. From then it was easy going compared with what we had endured. It was sheer luxury when we settled into the Hotel Victoria in Johannesburg and had a hot bath and dinner at a table with a white table cloth.

After a heady year of running wild on Christmas Gift Farm I was finally declared fit enough to return to the starched confines of school, the thought of which distressed me no end. The Old Man, however, was adamant that I obtain a good education and by then I knew that a sudden recurrence of those 'giddy turns' would be rather pointless for he had the measure of me. The woe-is-me-act may have once weakened Auntie May's resolve but with The Old Man it was like oil gliding off granite.

So with a heavy heart and my incurable distaste for lessons I grudgingly resumed my schooling in Gwelo where it came as no surprise that, academically, I had fallen way behind other children my age. I had no option but to knuckle down, with The Old Man observing implacably from the sidelines. Although I struggled in the classroom all my running, cycling, swimming and riding on the farm paid dividends on the sports field where I soon ranked as one of the school's best all-round athletes.

For a while I attended the local school, sometimes riding in on my pony which I left tethered to a jacaranda tree outside my classroom. Then The Old Man decided that only a stint at a boarding school in Johannesburg would get me out of my tomboy habits and instil in me the more refined manners expected of a young lady.

Initially I was dreadfully homesick but I endured by channelling all my energies into sport and the gymnasium. I also discovered that of all my school subjects the one that appealed to me the most was art and I was found to show some talent. With the teachers' encouragement I was then able to take art as an exam subject and later obtained an 'A' and first-class certificates.

My first school holiday back on the farm coincided with another long-awaited homecoming. When my mother married Harry Cumming she knew that in accordance with his divorce agreement his children would return from England to spend a year with their father in Africa. And so it was that on my holiday I was to meet my stepsister Dorothy and my stepbrother Roualeyn for the first time. Mollie, the youngest, had decided to come out later.

After the initial shock of finding myself part of a blended family I rather grew to like the idea of having a brother and sister. Dorothy, the eldest, was twenty-one and wore horn-rimmed spectacles which I coveted madly as I thought they were so ultra-chic. She was a teacher and I absolutely adored her, even though I must have been a royal pain at times for I was like her shadow, trailing her everywhere and emulating absolutely everything she did.

Roualeyn was eighteen and took little notice of me at that stage. He had a tough time of it at first. His father was rather disapproving of him and his affected ways for he took to wearing his kilt, a Gordon tartan, on most occasions and had great fun boasting to all the girls that he wore nothing underneath it (I don't think he was fibbing!). Roualeyn had clearly been spoilt by his mother. When he came out to stay with us on the farm his luggage contained the much-talked-about kilt and half a dozen white flannel trousers (he believed you only played tennis in white flannel trousers) and a dinner jacket, which was quite something for a boy so young. Poor Dorothy had only a couple of gingham frocks.

The Old Man in his taciturn way, though, instantly set about making a man of his only son and, with two of my uncles from South Africa, arranged a huge hunting trip that was to initiate Roualeyn to the rigours and challenges of Africa. I silently commiserated, for I was well acquainted with The Old Man's exacting drills.

To my great delight I was included in the hunting expedition. Even Auntie May, who had now moved to Christmas Gift Farm with my grandfather following the death of my grandmother, came along and was put in charge of the cooking.

I couldn't contain my excitement for it was my first hunt. It took us weeks, as we literally trekked into the never-never, as far as Portuguese East Africa. The men had to shoot for the pot every day and the cooks had this wonderful method of threading the meat onto long sticks before roasting it over an open fire. The results were always mouth-wateringly delicious, especially after a long, action-packed day in the sun.

It was bush-bashing in the finest tradition as the sweeping African plains were then still teeming with wildlife. This was some time before the scourge of wholesale poaching and the greed for trophies all but decimated the land's big game. And it was pretty rough-going. Bitumen was a rarity and we had to traverse swollen rivers on pontoons and followed what passed for tracks until it was time to set up our daily camp.

Mosquitoes posed the greatest threat because of malaria, and our African staff had to ensure that everything was mosquito-proofed. They also ensured that fires burned all night long to keep the lions and hyena at bay. I used to love lying snuggled in my camp bed where I'd listen intently to all the orchestral sounds of an African night – the low, sonorous rumble of lion in the distance and the screeching and scratching of myriad unseen creatures that lurked just beyond the campfire's lasso of light.

One day Roualeyn and an uncle went tracking an old kudu bull they thought had been abandoned by its herd. They were missing for three days until one of our trackers eventually found them. They were both in a terrible physical state and had to be rushed to the nearest hospital where they were treated for malaria.

Sadly the incident brought our hunting safari to a premature end but Roualeyn had been blooded into big-game hunting and discovered, albeit painfully, the cardinal rule in bush survival –

never venture far without adequate protection. The African bush is unforgiving of foolhardy exploits.

To everyone's amazement Roualeyn decided to stay and make a new life for himself in Rhodesia. Dorothy's future, however, took an ill-fated turn when The Old Man found out that she had fallen in love with her second cousin Neil, our farm manager. He was highly opposed to the relationship and when the year was over Dorothy elected to return to England where she worked as a teacher for many years. I thought it a great pity, really, for they were deeply in love. As it turned out Dorothy never married and died quite young somewhere in Switzerland and Neil had a disastrous marriage that ended in a very messy divorce.

As for Roualeyn, his father put him to work in Meikles Store, where he was given a rather lowly position. But he gradually proved himself an astute and capable young man and soon branched out on his own. When Mollie the younger sister came out to stay, Roualeyn was able to introduce her to all his friends and take her around the country. She had a wonderful year and received several proposals but went back to England, where she eventually married and settled down.

Finally, after what seemed an interminable spell in the confines of boarding school I matriculated and returned to Christmas Gift Farm, overjoyed at the prospect of never having to wear a panama hat or a uniform again. Now, I too, would sample the giddy delights of adult life.

For a while I had toyed with the idea of becoming a vet, but The Old Man was appalled by my career choice. In fact, he was horrified that I should even contemplate doing anything quite so unseemly for, in his very words, 'no lady becomes a vet'. Looking back now, I can see I would have been ideally suited to the job because I love working with animals. I had, and still have, wonderful instincts when it comes to animals. Ever since I can remember I found I could communicate with them and being an only child they were my constant companions. It was often said that at times I seemed to have a closer rapport with animals than with humans, something I always took as a compliment even though I'm sure it wasn't always intended as one.

But in those days it was unheard of for women to become vets. So I ended up in quite a quandary over what to do with my life. I flirted briefly with the idea of becoming a gym instructress because I was rather good at it and I had liked our gym mistress. Again, my idea was squelched; the family fearing that becoming a gym mistress would leave me musclebound and unable to have a family. It all sounds quite ludicrous now but that was how they thought in those days.

After that it was back to the drawing-board and, strangely enough, it was drawing that happened to be my forte at school and I took inordinate pride in the fact that I got honours for it in my matric year. So when I announced that I wanted to go to art school the idea was, to my surprise, enthusiastically sanctioned by The Old Man. There was a proviso, however, and one that even more surprisingly involved no hardship. Before I was to enrol in the Johannesburg art school I was to take a trip abroad – with my mother and Auntie May acting as chaperones – where it was hoped I would gain some insight and wisdom from the great masterpieces in the European galleries.

And so it was that in 1932 my mother, Auntie May and I set sail from Cape Town on board the *Dunbar Castle* amid much festivity. We took our cue from the other passengers and threw streamers down onto the dock, waving excitedly to The Old Man and friends until they disappeared from view and the breathtakingly beautiful Table Mountain, with its distinctive frilly tablecloth of cloud, receded into the distance.

Apart from a horrific episode of seasickness when I all but pleaded with my mother to make the captain take us back to port, we had the most glorious passage which took us about three weeks. There were endless deck games and parties and I met a fellow called James who partnered me to most of the dances. We entered a fancy dress dance together and he went as the Forgetful Gentleman who had misplaced his trousers (but thankfully wore a pair of boxer shorts) and I was a bluebird. Auntie May, in her inimitable fashion, had set about making me the most beautiful costume and, needless to say, I walked off with the first prize.

As it turned out I spent a good deal of time with James during the voyage and when we docked at Southampton I fancied myself in love with him. He was a university student and was about to embark on further studies in London. As he had some time to spare before commencing his academic year we invited him to accompany us on some of our travels. We hired a Riley car and James then drove us around England, Scotland and Wales.

We swam in Loch Lomond one evening and it was bitterly cold, so we slipped out of our wet bathing suits and were suitably covered by our raincoats, or so we thought. Suddenly I couldn't help but burst out laughing when I saw that the piccadilly slit of James' raincoat revealed a pair of white buttocks to me. He was clearly not amused and I think that was the beginning of the end of our friendship because it became quite apparent to me that the young man lacked a sense of humour. On top of that he betrayed what my mother considered a rather mean streak. One evening he took me to the theatre in London and afterwards my mother was cross because I had let slip that James had neglected to buy me a box of chocolates. Actually I cannot remember ever receiving anything from James – no chocolates or flowers. He was quite miserly and I eventually came to realise that he didn't pass muster as a suitor.

Not that it left me broken-hearted. On the contrary, I was having too much fun to give the humourless James much thought after that, for the next stop on our itinerary was gay Paris. Auntie May refused to fly so my mother and I set off from Croydon on board a Helena aircraft which looked like a corrugated-iron contraption rather than a plane. And no sooner were we seated than my mother opened her newspaper and saw the panicked headline PLANE LOSES WING . . . She spent the entire flight with her eyes fixed on the wing, willing it to stay on!

I fell instantly in love with Paris. We spent hours at the Louvre, marvelling at all the masterpieces The Old Man had been so keen for me to see. The only disadvantage was that I had insisted on looking the part of a sophisticated young woman and wore a pair of new high-heeled shoes I had bought in London and thought rather grand. After hours of clip-clopping along in them my feet were in agony. I was almost in tears when I saw a woman walking in her stockinged feet, clutching a pair of shoes. 'Ah, a fellow victim,' I thought, and so keen was I to escape the pain I instantly followed suit. My mother was absolutely mortified and strode ahead, pretending not to know the waif in the stockinged feet.

I was soon forgiven, though, and we had a terrific time exploring Paris. We went to a nightclub which I thought was disappointingly tame, then to the Follies where I saw Josephine Baker wearing nothing but gold paint and we also took the obligatory trip up the Eiffel Tower where a man in the lift did a cutout portrait of me.

We also went on a quick tour of Switzerland before returning to Auntie May in England. Sadly, our wonderful European sojourn finally came to end. Before setting sail for Africa I was determined to complete my new sophisticated look with a perm. At a hair salon in London my hair was duly wrapped bit by bit in something resembling coarse loo paper and wires, which were then attached to a machine. I sat and baked for what seemed an eternity and to my horror the end result was an unmitigated disaster. I had to live with the crinkled mess for months and my fury was further compounded when The Old Man greeted me with the words 'Hello, Curly'.

Notwithstanding the calamitous curls, the months abroad had achieved all that The Old Man had hoped for. I came home a maturer and more self-possessed young woman who had finally dispensed with the boyish shorts and mannerisms.

I also gained an admirer, a married man called David whom I had known since I was at school. He was a superb rider and we used often to go riding and shooting together. One day my mother discovered a photograph of him taken in uniform during the First World War. She found the photograph where I had hidden it, at the bottom of my make-up purse and immediately told The Old Man. He subsequently accosted David, who was seventeen years my senior, and demanded to know what was going on. David reassured The Old Man that it was all perfectly innocent and that I had simply developed a crush on him and had requested a photograph. Thus what began as a childish infatuation developed into a unique and lasting friendship that would continue my whole life until David's eventual death.

Shortly after our overseas trip The Old Man organised the construction of a new double-storey house for my mother, which was built on another part of the farm near the citrus orchards and irrigation dam. It was beautifully and spaciously designed with a sundeck where The Old Man used to sunbathe in the nude.

We always seemed to have visitors on the farm and many of my friends loved to stay over. We had a boat on the irrigation dam where we would swim and amuse ourselves for hours. Also, I taught several of my friends to ride and once they gained enough confidence we'd set off for long rides across the veldt where we often spotted kudu and some smaller antelope.

When it was time for me to start my art course in Johannesburg it was with none of the apprehension I had when I was sent off to boarding school. I was now a young woman, eighteen years old and on the cusp of an exciting new life in the big city. For the first time I left Christmas Gift Farm without tears and brimming with self-assurance. The Old Man had finally succeeded in what he had set out to do all those years ago, since I now took pride in being an independent young woman eager to take on exhilarating and new challenges.

Chapter Three

ALL THOSE HORSES

A major hurdle immediately presented itself at the outset of my art studies in Johannesburg when, to my chagrin, I found myself living in circumstances not altogether conducive to a worldly-wise young woman.

At my family's insistence I had agreed to move into a residence with scores of other students but, not surprisingly, soon began to chafe at the fun-crushing restrictions. The place was horrifyingly reminiscent of boarding school and after my blissful, liberating trip abroad I simply could not readjust to communal living. I tolerated it for a while to please my family but then, with another student, determinedly set out to find a more suitable place. At first my parents were opposed to the idea but after several entreaties and a promise that I would not neglect my studies, they finally agreed to the move.

We found a huge room, more like a bedsit, that was up for rent in a double-storey house in Berea Road, Hillbrow, which was then a bohemian part of town. It was perfect – our very own students' pad. The landlady provided us with boiled eggs, toast and a hot drink in the morning and we had sandwiches and fruit with the other students during our lunchbreak at the art school. Dinner was a different matter – we often made up a party and went to a restaurant or to the theatre, followed by a late supper. My parents had increased my allowance to help me pay for the rent but there were many times I found myself having to count the pennies.

Fortunately there was a small boarding house near us where, if money was short, we could have a light meal for one shilling and sixpence.

We did a lot of entertaining there, often to our fellow tenants' dismay. Our gramophone took pride of place on the large dining room table and it tended to work overtime at weekends when friends dropped by. One day, after a tenant complained about the noise, we replaced the gramophone needle with an acacia thorn so we could still hear enough to dance without disturbing the neighbours.

Naturally, as a popular and fun-loving student it didn't take me long to become intoxicated by the fast-paced life in the big city. We partied, danced and lived the charmed life of the young and unencumbered. We didn't have a care in the world other than to savour every joyous moment. And despite all the rousing revelry and *joie de vivre* I managed to keep my promise to my family and diligently attended all my art classes. Everything seemed to go swimmingly except I missed my horses terribly and longed to get back in the saddle.

I can still recall vividly the first time I was put on a horse at about three years old. It was when my mother took me on a trip to a farm outside Somerset East, where she was to deliver a baby. Even after so many years I am able to call to mind how it felt sitting on that horse because it just did something to me. I couldn't stop patting it and talking to it. There was a small boy, most probably the farmer's son, whom I called Huff (although I don't think that was his real name) and together we sat astride the horse. Someone took a photograph of the two of us, dear Huff – the first man in my life – and myself, with this big bow in my hair, sitting ramrod straight and beaming from ear to ear. I have treasured that photograph all my life. It serves as a sepia-stained reminder of the day my love of horses was born.

After that, whenever I went to stay on a farm, I'd beg and plead to be allowed a ride on one of the horses. Even back home in Somerset East I would go with Mary, my dear friend, to her Uncle Bill's farm where there were big, frisky horses. We weren't allowed to ride them unfortunately, and had to make do with a couple of donkeys. I didn't mind because all I wanted to do was ride. And ride we did, even on those obstreperous donkeys. We managed to make them go at quite a fair lick while pretending to be a couple of cowboys charging fearlessly across the countryside. Not without mishap, though, for on one occasion my donkey bolted with me and then stopped dead in its tracks before a ditch, unceremoniously hurtling me into a thornbush. My behind and pride were hurt and with a sympathetic Mary looking on I tried vainly to fight back the tears. They were not so much tears of pain as tears of defeat from suffering my first ignominious fall – from a donkey.

The spill did nothing to dent my enthusiasm for riding. On the contrary, I sedulously set about mastering the correct posture and techniques for cantering and trotting, and I was completely self-taught. Once, while out riding on my own on yet another farm, I saw one of the farmers rising to the trot which so impressed me that nothing would do but that I emulate him. I watched him closely, made a mental note of every move, and then spent all afternoon gently coaxing my horse to obey each aid until I, too, managed to rise to the trot. The farmers mostly had horses that tripled, which was a special gait of cantering with the hind legs and trotting with the fore. Again, after observing their techniques I'd put my horse to work, growing more and more confident with each equestrian triumph.

I don't know what it was about horse-riding that I found so appealing and exhilarating. Maybe it had something to do with the sense of power it gave me. I was always the shortest of everyone I knew but once I sat astride a horse with the reins in my hand I felt possessed of a strength and fearlessness that somehow compensated for my five feet (fifteen h.h.) in height. And, admittedly, I felt that I was also very good at handling horses, no matter their temperament or size. It came to me quite naturally for I relied mostly on instinct. Of course there were some spectacular spills but I can't remember ever having to beat a horse or losing my temper with one, such was the rapport I developed with them, bar a few notable exceptions.

When I moved to Christmas Gift Farm, The Old Man gave me my first horse, an old roan named Mick who had been ridden from South Africa with the Pioneer Column at the turn of the century. He was one of the few horses that survived horse sickness and, according to The Old Man, it meant that Mick was 'salted' – he had become immune to one of the deadliest horse diseases in Africa. As it turned out, dear Mick lived to the ripe old age of forty and proved to be a calm and tolerant companion. We spent many happy hours riding around the farm and I taught my friends to ride on Mick. Sometimes he would carry three of us bareback to the dam and then stand waiting patiently while we cavorted in the water until it was time for him to take us home.

After Mick died The Old Man bought me a horse which he named Money because he was of the view that 'nothing went faster than money'. Alas, Money proved a grave disappointment after my beloved Mick. He had been an unsuccessful racehorse and from the outset we failed to hit it off.

One day, while riding Money on the nine-hole golf course we had on the farm he suddenly turned tail and bolted for home. I was only twelve at the time and, true to his name, Money went so fiendishly fast that I got my first taste of sheer terror. I held on for dear life, hoping he would stop at a gate and cattle grid that lay ahead. Instead, the blighter flew over it, with me desperately hanging on. When we charged to the stables I jumped off and unashamedly burst into tears, vowing never to get back onto Money. The Old Man was quite alarmed and pronounced what I had known all along – Money and I were simply incompatible.

After that experience nothing would do but that I be allowed to handpick my own horse at the livestock sales in Gwelo where, unaccompanied, I gamely proceeded to bid for a bay horse with a white blaze. And so it was that at the precocious age of twelve I bought my very own horse for the princely sum of twelve pounds. I christened him Robin Hood but he was commonly referred to as Robin by everyone on Christmas Gift Farm. I had him for years and years and utterly adored him, although, in all honesty there was nothing special about Robin. Fact is, he was quite an ordinary, dependable old horse, a real hack, and I would never have entered the show ring with him. He never pulled a Money stunt on me and because he was so mild-mannered and consistent, I became a more confident and accomplished rider over the years.

When I was on the farm, hardly a day went by without me saddling up my horse and going for an enjoyable ride. At weekends my friends knew jolly well that if they came over to stay they had to ride some of the farm's hacks. I could never understand anyone not wanting to ride and always insisted that even the most timid and fearful give it a try. I guess even then I was a very good teacher for with a lot of gentle persuasion the most reluctant of riders would soon be won over.

So, understandably, after months of tripping the light fantastic in Johannesburg I was craving a brisk and invigorating ride in the countryside. Finally, one glorious Sunday morning, a friend took pity on me and accompanied me to Moreton's School of Riding, which was located near the goldmine dumps at Booysens. It wasn't one of the more prepossessing areas of Johannesburg, but I was overjoyed at the prospect of spending a day out riding. I had never been to a riding school so I didn't know what to expect. I certainly had not expected to find so many people milling about, all of whom came meticulously turned out in loud checked jackets, jodhpurs and polished boots. Riding on Sundays at Moreton's was evidently considered quite a social affair.

I joined a party which included one of the instructors, and went out for a cross-country ride that took us along bluegum-lined sandtracks all the way to the Baragwanath aerodrome. Many of the riders were rank beginners so when the said instructor – one of three brothers who ran the riding school – complimented me on my riding and invited me to come back the following Sunday for a ride I accepted with alacrity, unaware that he had an ulterior motive.

After I had been out on another long ride the next Sunday the instructor called me over and introduced me to a flamboyantly dressed couple. The woman's name was Mrs Clough Wilson and she was decked out in a full-length fur coat and extraordinarily high heels. Mr Wilson wore a hacking jacket with a check so loud that what was no doubt intended to be a fashion statement was tragically reduced to an optical assault. We exchanged pleasantries for a while and then both the instructor and myself were invited out to lunch.

The Wilsons lived fairly close by and over lunch they said how much they wanted to show their prized hack Molly at the Rand Easter Show. Now the Rand Easter Show rated as a premier event in South Africa, drawing thousands of competitors and visitors from across the country as well as from neighbouring states. Unfortunately the portly Mr Wilson was deemed too heavy for Molly and Mrs Wilson's less than impressive equitation skills would not have withstood the demands of the show ring. So when they asked me if I would like to show Molly, I agreed without a moment's hesitation. This was an opportunity of a lifetime and even though I had never been in a show ring before I was not in the slightest bit daunted by the challenge that loomed ahead.

On the other hand, Arthur, the instructor, was not nearly as confident for we had only a few weeks to prepare for the show. Nevertheless, he felt I would be suited to the Ladies' Hack class. But before embarking on the rigorous training schedule mapped out for me in preparation for the big event, I succumbed to a rare bout of vanity. I knew that if I were to leave a lasting impression with the judges I needed to look the part. My student's allowance was such that it didn't allow for any extravagance but I found a pair of second-hand boots, a pair of breeches, a jacket and a bowler hat. I also splurged on a distinctive bow tie, which later became some-what of a signature.

My training for the ring had no call for glamour. Indeed, it was dusty and gruelling work but I loved every sweat-stained minute of it. I spent hours and hours going round the ring with Arthur acting as judge. I was shown how to execute an extended trot. Then came the figure of eight and having to change legs (where the horse is asked to change from leading on the near fore to the off fore).

It was painstaking and repetitive stuff and I was required to spend all my weekends and every spare hour I had on weekdays practising in the paddocks at the riding school. An added complication was that I could not afford to be caught skipping any of my art classes for fear of provoking The Old Man's wrath. I devised a system that involved taking my riding kit to school and as soon as I finished my last lesson at three in the afternoon, I'd bolt for the change rooms, get into my gear and then make a dash for the tram. It allowed me to get a couple of hours' training in before sunset.

Finally the great day arrived and, astonishingly, I experienced none of the pre-competition jitters normally expected of a beginner. Rather, after so much intensive preparation I couldn't wait to get into the ring and put Molly through her paces. And, if I may be excused just a soupçon of smugness, I think the pair of us almost immediately stole the show, so to speak.

There I was, dressed to kill in my highly polished boots and colourful bow tie and possessed of all the self-assurance one would come to expect of a more seasoned rider. Certainly I entered the show ring ranked as a novice equestrienne, but as a rider I felt I had finally made it to the big stakes. I was drawn to that arena like a moth to a flame, and, remarkably, I can still hear the music and visualise the faces of the judges as Molly and I proudly trotted by.

Ours was a flawless workout and to wild cheers and applause from a sea of spectators we were given first prize, a red certificate that, in keeping with custom, I had to hold in my mouth as we took our victory lap. The Wilsons were beside themselves with jubilation, but not to the extent that they felt compelled to part with some of the prize money as a token of appreciation. I said nothing about it, however, for my reward was winning at something which I had never attempted before.

When I returned to Moreton's the following weekend, still glowing with triumph, it was to find that Arthur and his brother Willie had more ambitious plans in store for their star rider. And this time they included showjumping. I had never jumped a horse, well not intentionally, that is if one disregarded the terrifying incident when Money jumped the cattle grid. But Willie seemed certain that I had the makings of a champion. All that was needed was for someone to show me how to stay in the saddle while my horse set out to clear a hurdle at full speed.

Showjumping is not an activity recommended for the faint-hearted but Willie was Moreton's jump specialist and he took some pride in his effective, if somewhat unconventional, teaching methods. So I was duly put on a horse called Tommy but not allowed reins or stirrup irons. Then, after a few cursory pointers, I was led to what was supposedly the 'jumping lane'. All it had was a makeshift two-foot high brush jump that, in time, I grew to know very well. There was no talk of going about it gently and before I knew it I was charging down the lane followed by a crowd of African grooms yelling and chasing the horse. To everyone's surprise, mine included, I stayed on. I think I must have made quite an impression on Willie because he then blithely announced that I was to train to compete in a showjumping event at the forthcoming Johannesburg Show.

With that it was back to a new round of training sessions and attempting to scale ever higher jumps. To help soften the horse's landing and to cushion my falls the stablehands had constructed a bed of dry manure on the landing side of the jump. Needless to say, I soon grew accustomed to the taste of manure.

Now that my riding had so unexpectedly progressed to competition level I needed to acquire a horse of my own, one that would make an ideal partner in the show ring. Enter Barbara, a wonderful mare with an enigmatic past. After a year of thriftily saving every spare penny I bought Barbara from Willie and was told that she had the dubious distinction of having once terrorised royalty. Apparently she had bolted with the Prince of Wales Edward VIII, when out hunting and afterwards had made it quite clear only female riders were welcome on her back.

Barbara was exactly what I wanted. She had a reputation for never refusing jumps but, by the same token, she also proved extraordinarily difficult to control because she was so fast. On one occasion she bolted with me when we were out riding on a track to the aerodrome. She took off suddenly and headed straight for the main road to Vereeniging. It was an exact replay of my near-disastrous ride on Money and again I could see a gate ahead. Only this time I knew that if I failed to make her stop and she cleared the gate, we would be on one of the Witwatersrand's busiest highways.

Miraculously I managed to yank her around hard but then suddenly felt a searing pain in my leg. I hadn't noticed the barbed-wire fence until it had cut through my boot and ripped at my flesh. Thanks to Barbara I suffered my first serious war wound, one that left a rather impressive scar for life. Bloodied and furious I got back on the mare, determined to control her errant ways. Indeed, with time we became a formidable, well-matched duo for no jump seemed too high or impossible to clear when we put our hearts and minds to surmounting all those obstacles in the show ring.

After our successful debut at the Rand Show in Johannesburg, however, there was a minor hitch. A photograph showing me jumping the post and rails appeared in the Johannesburg newspapers with the caption 'A Lady From Rhodesia'. Unfortunately the newspapers back home picked up the news and this was the first my parents knew of my showjumping pursuits. Predictably they were not amused and expressed concern over my studies. I managed to placate them by stressing that I had attended all the required art classes at school and that my riding was restricted to my recreational hours.

At that stage of my young life I had a boyfriend named Arthur back in Rhodesia. He was the most charming of men, an excellent all-round sportsman who played hockey for Rhodesia and was, most importantly, a very good rider. We both rode with the Gwelo Hunt Club and I think everyone assumed that Arthur and I would someday be married. He clearly adored me. Certainly he would have made an ideal husband: he was successful, good looking, devoted and very generous. He gave me a tennis racquet, a ciné camera and a horse called Tip Toes. All these gifts, although overly generous, were deemed quite appropriate until, to everyone's amazement, he presented me with a Ford Model A car. My mother was appalled and promptly put her foot down. A young lady could not be seen to accept so lavish a gift. Her solution? That I buy the car from Arthur out of my own pocket money. So, in accordance with etiquette I parted with thirty-three pounds – a huge sum of money in those days – and became the owner of a very stylish racing-green car.

And so it was that my mother and Arthur, after learning of my success in the show ring, came to Johannesburg to watch me compete at the following Rand Easter Show in 1935, which was opened with much fanfare by General Jan Smuts, the Boer War hero who became South Africa's prime minister.

This time round I did pair jumping with my instructor and showed a hack and I won again. But the highlight was the jumping event on Seagull, a horse belonging to the riding school. We won first prize. Then, to top all that I won second prize in the same jumping event on my horse Barbara, an extraordinary feat – first and second prize in the same jumping event – and to wild cheers I rode out victoriously on Seagull, leading my Barbara and this time clutching two prize tickets in my mouth. The loudest applause, apparently, came from my mother who sat just behind General Smuts. Later she told me how tempted she was to gently tap him on the shoulder and boast, 'That's my daughter riding round the ring with her prize tickets.'

After that there was no holding me back. I had become completely hooked on my riding, to such an extent that I moved out of my student digs in Berea Road and into the stables at the riding school. I stayed in a tiny room in the yard, certainly no place for a young girl, but as I had to prepare for so many events my new living arrangement enabled me to spend all my free time riding. And horses and competing became my life. Every morning, without fail, I'd wake before dawn, work the horses and then take a bath in a nearby house belonging to the stables before catching the tram to art school. I couldn't have lived any rougher but I was in my element.

Then one day a friend, the family's solicitor from Rhodesia, took me out for dinner. He was dreadfully prim and proper and was absolutely taken aback when he discovered that I was living in such woeful conditions. Not surprisingly, word was soon passed back to my parents and all hell broke loose. The Old Man immediately dispatched my kind married friend, David, to investigate what I was up to. He, of course, was highly amused to find that I had found the best possible way of continuing my studies as well as pursuing my dream of becoming a champion equestrienne.

I was deeply indebted to him for apparently on his return he managed to put The Old Man's mind at rest. In fact, shortly afterwards it was arranged for me to rent a more salubrious room in one of the old mining houses up the road from the stables. It made for a perfect arrangement – one that gave me more valuable time to concentrate on my riding. At that stage I was preparing Barbara for oncoming jumping events, including the high jump. We would ride out to the mine dumps, which were very steep but ideal to muscle up the horses and ourselves. We'd take the easier approach to the top of the dumps and then go down the extremely steep slopes. It required great concentration because it was essential to go down in a straight line, therefore maintaining perfect balance.

I found the exercise exhilarating and one day, after making it down without incident I came across two strangers, on horseback, chatting away to my instructor. They were brothers, Anthony and Peter Holmes à Court. After being introduced I found them to be very charming, although Anthony was the one who did all the talking and Peter was extraordinarily shy. He hardly said a word while we rode back to the riding school. He was however, extremely handsome. Lean and tall, about six foot three inches, with broad shoulders, brown eyes and dark hair. What attracted me the most, though, was his combustible dry wit. He always made me laugh whenever we met at the stables in the ensuing weeks. Sometimes he would give me a lift home after riding or take me out to dinner, but it soon dawned on me that romancing was not Peter's major suit.

In fact, on meeting him there was no impulsive love affair. Instead, ours turned out to be an unusually timorous courtship mainly due to the fact that he was so shy and retiring. I think it took months before Peter eventually summoned the courage to kiss me.

I remember the occasion so well. Peter had a little red sports car which we loved to take on long drives along the outskirts of Johannesburg. We got back late one night after our customary drive and had a cup of cocoa in the room I rented near the stables. Only this night he deviated from the norm in that just before departing I got a goodnight peck on the cheek. I was so stunned and surprised and before I could say anything Peter had fled to his car.

He was certainly very different from most of the other men I knew. I guess, looking back, I found his aloofness rather intriguing. At the time he was working at the Johannesburg Stock Exchange, a job he managed to secure almost immediately after arriving in South Africa. Peter had initially joined the Royal Navy as a young cadet but when his ship called in at Durban he fell instantly in love with Africa. Shortly after his return to the United Kingdom he left the navy and moved to Johannesburg, where his brother Anthony had already established himself. Although his mother was of aristocratic breeding and he was related to Lord Heytesbury in England, Peter never flaunted the fact that he was a blueblood. On the contrary, he was refreshingly unpretentious and could not abide any form of showiness.

Fun to him was driving around in his red sports car – it was his pride and joy. Our long trips would normally include a swim somewhere or a visit to a friend's farm. He would never let me wear a hat because he liked to see my hair ruffled in the wind and he absolutely loathed lipstick and nail varnish. Sometime later his hate-list included night cream, and I was warned that he would never go to bed with me if I wore cream on my face! But for all his idiosyncrasies, I fell hopelessly and madly in love with Peter. Strange, how the course of true love can never be predicted. I had Arthur in Rhodesia who was everything a woman could hope for and seemed so wonderfully uncomplicated and there I was, falling for someone who was emotionally remote and an appalling dancer. Peter did pass muster on the two most important fronts, however – he loved riding and he adored animals. I simply couldn't be with a man who didn't share my love of animals.

I think the first time I got an inkling that we were a serious item was on the night of the Rand Light Infantry Ball. I know it was on Friday 19 October 1934 because I still have the dance card. Peter's name appears for nine dances out of sixteen. It was also on that night he gave me my first passionate kiss without bolting afterwards! After that I started seeing more and more of him and my life became fiercely busy what with my riding, all the partying and dancing, and having to prepare for my final exams at the art school.

Then came the Christmas holidays, which I was expected to spend with the family on the farm. Peter suggested that I invite him up for a holiday after the New Year. When I broached the idea with my family they were more than happy for him to come and stay with us. No doubt they were curious to see what he was like for I had often made mention of him in my letters home. Actually, the first time Peter planted a kiss on my cheek I excitedly wrote in a letter to my mother, 'Guess what? Peter pecked me goodnight.'

Now it was all but a foregone conclusion that the man who stole my heart was about to endure an intense appraisal at the hands of a forbidding triumvirate – my mother, Auntie May and The Old Man.

Chapter Four

FOR THE LOVE OF PETER

Once back home on the farm I tried to lose myself in all the things I normally loved doing but always my thoughts turned to Peter. I missed him desperately and counted the days to his arrival. The day he was expected at Christmas Gift Farm I spent hours at the window on the lookout for his red sports car. When I finally spotted it coming up the drive I flew out of the house, trailing words of censure from my mother: 'You should not show too much enthusiasm, that should come from Peter,' she called out, her cautionary words muted by a thudding heart and young love.

Peter, of course, emerged from his car with his composure intact. He was, after all, an unruffled and correct Englishman to the core. But I was more than delighted to see him and after quick introductions tea and ham sandwiches were served. Later that afternoon I wanted to show him around the farm so we took the dogs for a walk. It was a glorious day and I felt giddy with joy for I had no doubt that the triumvirate had taken an instant liking to Peter. We had, thankfully, surmounted a major hurdle and I had a hunch that our time together on Christmas Gift Farm would mark a special turning point in our courtship. I did not have to wait too long for evidence of this.

At first our days were taken up with exploring the farm together. Peter and I would set out for long rides before breakfast, the best time to go game-spotting before the searing midday sun sent man and beast in search of shade. And, of course, all my friends wanted to meet Peter so there were umpteen parties and picnics. But what we enjoyed the most was swimming in the dam at the orchard and chatting away in the summerhouse. It was there that Peter, in a roundabout fashion, said that he thought it time he told my family that we should become engaged. I took that for a proposal.

When, finally, Peter took the plunge and told my family of our engagement plans they were thrilled and gave us their blessings, but The Old Man insisted on a two-year engagement because he felt we were still too young to get married. Moreover, I had an art course to complete. I was twenty years old and Peter was three years older. At that age two years seemed like an interminable sentence but we weren't game to challenge The Old Man. We were also determined not to let the prospect of so protracted an engagement put a damper on our celebrations and ended up having a fabulous party on 23 January 1936 where I proudly flourished my small engagement ring.

The announcement of our engagement appeared in several newspapers in Rhodesia, South Africa and England.

I was rather amused when Peter read me a letter he had written to his mother informing her of our engagement:

> 'We have just become engaged. Ethnée and I have known each other for a couple of years. She is only five foot, full of energy and a superb rider and showjumper. We met when we were out riding. She is at the Art School in Johannesburg, we ride together most weekends. She is fair and has freckles.'

Not what one would call an especially expansive letter but it was in keeping with Peter's diffident style. I then wrote her a letter myself, one that included a lot more detail as well as photographs that I hoped would satisfy her curiosity about the freckly, fair-haired girl her son intended to marry. Unfortunately the ensuing war years prevented us from ever meeting but we kept up a regular correspondence and I knew she treasured my letters until the day she died.

Before our holiday drew to a close Peter and I decided to return to Johannesburg together. The Old Man resisted the idea at first but to Peter's credit he eventually managed to win him over. For all his reticence Peter could be devastatingly persuasive if he set his mind on something, and on that score he and The Old Man were evenly matched. We notched up one more victory when, just before departing in Peter's sports car, The Old Man agreed to my request that I be allowed to live in a flat of my own. I felt that being engaged it seemed far more appropriate to have a place of my own.

I soon found a flat at number 67 Downing Mansions, Eloff Street, which proved wonderfully convenient for work and play. Peter was able to walk from his office at the stock exchange and have lunch with me, which was always a jam sandwich and a glass of milk. In those days we had our ice boxes in the corridor and had to order our milk from the landlady.

Cooking, however, was not my forte, and never has been, which meant that we went out for dinner most nights. But shortly after I moved into my new flat I had invited a friend over for a 'house warming' dinner. In the absence of anything that could even approximate culinary competence it was thought best that everything be bought ready-prepared. We bought a chicken, bread rolls and other goodies, some wine and set a lovely table. We thought we were rather smart and despite those few essential short cuts my first dinner party was declared a great success.

The same, however, could not be said of the way the evening drew to a close. When we went downstairs to take Isabelle home there was no car. Peter's sports car, his pride and joy, had been stolen. The night ended with Isabelle having to catch a taxi home and with us reporting the theft to the police. Next day they found Peter's car in a ditch 500 miles away.

But in the main, life could not have been sweeter. I was taking extra craft classes with a very talented woman whose small studio was only a block from my flat. Her friend, who shared the flat with her, did all the housekeeping and made little biscuits and fruit drinks for us during the class. I liked both women very much and certainly benefited from the private tuition. In fact, I submitted several articles for their arts and crafts stall at the Rand Easter Show 1936 Empire Exhibition and subsequently was swamped with orders that helped supplement my allowance. I was blissfully unaware of my teacher's personal arrangement until someone quipped, 'How are you getting along with your lesbian chums?' Not that it made the slightest difference. I liked them both and our friendship continued over the years.

Only eight months into our engagement, the two-year restriction proved more than flesh and blood could bear so Peter and I prepared, yet again, to put our case to my family. There was a long weekend in October and Peter was unsure when next he would be able to take time off work, so, if permission was forthcoming, we felt it would make for an ideal wedding date. After much deliberation my family not only relented but promptly set about planning for a huge and lavish affair in Rhodesia. And, naturally, it was assumed that the reception would be held at Christmas Gift Farm. Peter, to put it mildly, was horrified. He had hoped ours would be a quiet wedding in Johannesburg.

He got his way although my family must have been deeply disappointed at being denied a fairytale wedding on the farm. But with characteristic grace they accepted our plans for a more subdued wedding at St Martin's-in-the-Veldt in Johannesburg on

Friday 2 October 1936. As the wedding ceremony was set for 10a.m. on a working day we anticipated that several of our friends would be unable to attend. As it turned out everyone came to the church but some, sadly, had to give the reception a miss and return to work.

My mother welcomed everyone but later asked me, 'Who on earth were those strange women, one with an Eton crop and bobby socks, and the other dressed up like a lamb?' I had to quickly fill her in. They were, I explained, my great friends who had been giving me extra craft lessons. Heaven only knows what went through my mother's mind. I suspect she was rather disapproving of her daughter associating with such eccentric-looking women.

It turned out to be a wonderful occasion. My dear friend Cath was bridesmaid and helped me dress for the wedding. I remember becoming quite anxious over having to wear high heels. If I had had my way I would have been married in my riding breeches and boots. Cath insisted I make an effort, however, and she went to endless trouble with my make-up and hair before I was taken down the aisle by a very proud and happy Old Man.

I still have the clipping from the *Star* newspaper which reported our wedding as follows:

> The dainty bride wore a two-piece of creamy silk Tolynaise, the tailored lines of which were followed by her Baku hat to tone, severely simple in style. Miss Cumming carried a lovely sheaf of delphiniums in two shades of blue. When the bride and groom left by car for a short motoring trip to the Eastern Transvaal, Mrs Peter Holmes à Court travelled in a tailored Donegal tweed costume, with soft brown felt hat to match.

After the reception Peter and I drove to Waterval Onder where we spent our honeymoon weekend in a thatched rondavel [a circular one-room building] at the Wayside Inn. It was a blissful retreat near a river that had some wonderful pools for swimming. We found an idyllic spot where we could sit under a waterfall and sunbathe on the rocks. We also managed to hire two very good horses and spent much of the day out riding. Later we had to change for dinner, which was quite formal and served in a dining room decorated with scores of African masks and spears with clay pots containing massive arrangements of wild proteas. It made for an unusual ambience but I loved the place and cherished the memory of our time there all my life.

Unfortunately as honeymoons go, ours was all too brief. So brief, in fact, that when it was time to return to Johannesburg the bill came to the grand total of four pounds, four shillings and sixpence! Nevertheless, we were keen to get back and settle into our first home which was called Greengates, a small cottage that came with two acres of overgrown garden and an orchard. It also had a windmill and a garage at the edge of the property which we later converted into a mushroom house, where, with expert guidance from a neighbour, we began growing our own mushrooms. It became quite a thriving little business and Peter used to sell supplies to his friends and colleagues at the stock exchange to augment his salary of seven pounds a week.

There was no refrigerator in those days and all perishables were placed in the cool larder under the windmill which was kept cold by water dripping onto its thatched roof. Our stove was a small paraffin two-burner which I never learnt to master, and as I seem to recollect our first breakfast was an absolute disaster. The first couple of days were spent adding finishing touches to our new home and getting accustomed to being Mrs Holmes à Court. I busied myself doing all those wifely things such as filling the house with flowers from our garden, writing to thank family and friends for their wedding gifts, completing all the unpacking and then finding domestic help.

We had engaged a maid by correspondence and when she arrived at Greengates we were rather taken aback as she seemed so frail. Her name was Sarah Simmonds (not to be confused with Sarah at Christmas Gift Farm) and she proudly informed us that she was the half-caste daughter of an Irishman and a mixed race mother. Contrary to first impressions she proved more than capable of coping with the work and before long became a devoted and valued member of our household. Furthermore, to my great relief, she excelled as a cook.

But our haven was not considered complete until we had built a stable for my horse, Barbara. In fact, we ended up building two stables because a friend wanted to board her horse, Wonderbar, with us. It made for an ideal arrangement because it enabled us to share the services of Moses, the groom-cum-gardener. Also, as our house was near the Inanda Polo Club, which in those days was surrounded by a lot of open country, we had easy access to excellent riding terrain.

At weekends, Peter had the use of Wonderbar, which meant that we could go out for long rides together. We were blissfully happy and for all The Old Man's dire warnings about us being too young we soon slipped comfortably into an untroubled married life. On weekday mornings I used to drive Peter to the bus stop in the nearby suburb of Rosebank and then collect him from there after work. In time I became quite a familiar sight for I had Charles, our Persian cat, reclined on the ledge at the back window and Andrew, our little dog, perched on the seat beside me.

Meanwhile, we continued to renovate and improve our house. We added a small above-ground swimming pool and then another bedroom which we intended to be the nursery. As it turned out we didn't have to wait too long before it became occupied. I fell pregnant within a couple of weeks of marriage but I would not let that deter me from devoting a lot of my time and energy to riding. I rode almost right through a problem-free pregnancy but at my riding friend's behest I stopped just a few weeks shy of Robert's birth.

On the morning of 27 July 1937 I told Peter that I thought it time to go to the nursing home. We phoned our doctor, who also happened to be a personal friend, and were assured there was no need for haste. However, as we lived some distance from the city he thought it prudent to get to the nursing home in good time.

On arrival we were met by a rather haughty sister who felt that because it was our first baby we were panicking needlessly. I was then relegated to a room with two beds where I was left on my own with a pile of books and magazines. Fathers were then not permitted to attend deliveries so Peter left me there and went to work.

By lunchtime, when Peter came to see me there were still no signs of progress. But no sooner had he left than I had to reach for the bell. 'Sister Haughty', no doubt unimpressed that I hadn't let go the bell until she made her reluctant appearance, yanked back the blanket and then grabbed for the bell herself to alert the doctor. I never saw the labour ward or my doctor because it was down to Sister and me to bring my firstborn into the world.

I remember looking down at my watch, a twenty-first birthday present from my mother, and making note of the time. It was 2.45p.m. As labours go I must have set a record time for within minutes she held up my screaming, red-faced son by his feet. The first thought that struck me was that he was so long and would no doubt grow to be as tall as his father.

Childbirth then was nothing like it is today; despite a textbook delivery I was made to stay in hospital for the required ten days following our son's birth. Not that I minded, really, for I lapped up all the attention. My ward soon filled with flowers and gifts as a procession of friends came to have a peek at our son. The lesbian couple from my art school days were among the first to set eyes on Robert and let slip a typical remark: 'Nice baby, looks like a long piece of biltong.' When I was finally allowed to leave the nursing home it was in my smart Donegal tweed suit that I had worn as my going-away outfit after the wedding. It had taken me no time at all to regain my figure, a miracle I immediately attributed to all the riding I did throughout my pregnancy.

Child-rearing, though, proved nowhere near as uncomplicated and my mother, the accomplished maternity nurse, came down from Rhodesia to give me a much-needed hand and to teach me the rudiments of babycare. I can remember once being at the end of my tether and remarking, 'If I had a foal I would know what to do. But a baby?' Fortunately Robert was an easy and delightful baby and he used to love lying under the shade of a tree in our garden, surrounded by all our pets. He expressed no interest in his woolly toys but would delightedly gurgle away when our cats and dogs came and stood guard.

On 15 August he was christened in the same church in which we had been married and with water from the Nile that one of my uncles had bottled during the First World War. He said it would bring good luck and wanted all his grand-nephews and nieces to use it. We did so with both our sons.

I was back in the saddle almost immediately after Robert's birth and when he was but a few months old I'd take him for gentle little rides on Barbara, making sure to hold him tight. He absolutely loved it, giving every indication that like his mother and father he was born to ride.

Shortly after Robert's first birthday, however, we made a decision to move back to Rhodesia. At the time Peter was earning seven pounds a week working at the stock exchange and received a small allowance from his late father's estate. The Old Man also gave us a small allowance and some shares in the Meikles Stores. It may not sound much but in those days it was more than adequate. We had our servants, our home, a car – which my adorable Auntie May gave us – and our horses. But The Old Man was of the opinion there was not much of a future for Peter on the stock exchange and, now that we had the added responsibility of a child, offered to set him up in business.

Peter took a fleeting trip to Rhodesia to discuss the matter with The Old Man. As it turned out my former boyfriend, Arthur, was managing the Gwelo Newsagency for a friend who had put the business up for sale. It was a thriving concern which was located directly opposite Meikles Store in the main street. Without hesitation, Peter bought the Newsagency, after The Old Man agreed to stand security. He bought it for a staggering £3000. I was delighted for I was keen to move back to Rhodesia to be close to my family. Arthur was a tremendous help in starting Peter off on his business venture.

Unfortunately the move was not without heartbreak. We had hoped that our maid, Sarah, who had grown very attached to Robert, would be able to accompany us but she was reluctant to leave her family and expressed grave fears about moving to 'lion country'. I was deeply upset by her decision for we had come to adore her. In fact, we corresponded for many years and always sent her money at Christmas so she could lash out on a bottle of her favourite sherry, one of her enduring weaknesses.

Then there was the equally heart-rending uncertainty over what to do with my beloved horse, Barbara, who not only had a bad leg but was then getting to the end of her days. For a while we had tried to breed from her and I had a wonderful, sentimental notion that she would have a foal when I had my baby. Well, sadly, that was not to be. Luckily our vet kindly offered to take care of her on his farm. I was enormously relieved for she had played such a vital role in my life and together we had conquered many championships in the show ring. I could never have done all that without her and in return I wanted to ensure she enjoyed an honourable and secure retirement.

With Barbara's welfare taken care of all that remained was to find a buyer for Greengates. As fortune would have it, we ended up selling for a good price to the first person who came to view the cottage. That taken care of we then loaded all our furniture onto Christmas Gift Farm trucks and followed in the car with Robert and all our pets.

When we finally arrived back on Christmas Gift Farm it was to find a wonderful present from The Old Man awaiting us – eighteen acres of prime land along one of the boundaries of the farm and about two miles from my parents' homestead. I was beside myself with excitement for it meant that we were able to design and build our very own home. We knew then that it was going to have to be somewhat larger than Greengates as I was expecting our second child.

While our thatched cottage – which we were going to name Heytesbury after Peter's ancestral home in England – was in the process of being built, we lived with my family in the main house. It was here, one morning, while we were all enjoying tea on the verandah that our breezy banter was suddenly brought to a gasping halt by a bulletin on the wireless. 'A state of war exists.' It was 3 September 1939 and with that brief, portentous announcement icy tentacles of fear began to tug at that part of me where a new life pulsed, unaware of the turmoil ahead.

Chapter Five

A CALL TO ARMS

A month after Germany invaded Poland, our son Simon was born following a brief battle of his own. My waters broke early in October and on my doctor's advice I was rushed to the nursing home in Gwelo where I expected a repeat of my first uncomplicated and speedy delivery. Instead I ended up spending a fortnight in the nursing home anxiously awaiting the onset of labour. The long wait almost drove me to distraction and in desperation Peter and I would go for drives over bumpy farm roads every night hoping it would expedite matters.

No such luck. I'd be returned to the ward every night with not so much as a sign from our baby that it wished to enter the world. Eventually our doctor, who was due to go on holiday, brusquely – and literally – took the matter in hand. I was taken to the labour ward where he proceeded to use interventionist methods to try to turn Simon. When all his fiddling failed to produce the required results it was decided to induce labour.

Only then did obstetric procedures slip back into an all too familiar pattern as no sooner had the doctor departed, no doubt thinking it would take some hours, than it was back to just me and a very flustered sister on duty to deliver my child. Although Simon was born a little prematurely on 26 October 1939, it didn't take him long to recover from so brutal a début and he quickly put on the required weight. I did not fare nearly as well and it soon became evident that there was internal damage. My mother was livid when she discovered that my condition was the result of an impatient doctor wanting to hasten the delivery so he could go on his holiday.

Somehow, though, I managed to get my little family all settled into our new house and there we survived a less than festive Christmas since so many of our friends were being conscripted and sent to the war in Europe. When my health showed no signs of improving my mother offered to take me, the children and their nanny, Joey, on a short holiday to enjoy some sea air, hoping it would help revive me. I remember feeling terribly ill on the train journey to Somerset West near Cape Town, where we were to stay with some friends.

On our arrival my mother arranged for me to see a specialist in Cape Town. He soon confirmed that I had suffered serious internal damage and had me admitted to the Salvation Army's Booth Memorial Hospital in Tamboerskloof for emergency surgery. It all happened so quickly and caused my little Simon enormous distress because I was no longer able to breastfeed the poor mite. I persuaded my mother not to tell Peter of the operation as I did not want him to worry needlessly – a decision that in retrospect proved rather unwise.

After the operation I became so gravely ill that at one stage they feared I would not pull through. My mother, at my cousin Dr Paul Oates' urging, quickly cabled Peter to let him know what had happened. At the time my cousin Paul was based at the famous Groote Schuur Hospital in Cape Town, where some twenty years later Dr Christiaan Barnard and his team performed the world's first successful heart transplant operation. While Peter drove down from Rhodesia like a demon possessed I slipped in and out of consciousness, oblivious of what was happening around me. When I finally emerged from the haze it was to find a large foot propped up on my bed. It belonged to Peter, who had kept a bedside vigil from the moment he had arrived at the hospital after driving almost non-stop for days.

With Peter by my side I made a slow recovery but he had to return home to tend to our business after I was declared well enough to be discharged. I was ordered to stay behind with my family as the doctors felt I was not fit enough to endure the long trip home. They thought it best that I spend more time at the coast with my mother and sons until I had regained my strength.

For several weeks I did nothing more exerting than soak up the morning sun on the beach opposite our hotel in Somerset West and rest in my room in the afternoons. Finally, after a three-month absence from home, I was given the all-clear to make the train journey back to Gwelo.

I arrived to find much had changed in the short time I had been away. Our newsagency had been badly affected by a paper shortage due to the sinking of so many ships bearing supplies for the colonies. Then, to exacerbate an already trying situation, Peter received the dreaded cable demanding that he report for duty at the Simonstown naval base in South Africa. For a while we had been lulled into a false sense of security and clung to the hope that as Peter had his own business and a young family he may have qualified for a special dispensation. It was not to be and with hardly any time to spare all he was able to do by way of a contingency plan was to put his manageress in charge of the business. With that my young husband was gone.

Following his departure nothing seemed to go right. Firstly, Peter's beloved dog, Andrew, mysteriously disappeared, never to return. Like The Old Man I have always been a firm believer in ESP and I suspect the little dog, a cross scottie and terrier, sensed that his adoring master wouldn't be home for a while. I had read many such stories of animal ESP, the most extraordinary involving the legendary Egyptologist, Earl Carnarvon. Apparently, at the moment of the Earl's death in Cairo, his little terrier in England sat up on its haunches, gave a yelp, and fell over dead.

Nevertheless, I tried desperately not to divine Andrew's disappearance as an omen and to maintain a façade of optimism for the boys' sake. It became an almost impossible undertaking for within weeks of Peter's call-up his manageress announced that she too had joined the war effort and was being dispatched to Kenya to do a tour of duty as an ambulance driver. It left our business in such a parlous state that I had no option but to wade in myself.

There was no Peter to consult, only scores of files left piled on his desk, all containing documents concerning matters of which I had absolutely no knowledge. Suspecting that I was going to have to dedicate every waking hour of the day to saving the business, I decided to let our house and to move back in with my family. This arrangement helped ease some of the pressure and my mother and the nanny were able to look after Robert and Simon while I grappled with a commercial crisis.

I was in the Gwelo Newsagency office from 6a.m. every day until late at night, battling in the face of a shortage of supplies and rocketing paper prices. Fortunately I got invaluable support from Miss Mackay, a delightful woman who had been holidaying in Rhodesia when war broke out. She was unable to return home to Scotland as there was no transport for civilians. She took up temporary residence with my family and kindly offered to lend me a hand. She was a godsend both at work and at home, where, being a former schoolteacher, she gave Robert his first reading lessons. Even then Ki, as she became affectionately known to us, had an inkling that my Robert was destined for a stellar future. How right she was.

In spite of all our valiant attempts at maintaining a semblance of normality there was no escaping the turmoil and grievous loss inflicted by a catastrophic war. In the midst of so much global chaos we were dealt a savage blow closer to home in 1940 with the death of The Old Man, who had, over the years, been waging a private war against diabetes. His condition often caused the most awful seizures but with my mother's expert and devoted care they were able to keep it under some control. In those days insulin was in short supply and The Old Man was put on a rather strict diet, which seemed to do the trick. Although, I do remember times when he would have such terrible fits that my mother had to put a coathanger in his mouth to prevent him from biting his tongue.

As the years passed he suffered some serious setbacks and his health began to deteriorate to the point where he became a frail shadow of the crusty, taciturn man who had extended so much love and support to me as his adopted daughter. I had been a 'spoilt brat' when he bounded into my life and now, in the face of so much upheaval and uncertainty, the great Machelobe finally took his leave of a world being ravaged by war.

I was heartbroken, and his death came at a time when I so longed for his sage guidance and advice. Business had become increasingly difficult as more ships were being sunk and it was almost impossible to replace stock. Our newspaper sales had dropped dramatically, despite the recent opening of the Thornhill Air Station in the area. Then the newspaper company, which had been our main supporter from the outset, began using standover tactics and threatened to terminate the paper contract. I was at my wits' end and after a few months of tense, if not downright hostile, dealings I was more or less forced into selling to the printing company. I could find no way out because it was made abundantly clear to me that they would open in opposition to us and thereby place a stranglehold on all newspaper sales.

About three years after we had acquired the Gwelo Newsagency I signed everything away. It was my first salutary lesson in dealing with hardened businessmen. As a woman with no business experience to speak of I stood little chance of surviving such ruthless commercial combat. Nowadays it would be a very different matter. I may not have saved the business but I would have secured a much better price and certainly much better value for the stock. What made it especially difficult was having to explain by correspondence to Peter what had happened. The two advisers who had helped me in the negotiations did the same, informing him that I had done the only thing available to me. Our words would no doubt have come as cold comfort to someone who faced the prospect of returning home from the war with no job.

After Peter was called up we thought he would be primarily based in Simonstown, near Cape Town, but for six weeks I heard nothing from him. As it turned out he was almost immediately sent off on HMS *Orion* and the first I knew of this was when a message was relayed to me via the Red Cross in Johannesburg. I was able to ascertain that the ship was in the Pacific and that the crew were being transferred to HMS *Liverpool*, destination unknown.

The weeks and months seemed to drag by at an agonisingly slow pace and I lived for those frustratingly short and censored aerogrammes that would give me some comfort that Peter was well. Finally, in an attempt to preserve my sanity I set out to find something to help make our long separation bearable. As Peter was doing his bit for the war I felt it only fitting that I should do the same back home. I had heard that the RAF air station a few miles from Gwelo was recruiting women so I joined the first group of women to enlist. The day we reported for duty we were issued with khaki uniforms and a drill sergeant then promptly set about putting us through our paces on the square.

That was about the extent of my basic training as I was straightaway posted to the plotting office at the Thornhill Air Station where one of my first tasks was to draw various aircraft for the young pilots' aircraft identification lectures. I found this fascinating and perhaps very necessary not to have our aircraft shot down in error. I was given a large typewriter and my own desk in the office which I shared with Flight Sergeant Colin Campbell.

My work at the station became a wonderful but demanding diversion. We were in the office by five in the morning which presented me with some problems. Having two young children I was not required to live in barracks so it meant that I had to get up at four o'clock to allow me enough time to get ready and look spick and span in my khaki uniform. I spent a fair amount of time in the evenings ensuring that the collar of my shirt was starched and that my buttons and shoes were polished to blinding perfection. My obsessive attention to detail must have made some impression for I was often made to lecture to new recruits on their attire.

My duties at the station included typing letters and reports for the wing commander, which took some doing. Fortunately I had done a little typing when I ran the newsagency but it was not nearly good enough for the work I was now required to do. Furthermore, I was on the lowest pay scale, whereas a friend of mine earned much more purely because she was a qualified shorthand typist. Not to be outdone I signed up for evening classes, blitzed the course in record time and became the proud owner of Pitman's shorthand and typing certificates. I was also upgraded to top pay.

The mornings were the busiest time of the day in the plotting office as that was when the pilots took to the skies on their training flights. Later in the day, when things got a lot quieter, we'd head for one of the hangars and play badminton. I also took up golf with a foursome and, strangely enough, achieved a much better handicap then than I did after the war with the help of a golf pro.

It has often been said that during the war, people caroused and partied with an almost frenzied abandon, perhaps fearing there would be no tomorrow. Certainly I had enormous fun with the friends I made out at Thornhill Air Station, but even the laughter and revelry couldn't mask the heart-rending tragedies of war. We had countless farewell parties for the young pilots who were posted to distant shores after their six weeks' training at the station, and many never returned. There were also those hapless souls who never made it to the warfront, like the charming young pilot who decided to impress me with a bit of dare-devilry. He flew low over Christmas Gift Farm, tipped his wing, buzzed us and then to our horror crashed into a tree. He was killed instantly. It came as such a shock for he had had a cup of tea with me in the office that morning. He had been full of fun and anxious to have his posting.

On certain Sundays we would march in pairs to church. A friend of mine was the tallest and I was the shortest so we chose to be partners and to lead the troop. We thought this was hilarious. But the laughter, so brief and cathartic, was often no match for the tears. One of my saddest moments was when I had to break the news to my uncle that his son, my cousin Tom Oates, who was in the Fleet Air Arm, had been killed. Then, shortly before the end of the war, he received news that his other son, Jack, who was captain of his ship HMS *Alert*, had gone down with all his crew after the ship was bombed. Then there was my cousin Keith, my childhood companion, who saw his best friend shot down in North Africa. Keith suffered severe shock and was sent home on long leave. He never really recovered from that and became a very withdrawn young man after the war.

News of Peter, though, was almost impossible to come by and it caused me untold anxiety. Months turned into years and still no word as to when he would be able to come home. I got my hopes up once when, in one of his letters, Peter suggested I resign from the airforce and take on a part-time job in case he was granted leave at short notice. We had no such luck. Then I had word that Peter had been on HMS *Delhi* when it was bombed in the Mediterranean. It was frustratingly difficult to get all the information but I was able to confirm that my Peter was safe. A few men were killed in the attack but it was thought the casualty rate would have been much higher had it not been for the fact that most of the crew were up on deck when the ship was hit. Many men were injured, though, and had to be taken to the hospital in Gibraltar. Peter later told me that some of the men suffered from severe shock. He recounted a case of someone who was convinced there were crocodiles under his bunk and others who suffered awful nightmares that kept everyone awake.

When they finally got back to England Peter was sent to a hospital in Bristol where he was diagnosed as suffering from shell shock. Afterwards he swore blind that it was really a mental hospital, and that he had been treated for a nervous breakdown. Following treatment he was given sick leave and he went to stay with his mother. She in turn wrote me an alarming letter in which she expressed grave concern about his condition. He was chain-smoking, his nerves were shattered and he was having the most dreadful recurring nightmares.

But there was still no word as to when he would be allowed to come home to us. I resigned from the airforce in 1943 and took the boys to Bulawayo where I had a part-time job as secretary to a small company that ran a farming magazine, all just as Peter had requested. However, the cable that would herald his arrival and the resumption of a normal, married life was a long time in coming. My emotions were put through the wringer with all that waiting but in many respects it enabled me to prepare Robert and Simon for Peter's homecoming. They had no recollection of their father and to them he was the dapper naval officer who smiled back at them from a photograph on my dressing table. It would take some doing to get a shell-shocked husband and two little boys reacquainted and back on the family track. What I needed was for that long-awaited cable to arrive and make it happen.

Chapter Six

THE HOMECOMING

The cable I had so longed for eventually arrived on 10 June 1944. The cryptic message simply read: 'arriving Capetown Sunday 11th. My address c/o luut England HMS gnu capetown holmes'. Peter was homeward bound. I was so elated I don't think my feet touched the ground for days. Somehow, in my airborne state, I managed to get myself and the boys packed up in double-quick time and on the first available train to Cape Town.

As I was unsure how long we would be away there was no question of travelling lightly. We ended up with masses of luggage: Robert's bicycle which he insisted had to come along, lots of Simon's toys, all of Peter's civilian clothes and last, but not least, my saddle. I seem to recollect we took up almost all the carriage's luggage space.

On the journey down to Cape Town I secretly hoped that, for the children's sake, when Peter came to meet us he would be dressed in his smart naval uniform, as that was how they pictured him. I wasn't disappointed because as soon as our train steamed into the station I could see him towering over the crowd, looking distinguished but painfully thin in his smart uniform.

I was overjoyed to see him but, as he had his close friend Donald England with him, I had to resist making an unseemly fuss. Peter may have been away from home for nearly four years but in public he remained as emotionally guarded as ever. Later that night, however, in the privacy of a wonderful hotel suite and after some celebratory champagne there was no call for caution. My naval officer husband let it be known that he was well pleased to be home.

Within days we found a flat at Three Anchor Bay, a charming beachside suburb in the shadows of Table Mountain, which the boys immediately mistook for heaven on earth. Our apartment block allowed them daily access to a beach studded with large tidal rockpools and subsequently, no day was complete without Robert and Simon having spent hours wading through the pools and poking under the rocks to uncover well-camouflaged crustaceans. Looking back, I think those fifteen months we lived in Cape Town after Peter's homecoming were certainly the happiest of our married life. Peter had arranged a system whereby he worked three days solid and then had three days off. When he wasn't working he would spend all his time with me and the boys.

Often we would allow Donald, a gunnery officer at Simonstown, into our cherished fold. He was Peter's closest friend and they had been together on HMS *Delhi*. It was Donald who first alerted me to Peter's fragile condition. He told me they had shared a cabin on the ship returning to Cape Town and one morning, when Donald turned on his electric razor, Peter suffered a major anxiety attack and hid under his blanket. He thought the ship was being bombed. There was no doubt that Peter was still in a bad way since he suffered from terrible headaches and recurring nightmares. Also, whenever a plane flew overhead at night or a car backfired he would jump under the bed. His nerves were absolutely shot, but I hoped that given time and much love and attention he would gradually overcome his panic attacks.

Donald helped enormously by being there for Peter and also by giving me and the boys his unstinting support. He would often take us in his car on lovely long drives along Chapman's Peak Drive, one of the most spectacular scenic drives in southern Africa that had been carved into the rocky cliff face of Table Mountain. I always prepared a wonderful picnic and Donald unfailingly supplied the gin, which he managed to buy from the wardroom for something ridiculous like tuppence a tot. So constant and generous was Donald's supply of navy-issue gin that Robert and Simon cheekily took to calling him 'The Bottle Man'.

Both boys had started school at Lion's Crest, a small preparatory school at the foot of Lions Head Mountain and, at their father's insistence, caught the bus to and from school unchaperoned. Peter was adamant that our sons be taught to be independent from an early age. They seemed to have no problem with this until one day Simon arrived home from school on his own. Normally he would wait for Robert, who had a longer lesson, but on this day Simon soon tired of kicking his heels and decided to head home without his older brother, who happened to have both their bus fares.

Young Simon, not to be impeded by so trifling a practicality, promptly turned on all cylinders of his cherubic charm and found a kindly lady passenger who not only took pity on his plight but offered to pay his one penny bus fare. He arrived home flushed with pride at having sailed through his first lesson in independence at the precocious age of five.

As the weeks joyfully rolled by I kept looking with deep longing at my unused saddle. I was never completely happy without my riding and in Cape Town I knew no-one who had horses let alone a riding school where I could hire a good hack. I had just begun to despair of ever finding a place to ride when a friendly tailor came to my rescue. I had taken him a pair of my breeches to be repaired and we fell into conversation about riding. When I told him my horses were in Rhodesia and that I was on the lookout for a riding school or stables where I could hire a horse, he made mention of a Mrs Floyd.

There was a certain hesitancy in his voice which seemed to imply that Mrs Floyd was not an especially approachable woman. 'She is a very particular person and she can be very difficult. She either likes you or she doesn't,' he warned. But the redoubtable Mrs Floyd apparently owned excellent stables and some very good hunters. When the tailor gave me her phone number I thought it would be worth risking her ire if there was even a remote possibility of me getting a ride.

As soon as I arrived home I took a deep breath and dialled Mrs Floyd's number. The tailor had painted such an ominous portrait of her I imagined her to be quite a battle-axe. Her voice did little to allay my nervousness. 'Who are you?' she all but barked down the line. I quickly launched into my prepared patter, telling her about Peter's return from the war and that we were temporarily stationed in Cape Town, a long way from our beloved horses.

She asked a few terse questions and then subsided into an interminable and frigid silence. I expected her to hang up but to my utmost surprise she gruffly extended an invitation to come riding the following Sunday.

The woman we subsequently met as arranged on the platform at Kenilworth Station matched the stern, clipped voice. Tall and grey-haired, she strode into view like someone clearly accustomed to leading rather than following. Face-to-face, Mrs Floyd spoke in a sort of cursory shorthand as if expending breath on formalities was deemed too wasteful a pursuit.

'So here you are . . . How do you do . . . Come along . . . Had a bit of bother parking the car,' came the staccato phrases by way of a hurried introduction as she marshalled us along to her car. All my reservations evaporated, though, the minute we drove up to her delightful thatched house overlooking the stables. I could smell the horses and somehow my eagerness instantly ignited a common bond between us. Here was a kindred spirit, a woman seemingly more comfortable tending her horses than exchanging pleasantries with strangers. And when she saw just how excited we all were at the prospect of riding, she suddenly revealed a charm and a warmth that was starkly at odds with the irascible woman we had initially encountered at the station.

From that day on Mrs Floyd embraced my family like long-lost relatives and her domain became our home from home. Even on that very first day she paid me the ultimate compliment by allowing me to ride her favourite hack, Stella. She was a superb ride and a fast jumper, so like my Barbara, and we instantly developed a rapport. Peter rode Mrs Floyd's hunter and Robert was put on a small pony called Tony. In fact, it was on Tony that Mrs Floyd gave Robert, then barely seven years old, his first jumping lesson. Even then she predicted he had the makings of an exceptionally good rider. We spent almost all our Sundays at Mrs Floyd's and I think having us there became the highlight of her week. She adored Robert, who soon proved himself an extraordinary rider for someone so young.

One Sunday Peter decided to test Robert's independence by allowing him to find his own way to Mrs Floyd's. Getting to her place, which was some distance from our flat in Three Anchor Bay, involved catching a bus to Cape Town Station and from there a train to the nearest suburb. Mrs Floyd had agreed to collect him at Kenilworth Station, as she usually did for us. I was terribly apprehensive for he was so young but Peter couldn't bear the thought of our sons being mollycoddled. When Robert finally rang to inform us that he had arrived without mishap and dead on time I was quite weak with relief. I think even Mrs Floyd, the tough and unsentimental woman that she was, was enormously impressed by our intrepid son's navigational skills. So was I.

It became a sort of ritual for us to have lunch with Mrs Floyd after our long Sunday rides in the countryside. Simon, who normally had only a short ride in the paddock, much preferred to play with her bantams in the stable yard. No-one dared tell him that the lunch we all so enjoyed normally consisted of one of his beloved bantams. Simon's favourite horse at Mrs Floyd's was George Robey, a dear old toothless gelding that was completely white but had very large, soulful brown eyes like his namesake. Mrs Floyd's late husband, a dentist, had extracted all George's teeth after they had become infected and he survived on a diet of bran mashes, soft foods and grated carrots. Despite such privations he remained a sweet-natured horse and was much adored by many children, who were given their first riding lessons on him.

I became extremely fond of Stella, so much so that Mrs Floyd made the most magnanimous gesture. After an exhilarating ride on Stella she said, 'When the war ends and you have settled somewhere I hope you will be able to take Stella. She suits you and I wouldn't want anyone else to own her.'

I was so moved because I knew how much Stella, her most prized jumper, meant to her and yet she was willing to part with her. Obviously I was flattered but at that stage our future was so uncertain. I had no idea of where we were headed or what lay in store but, strangely, I always remembered Mrs Floyd's kind offer. Several years later I did indeed take possession of the brave-hearted Stella, but at that time my life was nowhere near as blissful as the one I experienced with my family that year in Cape Town.

The war had delivered to me a husband in the most fragile of mental states and a terrifyingly uncertain future. Our business had not survived the chaos wreaked by those distant battles and The Old Man was no longer there to dispense his wise counsel. Nevertheless, those months following Peter's return will always be remembered as the most blissful period of our married life. Cape

Town, with its serene and soul-subduing mountain, old Cape Dutch architecture and historic vineyards provided a glorious backdrop to those halcyon days. Locals had tetchily dubbed it the windy city, as whenever a ferocious south-easter – commonly referred to as the Cape Doctor – would shroud its sandstone monarch in cloud it would hold the peninsula hostage for weeks on end. Notwithstanding the times we were often compelled to cling to lampposts for dear life during those furious storms, we were in no hurry to depart the Cape's entrancing caress.

Indeed, we began to regard our little bolthole at Three Anchor Bay as home. The boys, however, thought no place could possibly be a home when it had no pets. Keeping a cat or a dog in the place was out of the question but to appease Robert and Simon we answered an advertisement for a tame budgerigar that was said to be in need of a home. Unfortunately, by the time we rang it had already found new lodgings. The owner, sensing my disappointment, quickly sweet-talked me into buying one of his young budgerigars and assured me the boys would have great fun teaching it to talk.

Enter Michael, a small green budgie who was delivered to us in a little brown paper bag. Initially I was opposed to having a caged bird but Michael soon proved to be no ordinary feathered friend. He was a real character and gave the boys endless delight. I loved having Michael around, especially while fussing about in the kitchen. I still rated as a near-hopeless cook and after several years of marriage had not conquered my aversion to slaving over hot stoves. So Michael was always a welcome diversion when I was preparing a meal. He was incurably inquisitive and rather fancied himself as my kitchen assistant. Unfortunately he once proved more of a hindrance than a help when he flew straight into a saucepan of stewed plums and emerged a sticky, horrible mess.

He made for quite an amusing addition to our family and under

Robert and Simon's tutelage speedily learned several words. They used to perch him on the lip of a large vase and talk into it, the booming sound attracting his attention. Within no time he began reciting words but always lost the plot with 'Peter Piper picked a peck' and in utter frustration would end up shrieking 'Oh! Bloodeee'.

Those days in Cape Town were a tranquil interlude and a godsend, for Peter's health improved immeasurably. When he was granted his first leave since his return from the war we decided to take a short holiday together, our second break in eight years of marriage if you include the weekend honeymoon. We arranged for the boys to stay in a small exclusive boarding school and spent the first night of our holiday at the famed Mount Nelson Hotel, an icon in Cape Town with its suffused pink façade, exquisite gardens and august colonial heritage.

As luck would have it our stay there that night on 13 May 1945 coincided with news of VE Day. Suddenly the privation of six years of war was forgotten in a frenzied burst of celebration one never expected to see staged in the sedate surrounds of the Mount Nelson. Patrons sang, hugged, cried and danced with robust abandon way into the night. All the bars were closed but Peter and I had packed a bottle of gin – from Donald's cache of provisions – and continued the celebrations in our room.

Early next day, feeling just a little jaded, we set off on our long train journey to the Wild Coast on the eastern coast of South Africa. The trip took us along the awesomely beautiful Hex River Pass which was often captured on canvas by the country's most celebrated artist, Tinus de Jongh. Years later we were able to buy three of his much sought-after paintings as a reminder of that spectacular journey. When we arrived at Butterworth, now a bustling little town in the Transkei, we were met and driven to an inn on what was then a very remote part of the Wild Coast. The small and very basic establishment was run by a former colonel who had retired from the armed services shortly after the First World War.

There was nothing but miles of pristine coastline, a river and gentle undulating hills. It was a place where one came to do nothing more strenuous or taxing than communing with nature. We loved it, especially Peter who was sorely tempted to set up a little pub of his own beside the sea. He became quite animated whenever we discussed the idea and thought it would be an ideal spot for me to run a small riding school for holiday guests and to act as their guide on rides along the beach.

Now that the war was ending we had some decisions to make about our immediate future which already presented us with a number of unforeseen problems. The most pressing concerned Peter's residency, because he had left South Africa before the war and had not been in Rhodesia long enough for him to become a permanent resident there. An alternative was to settle in England but at the time we weren't overly keen on the idea.

The matter was unexpectedly decided for us shortly after our holiday when Peter was instructed to return to Rhodesia to be demobbed. Not that it did much to dispel our feelings of uncertainty for we had nothing but my family to go back to. The Gwelo Newsagency was no more and while we were stationed in Cape Town we had sold our house in Rhodesia.

There was also the added complication of the boys' schooling. We had always vowed that our children would be given the best education we could afford, but that in itself posed a problem because there weren't too many good schools in Rhodesia. Most children were sent to boarding school in South Africa, then thought to have a superior education system. Unfortunately we had left it far too late to enrol our sons, something most parents did almost immediately after their children were born. However, one of Peter's naval friends, a man named Davey, made mention of the fact that he was well acquainted with the headmaster of Cordwalles, the preparatory for Michaelhouse School, widely regarded as the Eton of Southern Africa. Michaelhouse had long prided itself on having nurtured some of the best brains in the country and it was the alma mater of many leading politicians and business grandees.

We decided Robert and Simon deserved nothing but the best and thanks to Davey putting in a good word on our behalf they were enrolled at Cordwalles the following year. We would never come to regret having done so, even though it meant not seeing our boys for much of the year as Cordwalles was in Pietermaritzburg, Natal Province – a fair distance from the grass plains of Rhodesia. Peter was enthusiastic about them receiving such exclusive schooling as he believed it would instil in both boys the sort of leadership skills that would prove enormously beneficial to them in later years.

With the boys' education taken care of we once again packed up all our belongings and on 15 September 1945, just fifteen months since Peter's homecoming, we took a sad and tearful leave of Cape Town. I was quite heartbroken for I had grown to love the Cape, a place the explorer Sir Francis Drake was once moved to describe as 'the Fairest Cape in the whole circumference of the earth'. As the immutable silhouette of Table Mountain gradually faded from view I was suddenly overcome with sadness. Over the years I had become accustomed to painful farewells but watching Cape Town slip from sight unleashed an unfamiliar tide of emotion.

I was not to know that in the retreating shadows of that sublime mountain I was leaving behind the most contented phase of my married life. And as our train steamed inexorably into the hinterland it brought me ever closer to a spiritual darkness that would hold me captive for a long time.

Chapter Seven

CLEAR ROUNDS AND SPILLS

Peter's combat with his demons intensified soon after we arrived in what was then a cauldron of unremitting gloom. There were no jobs to be had in postwar Rhodesia and Peter, like so many men who had returned home from the battlefields, found himself cast adrift. Although he wouldn't admit as much, I knew it came as a crushing blow. He had wanted to regain some control of his life and to recover all we had lost during the war.

Initially we stayed with my family at Christmas Gift Farm which was wonderful because my mother was overjoyed at being reunited with her young grandsons. But later we were compelled to move to Salisbury because that was where Peter was to be demobbed. And it was here, as a civilian, that my husband began to walk the streets in search of work. For three weeks he was subjected to a host of job interviews. It felt more like three years. We both became so despondent and had all but given up hope when he landed a job as a travelling salesman for a firm that imported hotel ware and hospital equipment. In many respects Peter was totally unsuited to the job. He was still having problems with his health but there was no alternative. He needed the job and seemed determined to give it a go.

Friends of ours had kindly lent us their flat in Salisbury which was located opposite the racecourse in Rotten Row. Given our straitened circumstances at the time we thought the name of the street rather apt. Nonetheless, we felt confident that with time our situation would improve. So once Peter was furnished with a Ford van, a bundle of catalogues and some samples he headed north of the country with every intention of passing muster as a salesman.

I can still see Peter in my mind's eye the day he set off. He was clearly anxious and unsure of himself and my heart went out to him. I tried to encourage him as best I could but I knew that he felt like a fish out of water and that he was reluctant to leave home.

He covered a fair amount of the country on that first trip and would ring me every night for words of encouragement. I was deeply concerned for him but as it turned out Peter did exceptionally well and took several good orders from hotels that had run out of stock during the war years. He returned in such good cheer and sported an even wider grin when he received his first pay cheque and commission. But no sooner was he established in his job than we were faced with yet another unsettling situation – our firstborn's move to boarding school. It's something no parent relishes and taking Robert to Pietermaritzburg was certainly one of the most heart-rending things I have ever had to do.

The two of us travelled by train from Salisbury and found ourselves surrounded by mothers and a horde of excitable children who were being returned to boarding school in South Africa. I had never encountered anything quite so rowdy but I found it rather encouraging as they all seemed quite happy to be going back to school. We were met at the Pietermaritzburg Station by friends I had known in Rhodesia and after lunch we took Robert to Cordwalles. I was determined to make it as painless as possible for my young son and to ensure he settled in quickly. The last thing he needed was to see his mother getting emotional and tearful. I had a bundle of his favourite comics and a bag of sweets which I thrust into his hands before I kissed him goodbye. With that I hurried away so that my son would not see my distress. I left on the train that night so as not to delay the agony. I derived some comfort from the fact that my friends had promised they'd take Robert out on Outing Sundays.

For a year Simon attended a small kindergarten school in Salisbury and then he, too, joined his brother at Cordwalles. Surprisingly, both boys settled into boarding school without too many problems and did very well in their studies as well as in a host of extracurricular activities. They were also quite popular among the other boarders and would often bring friends home for the holidays. There were two long holidays during the year, but both the Easter and Michaelmas holidays were only ten days and usually the boys elected to spend them with their friends.

I remember one Easter, Simon was invited by the son of the bishop to spend the holidays with his family on the Natal coast. I was told by the housemaster that he had warned the bishop that Simon often swore like a stablehand and had been caught smoking on the playing field. This did not seem to bother the bishop for the invitation was not withdrawn and Simon ended up having a wonderful holiday with the family. Moreover, we were complimented on our son's impeccable manners.

The only drawback to having the children at a school so far away was that Peter and I were unable to attend all their school functions. One year, though, we managed to make it to their sports day and then took both boys for a short holiday at Salt Rock, a lovely resort on the coast north of Durban. As fate would have it, that was the one and only holiday we were to spend together as a family. Shortly after our return to Rhodesia we came to realise that Peter's earnings fell way short of being able to support us as well as pay for the boys' education. To try and relieve some of the pressure on Peter I took a job as a secretary.

I had hoped it would be similar to the work I had done at

Thornhill during the war but I was in for a nasty surprise. The job turned out to be such an utter disaster that I soon grew to loathe it. The man who ran the office was so insufferably rude and demanding that it didn't take me long to tender my resignation. It was Peter who inadvertently stumbled on something that held a lot more appeal than working for an objectionable boss. It was a small advertisement in the daily paper which read 'An instructor required to coach a young boy to ride and attain show standard. Apply for appointment.' I wasted no time in calling the number supplied. The woman who answered sounded delightful and we arranged to meet for morning tea at the Meikles Hotel the following day.

We hit it off instantly. She told me she had three sons and that the eldest was the one who was keenest to learn to ride. They were a close-knit Jewish family and both parents felt their children should be given every opportunity to pursue numerous interests. The children had already learned to play the violin and the piano and now they not only wanted their eldest to learn to ride but to reach show standard.

With my experiences at the Rand Easter Show I knew nothing was impossible but a major problem presented itself almost before I had drained my teacup. When I asked her where they kept their pony, I was met with a blank look. It appeared I was to teach a complete beginner, get him into the show ring and all without a horse. Now even to an optimist that seemed way beyond the reach of a miracle.

But I was determined not to be thwarted in my newfound venture. I had a friend who kept his horse at the racecourse opposite our flat. I was aware that he seldom had the time to ride and that the horse was mostly exercised by an African groom. When I approached my friend and asked him if I could use the horse for my weekly lessons he was more than delighted to oblige because it meant his horse would be assured a good deal more exercise. So with a borrowed horse called Punch and a young, earnest boy named Warwick I began to earn my keep as a riding instructor.

As Warwick had not been on a horse before I began by leading him around on Punch. That in itself should have been a simple enough exercise except that the horse suddenly took me by surprise and kicked me with great force on the behind. The pain was agonising and because the horse was shod it caused such terrible muscle damage that I have an unflattering imprint of that horseshoe on my rump to this day. I remember having to fight back the tears because I was not going to give my one and only pupil the satisfaction of seeing an adult woman, and an accomplished rider no less, reduced to tears. Notwithstanding that initial mishap it did not take me too long to get Warwick keen on riding. So keen, in fact, that he began campaigning for a horse of his own. But it was no ordinary horse the young man wanted, it had to be a dun-coloured pony.

Now where was I to find a pony of that colour? I could have found him a pony of any other colour but, no, master Warwick was quite specific. Well, by some fluke I managed to find him the pony he wanted, which was then named Titian. It was on Titian that Warwick finally made it to the show ring and won a clutch of prizes.

Following my star pupil's success my classes began to expand rapidly. Not only was I teaching Warwick's two younger brothers but somehow I had acquired eight other pupils – and all of them were being taught to ride on the long-suffering Punch. My generous, thoughtful mother eventually came to the rescue and bought me a lovely horse for my birthday.

Jonathan had originally belonged to the padre in Gwelo who had treated the horse more like a child. Apparently, when the padre went on his rounds Jonathan would nimbly follow him up the steps to the various front porches where he would then obediently await his master's return. They were very devoted to each other. When the padre was posted away my mother promised to find Jonathan a new and happy home.

And so it was that with Jonathan, Punch and a clutch of eager schoolchildren my fledgling business began to thrive. So much so that some of my pupils' parents urged me to establish a proper riding school. So, too, did the owner of Punch, who happened to have several acres of land a few miles out of Salisbury where he offered to build me a couple of temporary stables. These were erected almost overnight and consisted of nothing more elaborate than some poles and whitewashed hessian. But they did the trick while I concentrated on getting my new riding school up and running.

Luckily, it was then that Beryl Hallam Elton stepped into the frame. She had known Peter in England but had since married and settled near Umtali, many miles from Salisbury. I gathered her private life was somewhat complicated and that she wanted to move to Salisbury, where she hoped to give me a hand at the school. I was thrilled because not only was Beryl a qualified instructor, she also offered to bring six of her horses with her. In fact, soon after her arrival we became partners, named our business Elton Court Riding School and promptly set about making it one of the most popular riding schools in Salisbury. And it didn't take us long. Our pupils quadrupled within weeks and at weekends the young and the not so young would head our way to spend a day riding in the countryside.

We worked very hard but we loved every minute of it. As

instructors we also complemented each other since Beryl preferred to work with the fearless riders, the ones who seemed intent on pushing their luck, whereas I liked teaching the younger kids and the more nervous riders.

Beryl was not only a superb rider but a marvellously outgoing woman who, it must be said, had a rather unusual marital arrangement. While her husband was based on their farm up north she lived with her lover in Salisbury. It was an open secret and no-one seemed to have the slightest problem with it. She became one of my closest friends and with her around there was always cause for much laughter. However, Beryl often suffered from excruciating headaches that were attributed to a neck injury she sustained after a nasty spill from a horse. I remember once at the Bulawayo Show she came down with one of her dreadful headaches shortly before we were to ride in the matched hack class.

The event called for perfect synchronised riding and we were usually rather good at it. We had two horses that were very much alike and we wore identical black riding jackets, bowler hats and stocks. But on that particular day Beryl's headache was so severe she had to wear a pair of sunglasses. It meant I had to do the same. I thought we would never get through it judging by Beryl's condition, but somehow I managed to guide her along. Before we took off I quietly told her, 'Beryl, we're turning left here and then we're breaking into a canter. Ready!' And with that we were off. I don't know how we did it but we won. We couldn't believe it and afterwards fell into fits of laughter. And it was then that Beryl admitted she had done it all with her eyes shut, her headache had been so bad!

Meanwhile our school went from strength to strength – so much so that our financial affairs were nowhere near as dismal as they had been when Peter was the sole income earner. We were able to buy about thirty acres of land outside Salisbury and began building a replica of Heytesbury, the house we had on Christmas Gift Farm just before the war, with a thatched roof, open beams and a large fireplace. Beryl bought land opposite us where her husband supervised the building of a cottage and thirty stables.

He fenced off an acre for what was to be our new arena and permanent riding school. We had rapidly outgrown the temporary premises and felt that we had established a large enough client base to warrant an upgrading of our business. We had so many pupils and contracts with all the schools in Salisbury that it became necessary to buy a little twelve-seater van, which came in extremely handy. We ferried the kids to and from their riding lessons and to the various shows and pony club events around the country.

While our riding school continued to prosper, Peter was not faring nearly as well in his work. He returned from one of his trips feeling very depressed and complained that a lot of his teeth were loose. We didn't know then what ailed him and he ended up having most of his teeth removed. When his condition showed no signs of improving I urged him to go for a thorough medical checkup. After several tests his doctor diagnosed diabetes. I was shown how to administer his insulin injections, of which he had to have two a day. He was also put on a strict diet and instructed to take regular exercise. Looking back I think Peter had been suffering from diabetes for a long time and I suspect the stress and terror he endured during the war years had not helped matters.

Yet even under medication Peter's moods remained erratic. He had some very bad days and became quite irritable. They were the days I felt he had become a stranger to me. He was not the sweet, gentle Peter that I loved. Needless to say, we went through some difficult times. But I was hopeful things would change once we had moved into our new home. Also, Peter had resigned from his travelling job and had volunteered to do the books and to assist us in running the riding school. It made for a very convenient arrangement because Peter would then be able to supervise the school while Beryl and I went off to compete in the shows.

No sooner had we sorted out Peter's problems, however, than we experienced a terrible disaster at the school. We had been on the new premises about eighteen months when our stables caught fire. Apparently some little African piccanins had been playing with fire near one of the thatched stables and the whole lot went up in flames. It couldn't have happened at a worse time as the horses had just been brought in from the paddocks in preparation for the afternoon classes. Fortunately Beryl and the grooms were able to release most of them. There was a little grey mare, though, who was so petrified she refused to budge until one of the grooms braved the flames and pulled her out from a burning stable. Unfortunately she had been blinded and was so badly burnt that we had to have her put down.

While Beryl and all our employees were battling the flames I had gone to collect some of our pupils from a school ten miles away. When we were approaching the stables in the little van we saw the flames leaping up ahead. It was the most horrifying sight. The boys missed their lessons that day but they helped us clear some of the debris and spent much of the afternoon trying to calm the horses. All that survived the inferno were the tack room and the leisure area. It was a massive setback considering we had had such a charmed run up until then.

For a while we made do as best we could and managed to continue with the riding lessons. We had worked out a routine whereby the pupils had to go to the paddocks, catch their horses, groom them and saddle up. It was, we insisted, all part of learning to work with horses. There were many variations on this, all kinds of little exercises to help make it as interesting as possible for the kids while we decided what to do about rebuilding the school.

Finally it was thought best to construct a new set of stables on our land, only this time we were determined to do it properly. There were to be permanent brick stables, a feed shed, a hay shed and a pleasant entertainment area. Thankfully Peter offered to supervise all the building work while we continued instructing our pupils.

Then another setback. My dear friend and partner Beryl became seriously ill. Her chronic headaches had become so severe that she found it impossible to continue teaching. For a while she tried to soldier on but we knew she was fighting a losing battle. We felt the best solution would be for us to buy out Beryl's share of the business and then to find an assistant to help me run the school. It was not an easy decision to make and I feared things would never be quite the same again without Beryl's unwavering support. She had always called me Pard (for Partner) and when that partnership was officially dissolved she gave me a book as a present.

Sadly, Beryl returned to her farm near Umtali shortly before we made the move to our new and much more upmarket riding school. There was a jumping arena, an enclosed school, a free jumping lane and a number of other facilities designed to make the school more efficient. We had come such a long way from the few hessian whitewashed stables and now she wasn't there to enjoy the rewards of our labours.

For a while the school became quite a family affair with Robert and Simon doing their bit to help during the school holidays. Robert, as Mrs Floyd had once predicted, had developed into a very good and confident rider and when he was about twelve years old we competed in the pair jumping event at country shows. He had a splendid horse named Mr Jeremy Stickles which he jumped when he was home for the holidays and Simon had a piebald pony called Ukelele. One of my pupils, Rosemary, also had a piebald pony, Banjo, and she and Simon often rode together. Simon was a good rider but not nearly as competitive as Robert, who kept up his riding all his life and was later instrumental in forming the riding club at Michaelhouse School.

Following Beryl's departure I employed another qualified instructor and continued to expand the riding school, which had been renamed Rydal Court. I introduced a special ride for adults on Saturdays which took us to neighbouring farms and usually included a swim and a picnic. Not long before this I met Diana Rowe.

Diana had lost her nerve as a rider and had come to me for special instruction. She had a very beautiful horse but I soon discovered that it was entirely unsuited to so nervous a rider. Instead, I began taking her on a leading rein until she gradually began to regain her confidence. She became quite passionate about riding and on my advice sold her horse for another much older and quieter mare, Veuve Cliquot. Diana was determined to improve to the point of being able to compete in dressage events and began to work very hard.

Before long Diana became a much loved fixture at the school but it was more than her love of riding that repeatedly lured her there. Diana was what one would call the quintessential golf widow. Her solicitor husband spent almost every day on the green and when he was home he would take to practising his putting on the drawing room carpet for hours on end. Riding became her consolation and salvation. She literally threw herself into it and became such an accomplished rider she not only excelled in dressage competitions but began assisting me at the school.

We subsequently became very close friends. Indeed, it was

Diana who saw me through one of the bleakest periods of my life. When I look back I don't know how I would have managed had it not been for Diana's steely support. She first came to my rescue when my mother, who had been battling cancer, fell gravely ill. Diana offered to take charge of the school while I rushed to my mother's bedside. Within days of my arrival my mother died and on a cold June day in 1949 we buried her ashes near those of The Old Man, among the shrubs and trees she had painstakingly planted in the small cemetery on Christmas Gift Farm.

Her death left a terrible void in my life. All those wonderful, joyous years on the farm had suddenly come to a premature end. The lovely homestead, always resonating with laughter and music, would never be quite as inviting as it had been on the day I first skipped across its threshold. Life then seemed so blissfully uncomplicated and carefree. There was The Old Man, who had extended such love and care to both my mother and myself, the farm that pulsed with the magic of Africa and a future so ripe with promise.

I was not to know that with the passage of time would come so much pain that it seemed to make a mockery of all the dewy-eyed optimism I had possessed as a young girl growing up on Christmas Gift Farm. Ever since the war I had been accursed with loss. The loss of friends and relatives in battle, the loss of financial security and then the loss of my beloved parents. I had also lost a healthy and self-assured husband to that wretched war. The man who returned to me never quite recovered from it.

For all the sadness that seemed to dog me I fixed on the one and only thing that provided me with unending joy: my riding. The school gave me much more than a financial focus. It was the only constant in my life and I was hellbent on making it among the best riding schools in the country. Riding had become enormously popular in Rhodesia and two more schools had opened in direct competition with me. It meant I had to work even harder if I were to outshine my competitors. I decided that I would further my qualifications.

After making exhaustive inquiries I was told that the Cotswold School of Equitation in Kingham, Gloucestershire in England, not only offered the best course but was considered one of the finest equitation centres in the world. Although I desperately wanted to learn all there was to know about cross-country events and dressage I felt anxious about travelling abroad and leaving my family and business in the care of others. Peter could not have been more supportive or encouraging. He promised to hold the fort while I was gone and both Diana and the instructor I had employed to help run the school assured me they could cope with the workload. But deep down I had this sense of foreboding. I put it down to having to travel so far and alone and I kept reassuring myself that I would be home before long and armed with all the knowledge required to help me make my riding school prosper.

While I was away, Peter wrote to me almost every day, telling me how much he missed me and that the house was like a morgue. The boys had returned to school the day after I left and Peter seemed quite proud of the fact that he made them pack for themselves. Robert had packed his case about half-an-hour before leaving for the airport and consequently his jersey and various items had to follow by post. Simon, on the other hand, had everything in order. It seemed all was running smoothly at home and there was no cause for concern. I stopped fretting and threw myself into the course. I particularly enjoyed riding one of the instructor's horses over some practice jumps he had built in a field before competing at the famous Badminton Horse Trials in England. Some of them were such formidable jumps I think my eyes were shut and I left it all to the experienced horse.

On completion of the course I returned home brimming with all sorts of new ideas for the school. I talked of little else. Peter, though, seemed preoccupied and more withdrawn than usual. I tried not to get overly concerned and continued making great plans, one of which was to start running residential courses at the school. It was decided that we would use the wing of the house that Robert and Simon had during the holidays as a temporary dormitory until the building of a permanent one was completed. The courses proved extraordinarily successful. Within a week my students not only received intensive instruction but took an active part in the running of the stables. In the evenings there would be a film or a discussion and during one course we had great fun by going out for a moonlight ride.

It was amid all this excitement that one of my neighbours let slip that a few days before my return Peter had been to see a woman living nearby. At the time I read nothing into it, thinking that Bunny had been kind enough to invite Peter over to her place to make sure he wasn't too lonely. Bunny, together with another woman, rented a neighbouring farm house where they were known to throw some wild parties that became the talk of the bush. Sometimes we would be invited for the evening but I never quite enjoyed the parties. To put it politely, she was a divorcee, blonde, flirtatious and very attractive. She also thought nothing of disclosing some very intimate details of her love life to all and sundry. Having said that, though, men found her extremely attractive and very amusing. She also possessed a certain talent I lacked: she was a damn good cook. It was the offer of one of her cordon bleu meals that lured my Peter to her lair.

But I was far too busy with running the school to even suspect that Peter had been indiscreet. Instead, I charged ahead with blinkered determination to put into place the rest of my ambitious plans. I wanted to upgrade our horses and thought of Mrs Floyd's remark so many years ago in Cape Town. Stella, her wonderful jumper, would make for a superb asset to our school. When I telephoned her she was not only delighted to hear from me but repeated her kind offer to let me have Stella. She also informed me that she had another horse that would make an ideal dressage horse.

It was simply too good an opportunity to let pass and it was arranged that Diana and I and two grooms would drive down to Cape Town to take delivery of Stella and her companion. Peter, meanwhile, seemed curiously animated about the whole exercise and kept reiterating what a good idea it was and that there was no need to hurry back.

The trip down to Cape Town was long but far from tedious. Diana and I spent the journey discussing future plans for the school. Maybe it had become an obsession but we both loved our work and our horses. We spent a day with Mrs Floyd who, we discovered, at such short notice had miraculously been able to organise the horses' transportation by train. The grooms accompanied the horses all the way back to Rhodesia to ensure they made the trip without mishap since we were anxious to have them ready for the forthcoming Salisbury show.

When Diana and I returned home I could no longer avoid the signs. I knew straightaway that something was seriously amiss and decided to confront Peter. I made no bones about it. I asked him straight out if he was having an affair with Bunny. But he simply wouldn't talk about it. To me it seemed as if he had lowered a portcullis on his emotions. No doubt he had a hell of a guilty conscience for I had trusted Peter all our married life. But by going to Cape Town I had inadvertently played into both their hands.

I felt so utterly helpless and really feared for the survival of my marriage but how could I even begin to work things out with someone who wouldn't allow me emotional access? In fact, Peter was so bloody-minded about it all and sometimes turned very nasty when I tried to talk to him. To complicate matters further I had to prepare for the Salisbury show. Stella, I knew, would be ready after a little work but I soon realised the other horse required much more preparation if I were to enter him for dressage tests. Instead, I decided to show him in the Ladies Hack class.

We were all so busy that I hardly saw Peter at all. He was left in charge of bringing the hay and feed to the stables for the duration of the four-day show. The evenings, though, were horrendous. I would get home absolutely dead beat and then have to sit through dinner in utter, stony silence with Peter refusing to enter into a conversation with me. Somehow I managed to muddle through those exhausting days even though Peter remained emotionally out of reach. I clung to the hope that once the pressure of the show had passed we would be able to sort everything out and save our marriage.

But it was not to be. It was fairly late on the last night of the show that everything I had worked for so long and hard all but came crashing down around me. I was driving home and basking in our school's stunning success, when suddenly my headlights picked out Peter's van lying on its side in a ditch. With my heart in my throat I began scrambling about the wreck looking for Peter. All I found was the tack and various other items but no sign of my husband. He was waiting for me at home, whisky glass in hand and sporting some cuts and a barely contained rage. I couldn't get much sense out of him. I soon gathered that he'd knocked back a few whiskies which, combined with the shock, would undoubtedly have played havoc with his health.

I was even more confused and hurt when he said he didn't want dinner and would be going to bed – in the spare bedroom. And then, with a cold indifference he confirmed there was someone else and that while I had been studying abroad they had decided to go away together but thought it best to wait until after the show. Then, having dropped the bombshell, down came the shutters again. There was, he insisted, no point in talking about it.

I became so distressed and concerned that I called our doctor, who also happened to be a close friend, for urgent advice. He did not seem to take it at all seriously, consoling me with the words, 'Peter is at the dangerous age of forty. He'll have his fling and then come to his senses. I know he's a caring husband and father. Diabetics can be difficult customers but just hold on . . . and God bless.' His words failed to inspire hope. I knew instinctively that I was about to lose the love of my life. It was much more serious than a middle-aged man's momentary lapse of reason. Peter was clearly determined to pursue his affair with that woman.

Sleep eluded me that night, the longest night of my life. I kept trying to figure out ways of making my husband see sense. Desperate for support I called Diana who reassured me she would rush over at first light.

My neighbours beat her to it. I had always looked upon them as close friends of ours but it appears I had been duped. They came, they said, to take Peter with them to help him to recuperate. When I said that I was perfectly capable of nursing him myself they brusquely brushed me aside, took Peter by his arms, and helped escort him out of my life.

If it had not been for Diana I would have gone down in a heap. She chivvied me along and somehow, miraculously, we continued running our classes at the school as if nothing had happened. It was an extremely trying day but the staff were marvellous. No doubt they knew far more than they would let on and must have known for a while that something was awry.

That evening I took Peter some flowers but he refused to meet me. I was dumbfounded – that sixteen years of marriage should come to such a brutal end and without so much as a civil word by way of parting. The next day he sent the neighbours to collect his clothes and some books. After that there was no question of meeting to discuss how best to break the news to the boys.

My stepbrother, Roualeyn, soon got wind of what had happened and took it upon himself to confront Peter. Although his intervention was no doubt well intentioned it made matters far worse. He became really angry with Peter and demanded to know whether he was intending to abrogate his responsibilities or to pay some form of maintenance. Again, there was not so much as a flicker of emotion from Peter, let alone some reassurance that he would be there for the boys. Roualeyn was so incensed by Peter's cold indifference that he instructed me to pocket my pride and to immediately file for divorce. Even after having endured so much anguish I wouldn't hear of it. I held fast to the hope, no matter how absurd it seemed then, that Peter would come home. I was convinced that his mind had been poisoned by this woman because the letters he wrote me in the weeks I had been in England were filled with such love and tenderness. But on my return I was met by a hostile, ill-tempered stranger who seemed to delight in shutting me out.

Everything he did seemed so grotesquely out of character. After he walked out he refused to see me but deigned to send word demanding the full set of crested cutlery that we had been given as a wedding present. Fortunately I had the good sense to lock it away, together with a lot of other valuables, for they subsequently stole into the house while I was out teaching with every intention of helping themselves to all sorts of things. What he did help himself to was our joint bank account. He cleaned it out.

With that and no fare-thee-well Peter high-tailed it to Bulawayo with the new woman in his life. There, within a matter of weeks, they began passing themselves off as Mr and Mrs Holmes à Court. When Roualeyn passed on this information it was like a dagger in my heart, yet I still couldn't come to terms with it all. Deep down I believed that, given time and patience, Peter's sense of duty would prevail, even if it was just for the boys' sake.

At that stage they were unaware of their father's flight. In fact, shortly before the domestic tempest upended my world I had promised the boys I would treat them to a holiday. And I was determined to keep my word, even if a plundered bank account ruled out anything too extravagant. We stayed with my friend Peggy Whittaker and her family on their farm near Balgowan, a small town within easy distance of the boys' respective schools. It was there, sitting on her verandah, that I broke the news to Robert and Simon.

Simon never said a word. Not one. Robert, although stunned, said somewhat plaintively, 'Mum, don't divorce him. He'll come back.' After that the three of us made a concerted effort not to let what had happened put a damper on our holiday and for much of their Michaelmas break we stayed at Ramsgate, a small seaside town on the Natal south coast. But it was clear that both boys were deeply affected by Peter's desertion. Simon was strangely silent for much of the time and Robert just talked and talked about anything and everything that had absolutely nothing to do with the crisis we faced. We would go for endless walks along the beach and he would make fabulous and quite fanciful plans for our future.

Curiously, it was spending that short holiday with my sons that strengthened my resolve not to wallow in self-pity. I owed it to them to put a brave face on things and to ensure that our lives proceeded in as normal a fashion as possible. I had long been the sole income earner but I made a silent pact with myself that no matter how tough it was going to be, my sons would never be denied anything because of what Peter had done to us. It was down to me to chart my family's future. And I was determined not to fail them.

When I took the boys back to school I met both their headmasters and explained the situation. I also stressed that I would continue to pay for the boys' tuition and I would appreciate them keeping a watchful eye on them. I was certain that the boys hadn't quite come to terms with what had happened, especially young Simon. He was still at Cordwalles prep school whereas Robert, at fifteen, had already started at Michaelhouse. I think had they been together at the time I would have felt a lot more confident about leaving them to cope with it all.

At home in Salisbury I threw myself into my work still hoping that one day I would be surprised by Peter making a contrite reappearance. But the weeks crawled by without so much as a word from him.

I found that so utterly baffling. It was as if we no longer existed, that he had summarily snuffed us out of his life. His behaviour was deeply wounding. But I felt greater anger on behalf of his sons who had absolutely nothing to do with the way things had turned out in our marriage.

I wasn't going to let him get away with it so easily. I decided to confront him one more time to try and make him see sense. I owed that much at least to Robert and Simon. I took a trip to Bulawayo where he had found a job with a woodworking company. It was there that I managed to put a call through to Peter and asked him to meet me at the Grand Hotel so we could discuss future plans for our sons. I remember being on such tenterhooks because I was not sure he would keep the appointment. I was, I knew, clutching at straws but I was so intent upon appealing to that part of Peter where he was sure to have kept his guilt sealed up.

Surprisingly he did keep the appointment, but was no less opaque than he had been on those days before he left me. The conversation was strained and he suggested that the boys be put in government schools in Rhodesia, which would be much cheaper and involve no travelling expenses. I told him I wouldn't hear of it and that was about all we came to discussing. I left Bulawayo that afternoon despairing that the emotional divide between us was such that it would take a miracle to bring about a reconciliation. Yet I doggedly refused to relinquish the little hope I had of getting my husband back. And I vowed that when Robert and Simon came home for their Christmas holidays I would make sure Peter not only met them but give them a personal explanation for what had happened.

I set to work immediately and arranged a special outing to Bulawayo where we were to see an exhibition. I asked Peter to join us for dinner that night and he said he would meet us at the Victoria Hotel where we were staying. Feeling the need to bolster my already battered confidence I took the trouble to have a dress especially made for that night.

Peter, of course, never turned up. It was the final, most painful, insult I suffered at the hands of my estranged husband. That night he made it abundantly clear that he felt no compunction in having abandoned his young family.

Robert felt I needed cheering up so we went to the ballet that night. Simon preferred to go to bed and read. Robert was friendly with the son of the management – they were in the same form at school – so he rang him and asked if he could borrow his dinner jacket. This was duly arranged and Robert looked very dashing but had difficulty with his tie, just as Peter had always done, so I was expert at arranging a bow tie. Then suddenly Robert burst out laughing – he only had brown shoes. Once again he rang his friend, who proceeded to hunt for a large pair of black evening shoes. Very soon there was a knock on the door and the head chef appeared offering Robert his large pair of black shoes. We all thought this was hilarious.

Later in the evening Robert insisted that we go to a nightclub. I put money in his pocket and told him that he was my escort. It was a very entertaining evening. We had a splendid meal and Robert ordered wine and tipped rather heavily so naturally we were well looked after! I can still see the faces of some of the large-busted and well-turned out elite of Bulawayo and I am positive that they were saying, 'Oh, my dear, isn't she a cradle snatcher. She must be twice his age.'

We danced the evening away and I forgot my immediate problems. But after we returned home I was engulfed by a loneliness born of rejection and kindled by self-doubt. It was so all-consuming that it not only robbed me of reason but made me follow a course of action I came to bitterly regret for the rest of my life.

Chapter Eight

CHARLES AND CHOBE

During the war I met a man called Ian, who was unlike Peter in almost every way. He was a well-travelled journalist, a bon vivant and an absolute tonic at a time when there was little cause for fun and laughter. I found him a captivating dinner companion. He was entertaining and witty and, above all else, he danced like a dream. Yet for all our wonderful times together he knew that I was a happily married woman and deeply in love with my husband. My marital status, however, did not deter him from declaring his love for me during the course of our special friendship. He even went so far as to promise to take care of me and the boys if Peter did not return from the war.

That promise was all but forgotten when my beloved Peter came home and my friend felt compelled to fade from my life. But vulnerability, despair and loneliness in the wake of Peter's defection conspired to rouse old memories. And it was the memory of that distant promise that took hold of reason and spurred me into renewing contact.

I wrote to him care of his mother and was quite surprised by the prompt reply. He was stationed in Hong Kong, where he worked as editor of a major daily newspaper. He was clearly thrilled to have received my letter, although he said he was saddened by the news of my marriage break-up. At the time of writing he was preparing to leave for Montreal, where he had taken another senior newspaper job, and asked me to visit him there for a holiday, offering to pay the airfare.

The letter, the invitation and the feelings he said he still had for me acted like balm on my lacerated ego. I had felt so unloved following my painful separation from Peter that the very idea of being wined and dined on distant shores seemed irresistibly tantalising. After much discussion with my understanding friend, Diana, I accepted.

Ian had lost none of his winning ways and we ended up having a fun-soaked, joyous spell together in Montreal. We visited Niagara Falls, then New York City and Washington DC. Actually, it did not take long before his attentive ministrations did more than compensate for the hurt I had endured. They reignited my smile and restored to me a wondrous sense of well-being. I began to make peace with my lot in life. Nevertheless, I was absolutely staggered when at a rather lively party he suddenly announced to his friends that he would be following me back to Africa. It came as much as a surprise to me as it did to them.

After that it was as if events took on a life of their own and I became an unwitting spectator to them all. Admittedly I was quite flattered by my friend's attentions and his affection for me.

Soon after my return home, however, Roualeyn began to apply considerable pressure in his campaign to see me divorced from Peter. He kept harping on about how I had to accept the fact that Peter had gone for good and that I deserved a new chance at happiness. Even a very good friend of mine, a solicitor, passed some remark that Peter was openly living with another woman and that I should have more pride than to allow such an untenable state of affairs to continue.

I suppose it is fair to say that I was eventually pushed into filing for a divorce I didn't want. Peter, for all his sins, was still the love of my life. I wanted him back, no matter how long it would take for him to come to his senses. Oddly enough, I began to develop a fanciful notion that maybe the threat of divorce would jolt Peter into action. I couldn't have come up with a more foolish idea.

The court date was eventually set for early March 1952, only a couple of weeks after my return from Canada. Diana took me to the courthouse and I remember feeling sick with apprehension. Even then I was aware I had set something in train that would be near impossible to reverse. And today I still ask myself why I went on with it and why I let myself be pushed into something to which I was so bitterly opposed. For had I followed my own counsel and not rushed the fences I certainly would not have become entangled in an even messier situation. Yet for all my manifold misgivings I allowed myself to be guided through the legal process. Remarkably, the mother of my ex-pupil Rosemary was in court that same day filing for a divorce from her husband, and I remember telling her that coming into court was akin to being in the show ring and having to clear all the jumps.

Thankfully I knew the judge whose wife was a friend of mine. He was quite sympathetic and mercifully quick for within minutes I was granted custody of the boys but no maintenance. From that day on the boys – aged fifteen and thirteen – and I were on our own.

We had until 19 May for the divorce to be finalised and there was still, I thought, a likelihood that Peter would have a change of heart. But to complicate matters even more my friend asked me to marry him. Surprisingly, Robert and Simon encouraged me to accept his proposal because they liked him and were confident that he would make me happy. At that stage, though, I was nowhere near capable of making a clear-minded decision about my future. My emotions were still in turmoil and even Diana cautioned me not to rush into things. She knew that I was still in love with Peter.

Contrary to her reasoned advice and my own nagging doubts

I accepted my friend's proposal. Even having done so I stubbornly held to the belief that the news of my engagement would make Peter come charging back into my life and seek forgiveness. Alas, 19 May came with not so much as a word from Peter and the divorce was finalised. On that day too, my fate was sealed.

In many ways I wish I could completely disregard this woeful chapter of my life. But that's not quite possible because within months of his proposal and for all the wrong reasons I married Ian. It was, undeniably, a classic case of marrying someone on the rebound. Consequently, the marriage was all but doomed from the outset. Some of my friends encouraged me to start a new life with Ian, whilst others voiced their concerns about my hasty remarriage and even dear, sweet Mary was impelled to fire off a letter beseeching me not to go ahead with my wedding plans.

Unfortunately, I received Mary's letter only moments before I made my way to the registry office. Now, with the benefit of hindsight, I am certain that had I read it before I exchanged my vows I would have side-stepped the whole, horrible mess that ensued. For as destiny would have it I opened Mary's letter the first night of my honeymoon. We were staying at an inn where my new husband had gone to endless trouble to impress me. He had arranged for an intimate dinner to be served in the privacy of our room, which he had filled with flowers, and had ordered the very best of wines.

I had gone to the bathroom to freshen up when I remembered Mary's letter. I had, until then, not had an opportunity to read it. Her words hit me with a seismic force: 'You cannot marry someone whom you obviously don't love. You still love Peter. It will never work. This is advice from your old chum. Mary.'

Needless to say, I was reduced to a flood of pitiful tears while my husband patiently awaited my appearance for a lavish dinner that was rapidly getting cold. When I emerged it was to find that the charade would prove far more arduous to maintain than anything I had ever undertaken in all my adult years.

The following day, it all began to go horribly awry the instant we set off on our honeymoon to Lourenço Marques, the capital of Portuguese East Africa. For it was here that the sophisticated, affable man I had once found so entrancing revealed an over-fondness for liquor. Within days I lost every shred of respect for him and he had become an acute embarrassment in company.

On our return to Salisbury we moved into Heytesbury, the lovely thatched house I had designed and built with Peter, and tried to resume a seemingly normal, albeit strained relationship. My new husband got a job as a subeditor on a Salisbury newspaper, which meant he was required to do a lot of night shifts. I didn't complain for it suited me down to the ground. Days would go by without us seeing each other and it somehow helped minimise the tension. Eventually it became impossible to keep up the pretence. His drinking had gone from bad to worse and he had a number of car accidents while driving home under the influence.

Relationships, no matter how complex or troubled, are never easy to terminate and ending my second marriage was no exception. The day I suggested a divorce was difficult enough but, strangely, I felt a certain relief. Life had changed and I thought it would be fairer to go our separate ways. He was clearly devastated and couldn't stop weeping. He pleaded with me to be given one more chance to try and salvage our marriage but I knew there was no point. Our marriage had been a dreadful mistake and I was just so disillusioned and fed up with what had become such a travesty. Also, I was desperate to start afresh, to build a new life for myself and my sons. Ever since Peter had walked out on us we seemed to have careered from one crisis to the next. It was time to take control.

We parted and the marriage was finally dissolved. And in keeping with my resolution to turn over a new leaf I immediately put Heytesbury House on the market because it held far too many unpleasant memories. Once that was done I then set about having a new double-storey house built on a subdivision next to the stables.

While that was under way we rented a cottage and a rondavel on my friend Patrick Bromfield's farm. It was here that, as a family, we experienced some of our happiest times since Peter had left the scene and I ended my calamitous marriage. The boys came up from school for their Christmas holidays and shared the cottage with me. They absolutely loved it, especially Robert, who celebrated his seventeenth birthday there. Another occupant at the cottage was Claude, Simon's pet python. We had gone to some trouble to find Claude because shortly before Christmas Simon had expressed a wish to have a baby python as his present. As luck would have it, Patrick had heard that a nearby farmer had found a python with young in an ant-bear hole. So Patrick and I drove to the farm where the manager extracted one baby python for us. I don't recall where mama was. Patrick hid the python in a box under his bed and produced it on Christmas morning. Simon was absolutely thrilled.

Claude was extremely special to young Simon, who was fascinated with snakes. And when he returned to school I was given detailed instructions on how best to care for Claude, including making the python swim in the pool for his daily exercise. Mind you, not everyone was all that keen on dear Claude's presence. During a rather festive and jolly party at our place my friend Patrick decided to play a silly prank on my guests and produced old lethargic Claude. What he did not know was that there happened to be a fellow present who had a phobia for snakes and when he saw Claude the poor man, without so much as a peep, fell into a dead faint. It must have been awful for the guest, who was quickly attended to and Claude put to bed. Everyone else thought it quite hilarious and the party went on. So did the good times.

Fortunately for me, Rydal Court not only provided me with financial security but had long served as my emotional backstop during those troubled years when all else seemed to teeter on disaster. After two successive divorces I was keener than ever to make the riding school my sole focus while the boys were away at school. I met Charles Trevor, a successful civil engineer who had his own company in Salisbury, when he brought his horses to board at the school.

Like Diana, Charles became increasingly involved with the school and spent most of his free time either riding there or helping out. Within months the three of us decided to formalise our involvement in the school and to set up a company. Charles later gave me a horse, Bardolph, which I schooled for dressage.

We were the proverbial dream team and together kept coming up with new and better ways to secure Rydal Court's reputation as one of the best riding schools in Rhodesia. Such was our success that we soon began to outgrow the premises and started looking at larger properties with a view to expanding the school.

Eventually I sold my newly completed house and bought an attractive farm further out in the country called Gardiner Farm. Here we built new stables and a recreation area. Charles designed an interesting cross-country course for one-day events over terrain that included a river, natural banks, ditches and plenty of logs.

On the personal side of things, my business relationship with Charles gradually developed into something more serious. But there were some thorny impediments to formalising our relationship, caused in part by his separation from his wife. It was an extraordinarily difficult time for him and I suspect his involvement with Rydal Court helped ease the strain. After my own storm-tossed past I was equally keen not to rush into things and run the risk of making another terrible mistake. So while Charles was sorting out his private affairs I took my two sons and Diana on a fabulous safari.

I had arranged the safari with Patrick Bromfield, who took us down the Zambezi River in two small boats to his camp in a remote area below the Chirundu Bridge in Southern Rhodesia. Later this area became a popular safari camp after a road was built along the banks of the river. I had not had a decent holiday with my sons since the Michaelmas break we spent together in Ramsgate after I told them their father had left us. And Diana, my loyal friend who had stood by me through thick and thin, equally deserved a vacation.

The boys, of course, loved every thrilling moment of being in the bush and observing the wildlife from close quarters. Game-spotting is notoriously unpredictable but we were extremely fortunate on that trip. Hardly a day went by without us coming across some unexpected and spectacular sights. But the holiday was slightly marred for young Robert who mysteriously broke out in awful boils on his thighs. The itch was unbearable and he was in such distress that Patrick had to apply a special paste made with a mixture of sugar and soap on the boils. He vowed that it was a foolproof remedy but that Robert needed to stay out of the sun for it to take effect. So it was down to me, Diana and young Simon to continue our game-viewing.

No sooner had we set out from camp than we came across a large herd of elephants. With the wind direction in our favour we slowly and carefully began to move up close to where they were going about their business of stripping berries and leaves from the surrounding trees. I was just about to photograph one of the elephants through the long grass when Simon whispered with barely contained excitement, 'Mum, I can see his eyelashes'. I had never seen my son so mesmerised. He remained motionless for what seemed like an eternity just marvelling at the spectacle. I think it was on that auspicious day in the bush and seeing those awesome beasts that my son fell under the alluring spell of the wild. He would spend the rest of his life delighting in what became a strong and visceral tie with Africa and its animals.

Despite poor Robert's brief setback our safari holiday was the source of so many cherished memories and it was beyond doubt the best we had ever shared. Sadly, it ended all too soon.

In 1956, after treading an emotional tightrope for what seemed like ages, Charles and I were finally married. Dear Diana had, of course, long given us her blessing and on the day of our wedding she brought the champagne to celebrate. Forever on the move and always wanting to improve, we bought a less out-of-the-way farm in the Ruwa area, twenty miles from Salisbury, where Charles cleverly turned old tobacco barns into attractive Spanish type stables.

Meanwhile, Rydal Court continued to thrive. It had a good enclosed school, a free jumping lane, a dressage area and a cross-country course with an exciting water jump where many riders came to grief! In addition to these impressive facilities the school also offered a 'riding club' which involved trail rides, jumping instruction, a picnic lunch and perhaps a swim in the pool. The day would normally end with us gathered around a log fire and sampling some of Diana's exotic dishes. The riding club became extremely popular at weekends with people keen to spend the day out riding in the country.

We also arranged for a number of lectures and clinics to be held at the school. Our biggest coup, though, was getting Major Hans Handler of the famous Spanish Riding School in Vienna to come and run a clinic at our school. Ten of our top pupils could barely contain their excitement when they were chosen to participate and learn from one of the grand masters in riding. I was also extremely lucky in that he gave me private lessons on Bardolph.

Major Handler, for his part, was impressed with our school and the standard of our pupils. Indeed, one of the riders he singled out was young Rosemary whom I had first taught in the Elton Court days. When Rosemary started riding as a small girl I thought she would never learn to rise to the trot, but I was quickly made to revise my initial assessment. Later she proved herself a superb rider and a very successful competitor in the show ring. She competed in scores of dressage events in South Africa as well as Rhodesia. Some years later she took a Rhodesian Pony Club team to Australia.

By now, my sons were already in the process of charting their own futures. Robert had gone to study an agriculture and forestry course at the University of Auckland in New Zealand and then later moved on to Massey College, where he gained some prominence in their debating society. I received a call, reverse charges of course, in which he regaled me with all the details of a certain debate that won him much praise from a politician who said he would make a good lawyer.

Simon, meanwhile, was just nineteen and keen to pursue a career in wildlife conservation, and through our friend Patrick Bromfield was able to secure a job as an assistant in the Bechuanaland Protectorate's Game Department. The ruling was that they were not to take on staff under the age of twenty-one, which meant that Simon could help out but without pay. The prospect of working without pay would have dissuaded most young men, but not Simon. He was determined to gain all the experience needed to become a game ranger.

He seemed so certain this was his destiny that I agreed to pay

As a baby in about 1916 in Somerset East, my love of animals is already showing. I am holding Winkie my cat.

At three I helped raise money for the returned soldiers. I was given a tin and stood outside a big store with a smile and a clear, 'This is for soldiers!' I managed to fill my tin with donations.

The first time I sat on a horse, aged three, with my friend, Huff, and my proud mother wearing her starched uniform.

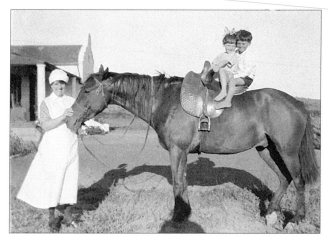

Friends and family at Christmas Gift Farm before setting out on a shooting trip, 1929. Left to right: The Old Man is wearing a pith helmet with Chum, his Rhodesian Ridgeback; cousin Colin Oates; Uncle Valentine; Auntie May wearing the hat and fur collar; Mickey Williamson (for whom The Old Man was guardian) holding Peter Pan the dog; Uncle Clarence Oates and Aunt Enid.

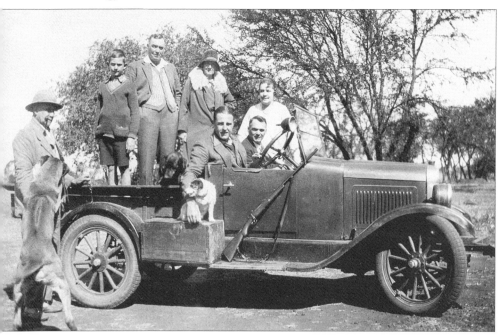

Christmas Gift Farm where I grew up, near Gwelo, Rhodesia, in about 1932.

A portrait of me at fifteen.

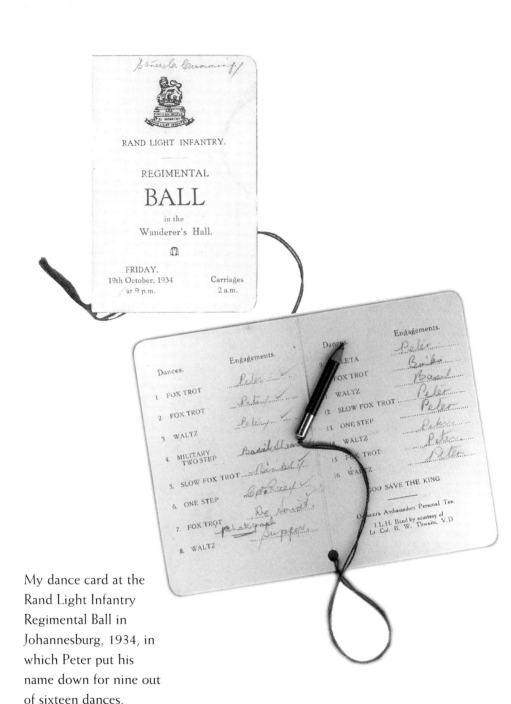

My dance card at the
Rand Light Infantry
Regimental Ball in
Johannesburg, 1934, in
which Peter put his
name down for nine out
of sixteen dances.

Barbara and myself competing at the Rand Show, Johannesburg, 1934. This picture appeared in the Johannesburg papers with the caption: 'A Lady From Rhodesia'. It was spotted by my parents who, up until then, were ignorant of my 'hobby' while I was at art school.

Our art school's float for the University Rag in Johannesburg, 1934. The slogan behind us reads, 'We are B.O. Hemians but "Mum" isn't the word'. We were of course referring to Mum deodorant! I am around the other side of the float and not visible in this shot.

Peter and I announced our
engagement on 23 January 1936.

CUMMING—HOLMES A COURT.
— The engagement is an-
nounced between Ethnee, daughter of Mr. and Mrs. H. R. Cumming, of Xmas Gift, Gwelo,
Southern Rhodesia, and granddaughter of the Rev. W. Oates,
of Somerset East, and Peter,
younger son of the Honourable
H. W. and Mrs. Holmes a Court,
of Devonshire, England. c2688/25

Our wedding on 2 October 1936. With my family (left to right):
Uncle Clarence Oates; Aunt Enid; Auntie May; young cousin
Gerald Oates; cousin Colin Oates; Geoff Deverall (Peter's best
man); Peter; step cousin Neil Davidson; myself; The Old Man;
Mother; bridesmaid Cath and step-brother Roualeyn.

My Peter, as an officer with the RNVR in 1943. This photograph sat on my dressing table while he was away at war and was a perpetual reminder of their father for Robert and Simon.

Peter with me and our boys in Rhodesia just before Peter went to war, 1941.

HMS Delhi, the ship Peter was on, was badly bombed in the Mediterranean in 1943.

Working in the plotting office at Thornhill Air Station, Rhodesia, during the war. F/Sgt. Colin Campbell is in the foreground.

In my Women's Auxiliary Air Services uniform
(about 1943). We were known as WAASIES!

During the war years, the boys and I spent most of our time at Christmas Gift Farm. I am on Bruce with Simon, Robert stands below with Billy Boy the Doberman and Bobby the terrier.

Among Simon's many talents was his photographic skill. This is one of his hand-coloured photographs of cheetahs.

Simon, Claude and myself in 1961 at the Game Department Stand – Francistown Agricultural Show.

Simon was in charge of the safari for Prince Bernhard of the Netherlands, Bechuanaland Protectorate, 1963. Simon is taking the photograph.

With Robert on his graduation day, University of Western Australia, 4 May 1966.
Courtesy *The West Australian*

Ronnie Critchley during the Middle East campaign (photographed in Egypt).

The Chobe Belle paddle steamer, steered by Charles.

Me with my Siamese,
Melloney, in her favourite
place prior to our
departure for Chobe.

Simon in Fiji, holding our dinner, June 1971 when I was sailing with him.

A menu I designed at Chobe River Hotel to celebrate the opening of the bar.

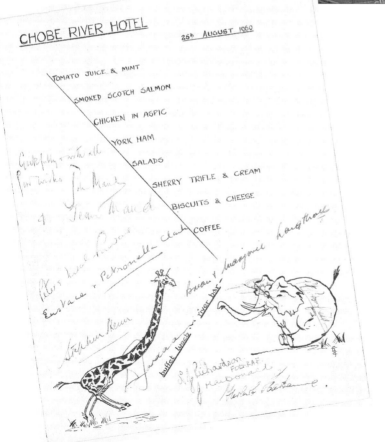

CHOBE RIVER HOTEL   26th AUGUST 1960

TOMATO JUICE & MINT

SMOKED SCOTCH SALMON

CHICKEN IN ASPIC

YORK HAM

SALADS

SHERRY TRIFLE & CREAM

BISCUITS & CHEESE

COFFEE

With Pago Pago, one of Heytesbury Stud's most prized thoroughbred stallions who lived to almost thirty years of age.

Robert's family at Middlebury College, Vermont for Peter's graduation, 1989. Left to right: Paul; Janet; Robert; Catherine; Simon and Peter.

Our filly Mercurial Madam won the WA Champion Fillies Stakes at Ascot, Perth in 1996.
Courtesy *Sunday Times Perth*

Ronnie with me on *The World Discoverer*, approaching Cape Horn, Antarctica, 1989.

June 1993 I visited Sara Henderson at Bullo River Station. I am sitting here in the bullcatcher with her dog, Jedda the Rottweiler and Jacque's Mugsie, the Jack Russell.

him a monthly allowance while he worked in his unofficial capacity with Patrick. When Simon turned twenty-one he immediately applied, as many others did, for the position and was accepted. What I found especially touching was that he thoughtfully returned his allowance the day he received his first pay cheque, together with a lovely letter of appreciation.

A couple of years passed and with both my sons away from home, Charles and I began to reassess our own future. Charles had retired from his construction company and we felt the time had come to take a less active part in the riding school. Diana, too, wanted to move on and concentrate on her dressage as well as have a bit more fun without the added responsibility of running the school. Before I let go the reins of a business that had seen me through some emotionally trying times, enabled me to have both my sons educated at Michaelhouse, one of South Africa's finest schools and to survive without financial support from my two former husbands, I decided to compete one last time in the Bulawayo Show. It was to be my 'swan song' after having won numerous prizes and trophies over so many years.

There to help carry me through this momentous occasion was Bushman, my seventeen-year-old horse that also boasted an equally impressive show ring record. We were the oldest competitors that fine day and what we may have lacked in youth we more than made up for with ageless cunning and grit. We won our jumping event after having to jump off three times against a couple of young men in the police team. The jumps were raised each time and we had to jump against the clock, which made for a thrilling contest. The crowd went wild and I think Bushman, sensing the electric atmosphere, all but sprouted wings and we flew over the jumps, taking most of them at an angle that saved us precious seconds. Bridget, one of my pupils, jumped Stella very successfully and then she bought her. I knew that Stella would have a very good home. At this time we did not have many school horses of our own as pupils boarded their horses with us.

After my triumphant curtain call Charles and I left our pets and horses in his daughter Jo's care and took to the road in search of a small inn that Charles had long fantasised about owning somewhere along the South African coast. Our quest took us to some glorious locations, mostly in the Cape Province. We became very excited about a charming inn near Stellenbosch and found ourselves making all sorts of grandiose plans. We would build stables there for our hunters and join the Cape Hunt Club. Everything seemed so perfect until, just moments before signing on the dotted line, our solicitor discovered that there were legal complications pertaining to a second bond. We both had cold feet and duly returned home disillusioned.

Waiting for us was a letter from Simon, who was then permanently based as a game ranger in Bechuanaland Protectorate. He was keen to have some of his belongings sent down to him, most notably his taxidermy equipment, numerous stuffed birds and snakes, his gun and his much-loved big white teddy bear, the same Teddy I had nursed when meeting Mary, which he gave to Patrick's five-year-old daughter Barbara who was so thrilled by the gift, she reportedly exclaimed, 'Simon, when I grow up I want to marry you!' (Teddy moved with the family to Rhodesia and many years later they all migrated to Western Australia. Today, Barbara's son, Oscar, is the proud owner of Teddy, although he is neither big nor white anymore!).

Charles and I thought it wise to take him the belongings ourselves for we were keen to visit Simon in Francistown. We duly set off on a very hot October day with Simon's possessions stacked to the roof of the car. We were invited to stay over with Patrick and his family. Simon, when not in his bush camp, had set up home in a small rondavel in the garden where he was kept company by two lion cubs. My son, it seemed, was still in the habit of adopting and befriending wild animals. (Actually, I cannot ever remember Simon not acquiring strange pets, be they reptiles or birds.) The cute little cubs, though, made for a welcome change from all the venomous snakes he was so fond of collecting. It was wonderful catching up with Simon and although he spent most of his time in the bush during the course of our stay it was quite clear to me that he was extraordinarily happy. He was where he liked being best – in close proximity to Africa's magnificent creatures.

And to some extent I understood his intense fascination with wildlife for there is something so spellbinding and alluring about the African bush that even Charles and I found ourselves in no hurry to return home. Patrick, fortunately, did not seem to mind us staying on and made mention of some government officials coming up from Mafeking for a meeting. They were, it seemed, so taken with my son and his dedication to his work that they wanted to meet his mother and had asked Patrick to bring us along for midday drinks.

It turned out to be a rather remarkable day. For a start the heat that October day was so intense that Audrey – Patrick's wife – and I had to dip our swollen feet in basins of cold water before we were able to squeeze them into our shoes. Applying lipstick, though, proved an impossible task for it had been reduced to the consistency of runny candlewax. Once we arrived at the party, relief from the brain-sizzling heat came by way of long, iced drinks served under high ceiling fans. It was through the subsequent haze of pink gins that I overheard the High Commissioner make some reference to a 'private enterprise' while in deep conversation with Patrick and another official.

Immediately I was intrigued, more so when I was told that the enterprise in question involved the development of a camp site and later a hotel in the new Chobe Game Park. The park was started for the Bechuanaland Protectorate government by Patrick, as Chief Game Warden, in 1956 with a number of African game scouts and then Simon joined him in his pioneering venture. Later that night we bombarded Patrick with questions about the area and what the government envisioned. Charles and I had been unsuccessful in our quest to find a small inn on the South African coast but a hotel in the wilds of Africa had an exciting ring to it.

We had never seen the Chobe River and I imagined it to be like the many sandy riverbeds we had passed along the way to Francistown. To get a clearer idea of where this supposed development was going to be I asked Patrick if we could arrange for a flight over the area. If we liked what we saw we would approach the government with a view to being involved in the proposed development.

We wasted no time. As soon as we returned to our home at Ruwa, we packed hurriedly and then drove to the Victoria Falls. There we met Patrick and chartered a Rapide aircraft. Luck was on our side for it turned out to be a near perfect day and we enjoyed excellent visibility. When we flew over the area I had my first sighting of the Chobe River. It was no dry, cracked riverbed but a magnificent waterway.

There were beautiful trees and a riverine area with lush grazing and an abundance of game. Further inland were waterholes, although some were dry as rain was not expected before November. We saw hundreds of lechwe antelope, a few rare puku and a shy pair of Chobe bushbuck. There was a pod of hippo lazing on the embankment and others just emerging from the river. We also caught a glimpse of giraffe heads above the trees, but the biggest thrill was sighting a herd of about two hundred elephant drinking and playing with their calves in the river.

And there was a magnificent spray of birds, including the carmine bee-eaters, brightly coloured malachite kingfishers, the lilac-breasted roller and we heard the cry of the fish eagle. We had seen from above a sublime slice of paradise and even before we returned to the gravel airstrip at Victoria Falls (now a busy international airport) we had made our decision. We would create something unique and develop a small luxury area for visitors to share this superb wildlife habitat. Thatched rondavels on the banks of the Chobe River and cooking facilities would be just the beginning.

Both Charles and I were so excited about the prospect of starting something from scratch in the wilds of Africa that we wasted no time in travelling to Mafeking, where Government offices were located, to finalise matters. Everything had to be done through the British Government, which took some time, but we were assured we could go ahead and build on the site we had chosen.

In November 1959, not more than a month later, we set off from our comfortable home in our new Landrover and with a caravan in tow. Competing for space in the Landrover on that long, slow journey was our African assistant, our three much-loved Siamese cats Melloney, Lydia and Ching and three dogs. It was rough going, especially the last part, because there were no roads to speak of. We followed sandy tracks for much of the way from Livingstone in Northern Rhodesia and these were made impassable in many parts by large trees that had been knocked down by elephants. We had to chop through the trees before we could proceed. I later discovered that apparently this was the original route David Livingstone took when he discovered the Victoria Falls in 1855.

Eventually we reached Kasane, the only settlement near the site, where we were to set up camp. The white population was three (we made it five): the local policeman Brian Langthorne, his wife and small son. Their sole contact with the outside world was by radio transmission twice a day. There was a house for government officials when they came up from Mafeking on business, or for fishing, and a pleasant camping site under some large mopane (pronounced ma-par-nee) trees on the riverbank. 'Facilities' were a small hut in which to store supplies, an area for outdoor cooking and a 'long drop' with no door! Home to us was our tent and caravan, which we set up under an umbrella of trees. It gave us the most superb view across the Chobe, famous for its tiger and bream fishing and we could see as far as the Caprivi Strip in South West Africa. Here we lived for six months, sharing our new habitat with vervet monkeys, an orphaned baby baboon and a variety of beautiful birds, and often larger wildlife.

We recruited builders from Rhodesia since there were little or no restrictions in those days on people moving from one country to another in search of work. We began making bricks, which were then spread out, covered with grass and left to dry in the sun. The scheme would have worked well had it not been discovered by elephants who thought this was done especially for their benefit. During the night they would come and eat the grass and trample all over the bricks. We made another attempt, in a different area, but the bricks were discovered by lions who left their huge pug marks imprinted in them. We couldn't afford more setbacks so we purchased a brick-making machine and bags of cement and began making sand and cement blocks. Once the first batch was completed we were able to set to work and build the first few rondavels, an ablution block and outside cooking facilities.

We had not long been at Chobe when Simon was sent there on

duty. One day I accompanied him in his Landrover to an area where the elephants were said to have been very destructive. He was to investigate and put in a report to the Game Department. While we were driving I noticed that the sack at my feet had begun to move. I mentioned this to Simon who asked me to be careful where I placed my feet as the sack contained Claude the pet python.

After travelling but a short distance into the bush I was quite alarmed when a young elephant suddenly burst out of the scrub and made it obvious that he felt he had the right of way. Simon reversed a few yards and then said calmly, 'It's all yours. Do continue, my friend.' I sat rigid with shock but Simon seemed so unperturbed, almost amused by the incident. He had an enormous respect for the law of the land and its animals and I don't think he ever feared them. Further down the track we met a herd of elephant and Simon continued very slowly and kept banging on the car door. On that occasion we were given the right of way. I wouldn't have dared risk anything like it.

Later we came to a lovely open area beside the river where a few elephants were grazing with some lechwe antelope. Simon parked the Landrover and then leapt out armed with his camera and tripod. I did not like the thought of being abandoned but before Simon disappeared he called out, 'It's all right . . . stay in the Landrover. The jumbos have very poor vision and they haven't a clue I am here.' He managed to get some excellent shots of the elephants that day.

Some months later I was told how Simon and three game scouts had been dispatched by the Game Department to shoot a herd of elephant that had reportedly been destroying the Africans' crops. Killing elephants did not appeal to my Simon. When he first joined the Department he had to shoot a marauding elephant, and he sent me a snapshot with the caption, 'I've vowed never to shoot another ele'. So when he was sent out again in pursuit of destructive elephants Simon decided to drive them away from the area rather than shoot them. He and the scouts ended up walking for days, until the scouts thought it was too much like hard work and gave up. So Simon went on alone until his mission was accomplished. He became lost, though, and it took him three days to find the camp. His scouts said that he was the bravest and most dedicated *Morena* (boss) they knew.

As for Charles and myself, we soon grew accustomed to having those magnificent beasts wandering up to our camp. They seemed to approve of our site under the shade trees on the riverbank and often wandered in to share it with our guests. This all added to the excitement of creating something unique in the wild. However, one American guest was not at all amused by having to share his quarters with the ever-encroaching wildlife. One day he seemed especially agitated and asked me to come and inspect his rondavel as there was 'something in the rafters'. It was dear Claude, sleeping very comfortably, and harmlessly. That was too much for our guest to bear and he promptly packed up and left. He was our only unhappy customer.

Once we'd taken care of most of the residential quarters we built a swimming pool on the edge of the river to provide our guests with some relief on those stiflingly hot days. Swimming in the Chobe was out of the question as it was infested with crocodiles and hippo.

While developing the game reserve camp the many locals working for us frequently requested we pick up goods for them when we went to Livingstone or the Victoria Falls to stock up on supplies. These mainly comprised sugar, soap, candles, bread and, strangely enough, Ponds face cream and 'Hold Me Tight' perfume.

As a result, we applied to Mafeking headquarters for permission to build a store. This was granted and the store rapidly became a very profitable extension to our business.

Transport soon began to pose a problem, however, not only for our guests but in bringing building materials to the camp. Charles figured the best way around the problem would be to have a pontoon operating across the river and he promptly set about building one. Being a civil engineer Charles constantly devised all sorts of new plans for the site, and supervised the building and construction work himself. The pontoon, driven by two outboard motors, was launched between Kasane and Kazangula on the Zambezi where Namibia, Botswana, Zambia and Zimbabwe come together. The pontoon soon became a roaring success. With transport taken care of we were able to speed up all the building work. After ten rondavels had been completed we built a larger one – No. 11 – for ourselves. It sported a modern loo, a six-foot bath and running water. Sheer luxury after endless months of camping.

By this time we had an efficient lighting plant and, after much negotiation, a telephone was installed. When the telephone technician arrived one hot morning, after driving from the other end of the country, his first words to me were, 'Who the hell has such influence to get a phone in this godforsaken end of the territory?' My answer was, 'We have. Come and have a cold beer.' The telephone was duly installed but ditches had to be dug around the poles to keep the elephants from rubbing against them and knocking them down.

We then built a huge water tank on a nearby hill so that water could be pumped up from the river, filtered and then gravitated back. Things were really moving. The next, but most important, phase was constructing the main building with the bar as the priority. Once that was completed the government officials came up from Mafeking to inspect our progress. When they gave us all-round praise for what we had accomplished in such record time we felt the occasion called for a major celebration. The bar was declared open and we served an excellent lunch with several bottles of good South African wine.

Guests started to arrive at our Chobe River Hotel from all corners of the globe. A famous singer of the day, Tessie O'Shea, and her pianist, Ernest Wampola, were among our first celebrities. She was known as 'Two Ton Tessie', a rather fitting epithet given that it took a major operation to get her settled in our fishing boat. But she was determined to catch some of the tiger fish for which the Chobe was renowned, and she did. In the evenings Tessie would make herself comfortable on the verandah and in the cool night air treat our guests to an impromptu concert. I still have a photograph of her, signed, 'To darling Ethnée and Charles: What a wonderful time I've had.'

Chobe was truly one of the most romantic settings in the world and everyone loved being there, myself and Charles included. In terms of location, the hotel was in the dress circle and for all its mystery and magic Africa never failed to stage an awe-inspiring show. Nearly every day began with a flawless sunrise which burst like a silent, crimson eruption on the horizon. And by day's end, after every living creature had been ceaselessly tormented by the heat, the sun would depart with much theatricality, sinking like molten gold amid the choral sounds that is Africa. There would be the haunting cry of a fish eagle, the hectoring barks of the baboons and the sounds of timid antelope retreating through the undergrowth. Darkness falls rapidly in the bush and before long the skies would be smeared with stars. Even today when I think back on Chobe my memories carry with them the pungent smell of woodsmoke and those distinctive, bewitching sounds of the wild.

It didn't take long for word of the magic of Chobe to spread. We became such a favourite bolthole that many of our guests would think nothing of making the ten-hour drive from Bulawayo, the closest town in Rhodesia, just so they could spend a weekend with us in the bush. Many of our clients were the white hunters from Kenya. They ran their safaris from our hotel and within a short time our venture began to turn to a profit.

In 1963 we had Prince Bernhard of the Netherlands for a safari. By then we were quite well established. Charles had built a small airstrip which enabled the Prince to leave his larger plane at Livingstone and rather than have to drive along those notorious sand tracks or cross on the pontoon, he, together with his entourage, flew in a smaller plane to our hotel.

The Prince was interested in collecting some specimens for a museum in Holland, most notably the pygmy goose, which would then be treated and packed to go to Holland. Patrick Bromfield was supposed to escort the Prince and his very large entourage, which included his doctor and his accountant, but at the time was too ill to undertake the safari. After years of working in the African bush Patrick had contracted scores of infectious diseases. He had come down with several bouts of malaria and bilharzia and they had exacted such a heavy toll that he had to have major surgery.

Patrick turned to Simon for help, who was more than thrilled to accompany Prince Bernhard. He was an utterly charming man and came to stay with us at the hotel for a few days before setting off into the wilds with Simon. He particularly enjoyed a fishing trip on our *Chobe Belle* paddle-steamer. Charles had built the vessel on an old hull and used the engine from an abandoned Studebaker car which had been towed all the way from Livingstone. The paddlewheel was about six feet in diameter and was fitted with twelve paddles. It proved to be an idyllic way to view game at very close quarters and we were able to float quietly near the bank in less than two feet of water. The Prince found the *Chobe Belle* offered him great relief for his bad back. While it floated down the river he'd lie stretched out on the deck!

His safari was the largest undertaken in the region. Simon had organised battalions of staff, who helped set up the cooking quarters and the deep freezes. They spent about three weeks out in the bush and when they came back the Prince declared it one of the most successful safaris he had encountered in Africa. He was also very impressed with Simon and his knowledge of animals and photography.

After he returned to the Netherlands we received some lovely letters from the Prince and from some members of his entourage thanking us for our hospitality. Simon had sent him some magnificent photographs of the trip since Prince Bernhard was disappointed with the quality of his own photographs. In return, the Prince sent Simon a beautiful Rolex watch that was a replica of the one he wore. He sent it via Pretoria in a special diplomatic bag so that Simon wouldn't have to pay duty on it.

Robert, meanwhile, found that studying agriculture no longer held much appeal and returned home from New Zealand with the idea of reading for a law degree. This posed some problems for there were but a few weeks to go before the new academic year started and he hadn't applied to any of the South African universities. After several calls to my cousin Dr Paul Oates in Cape Town, it was arranged for Robert to study law at the University of Cape Town. Robert was extremely lucky to get in to one of South Africa's leading universities at such short notice and I had my cousin to thank for that as he had no doubt managed to pull a few influential strings.

Robert rented a room near the campus and seemed to have

settled down to his studies when misfortune struck. I had a long letter from him telling me that after only a few weeks at the university he had suffered severe headaches and called a doctor who had him admitted to Groote Schuur Hospital. The initial diagnosis was malaria, then it was thought that he had typhoid but Robert kept insisting that he had glandular fever which indeed he had. The eventual diagnosis came as quite a shock. Robert, like his father, was a diabetic and had to be put on insulin. He spent over three weeks in hospital and was discharged and placed in the care of my cousin Paul and his wife Joyce.

He left the rented room, which I understand was rather miserable anyway, and spent some time with Paul and his family in their cottage at Betty's Bay, about fifty miles from Cape Town. I received a long letter from Robert telling me how fit he was getting with all the swimming and running on the beautiful beach and how wonderful it was being treated to home cooking. Joyce later managed to find Robert a flat relatively close to their home which enabled Paul to monitor the insulin and help put Robert back on his feet. For a while Robert kept up his studies but not to the exclusion of his many other interests, both social and business. Judging from all the photographs he sent me he must have attended every ball in town, always immaculately turned out in black tie and patterned waistcoat. He also started to dabble on the stock market and was, I was told, doing rather well, especially with brewery shares which he advised Joyce to buy. Indeed, she too did very well and thought my Robert was a wizard. He also frequented the racecourse and lost and made, but assured me that he and his friends had much enjoyment at little expense.

The next letter I received was all about 'the new business idea'. Robert and his school friend Robin had fixed on the idea of opening their own restaurant which was to be called La Corvette. At the end of the nineteen page letter there came a request for me to guarantee the business for £1000. Charles had already had a straight talk with Robert and told him that if he really worked hard and passed his exams at the end of the year I would continue to finance him at university, otherwise he had to get out and earn his own keep.

Robert assured me he would be able to reimburse me. The restaurant, he said, would have the best china and cutlery. The décor would be very nautical with brass cannon at the door and a genuine ship's lamp on the front desk which Robert had found in an antique shop.

My son was so full of enthusiasm but I needed a lot more information concerning the restaurant's financial viability so I telephoned him, asking for details. He said he had arranged for an overdraft but that I would need to guarantee the bank. Moreover, he was confident that he would be able to keep up with his law studies as well as run the business at night and at weekends. Once armed with all the information I made an appointment with my solicitor. His words were, 'You must have a lot of faith in your son.'

Robert opened La Corvette with some fanfare and there were forty-four bookings for dinner the first night. He seemed thrilled with himself and wrote,

'We serve the best food in Cape Town thanks to the chef, Cassiando. All our staff are Africans from Rhodesia, so they are pleased to be working for us. We treat them well and drive them home at night after the buses stop and we feed them on hamburgers. They work exactly eight hours. We pay them well but one mistake or sign of dishonesty means the sack without notice or pay to that day. It works well.'

The letter gave some indication of Robert the businessman. Robert the student, however, didn't fare nearly as well. He had been able to write two exams and had deferred others to February to allow him to run La Corvette. The law course was another three years and I was asked to continue paying his allowance for the duration of his studies as he was loath to sell his brewery shares. They were, he said, doing so well it would be a pity to sell.

All Robert's letters were full of La Corvette and he took immeasurable pride in the cuisine the restaurant offered. His specialties included select fillet cooked in wine and served flaming at the table. Several of my friends frequented La Corvette and were duly impressed. One night they requested to meet the chef in order to tip and congratulate him on the meal. Who should appear but Robert, having removed his apron and slipped back into his jacket. The chef, they were told, had been sacked for being drunk.

But as the months slipped by I sensed that Robert was having problems with his restaurant. The overdraft at the bank was worrying him, his friend Robin had lost interest and due to riots in Cape Town people were staying home. So with one thing and another Robert said he had decided to cut his losses and asked if he could give us a hand at Chobe while he reassessed his future. While at Chobe he intended to continue his law course with the London University by correspondence. Charles was not at all happy when I gave him the news but agreed to give my son a trial run. I sent Robert his train fare but he spent the money and hitchhiked with his little Corgi dog called Bridgette Bardog as far as Livingstone.

I went to meet him there. On our way across the river on the pontoon Robert, normally so garrulous, was struck speechless. He had never thought much of all our plans at Chobe but on that day I could see he had revised his opinion. As he looked up the Zambezi, Matilda the resident hippo popped up her head and gave him the once-over. He beamed from ear to ear then turned to me and said, 'Ethnée, this is fabulous'. He was even more impressed when we arrived at the Chobe River Hotel. He and Bridgette

Bardog made their home in rondavel No. 4. Within no time at all Robert was in the kitchen getting ready to prepare Christmas lunch for our forty guests.

Robert excelled himself by setting a long table with a huge ham, turkey, all the trimmings and vegetables. He carved the servings and everyone, including the waiters, entered into the spirit of Christmas at Chobe. It was a highly successful lunch and I seem to recall many bottles of wine were consumed on that day. Robert proved himself a great favourite with the guests and late at night he would often take a party into the large kitchen and turn out delicious omelettes which he tossed in great fashion.

I don't know how much studying was done because the hotel became busier and there was so much to organise. Charles and I took turns to take guests game viewing and we also had to supervise the hire of the fishing boats. Our trading store was doing extraordinarily well and Robert had come up with the idea of selling his freshly baked buns from there every day. That alone brought a considerable amount of trade.

After a couple of months we decided to open another store at Kavimba, beyond the game park. It involved quite a drive to keep the store stocked with supplies and one day I took Robert along for company. On the way back we had a frightening experience when we suddenly came face-to-face with a charging cow elephant. We had been talking so much that we failed to notice that we had inadvertently separated a herd of elephants and that a calf had been left on one side of the track. The mother was furious and with ears flapping and the most spine-chilling clamour began to charge our Landrover.

I had never reversed at such speed, which was not easy on the sandy track. Robert kept saying, 'Keep going, keep going, she's still coming our way.' Finally the cow was reunited with her baby and they hastily made their escape into the bush. We sat momentarily mute with relief and then Robert suggested that he should drive back. We were in the process of changing seats when there came a horrible scream from another cow elephant that had suddenly materialised behind us. Thankfully Robert put his foot down and got us away in time, but we were both very unnerved by the incident. All the way back to Chobe we drove slowly, scanning the bush for any movement or sight of another disgruntled elephant. Once we cleared the forested area and got into more open country we spotted three lionesses devouring their recent kill, a sable and behind a clump of grass a lion lay patiently awaiting his share. It was quite an eventful day but we refrained from regaling our guests with all the details for fear they would become alarmed and cancel the next day's viewing trips.

For someone who once so longed to be a vet I had my work cut out tending to the many orphaned animals we found at Chobe. The accepted view among conservationists is not to interfere with nature and to let the animals be, but I couldn't leave them to face certain death. Instead, I would do all I could to save them and then have them released back into the wild. But there were the few exceptions who preferred to stay with us. For instance there was Jeremy, a vervet monkey we reared after he had lost his mum. Little did we know what we had let ourselves in for as vervet monkeys are renowned for being the most mischievous of creatures. Jeremy turned from a cute little thing into a rebellious resident who delighted in terrorising our guests and staff.

The waiters began resenting Jeremy when he made a habit of scampering across their pristine white tablecloths with his dirty little feet. And he used to snatch money from the till and have us all in hot pursuit to try and retrieve it. He also caused some consternation when he ripped a hearing aid from one of our guests.

There was quite a to-do over that and Jeremy was fast becoming somewhat of a nuisance. The final straw came when, with lightning speed, Jeremy snatched a paperback from the hands of another guest. There was much shouting and many wild protestations but he skimmed to the top of a tree and cheekily began tearing up every single page in the book.

We were mortified. So much so that Jeremy was finally served with an eviction notice. We had tried to release him in the bush on a number of occasions, hoping that he would gain acceptance with the other vervet monkeys upstream on the Chobe. But somehow Jeremy always managed to find his way back to us. Charles, though, was adamant to be shot of Jeremy and had arranged for him to be released on a friend's game farm in Zambia. We assume he found a new home because he never made it back to Chobe.

Then there was darling Amanda, another little monkey we rescued from certain death. She was brought to us by one of the game scouts after her mother was killed by lions. She was pink without much hair and when I picked her up she held my hand very tightly and wouldn't let go. We reared her and bathed her in the washbasin and, like a baby, made her wear a nappy so she wouldn't cause an awful mess in the hotel. She was, thankfully, a lot better behaved than Jeremy and Charles bought her a little doll that if pressed would squeak. Amanda absolutely adored her doll and would nurse and rock it like a baby. She herself was much adored by all our guests.

We were fast becoming a very popular holiday destination among people keen to sample the seductive delights of the African bush. Robert was still determined to complete his law degree but knew that he would get nowhere fast doing it by correspondence. He decided to go to Australia or New Zealand because he felt there was no future in Africa. I agreed to send him an allowance on condition that he graduated with a law degree. He promised me that this time he would make sure there were no diversions and that he would see it through to the end. The day he came into the rondavel and gave me the kitchen keys was a sad one.

After Robert's departure we were fortunate in finding quite a good manager. Chobe continued to do well and we had completed a wing in the main building which had four bedrooms, all with a private bath. We upgraded our own living quarters and moved from our rondavel into a suite in the new wing which gave us a magnificent view over the river.

But for all its success and the exquisite surroundings, the workload at Chobe began to take its toll. We were growing and expanding at such a rapid rate that Charles and I were allowed very little free time to ourselves. On top of that we had the two stores that required constant supervision. It meant we had to make the long drive to Livingstone at least once a week. I often accompanied Charles because it was not a drive to undertake alone. One day, while on our way to Kazangula for mail, we stopped and gave an African a lift. Charles was driving and everything seemed quite normal until he started talking a lot of gibberish. He kept asking why lions were crossing the road and when the car started to zig-zag crazily across the track I knew something was seriously amiss. When I turned to look at him Charles had passed out at the wheel. Somehow I managed to reach across and jam on the brake without careering off the road. Thank heavens we had stopped to give the African a lift for I don't think I would have managed to move Charles out of the driver's seat on my own.

I drove as fast as the rutted sand track would allow me and once we got back to Chobe I phoned a woman at Kazangula whom I knew had been a nurse. She arrived in record time and was able to make Charles comfortable. Later, however, she confirmed my suspicion – Charles had suffered a heart attack. It was a warning to us both that we needed to ease off a bit and set about restructuring the way we ran the business.

Actually we had talked about building a little further up the river on the eleven acres we had been permitted to buy. Charles had thought of designing a cottage cantilevered over the river so we could watch the otters along the embankment and the elephants swim across the Chobe to the Caprivi Strip. And once we had put a good management team in place we would take some months off. He dreamed of getting a yacht and sailing in the Mediterranean with the two Simons: my son Simon and his son Simon. They had a lot in common as they had both studied taxidermy and photography and were keen to get involved in the making of wildlife documentaries.

Charles never realised these dreams. In April 1964 he took two very dear friends, Yvonne and Petey, from Cape Town out in the boat for a day's fishing. They pulled in to a small island where the girls wanted to go for a walk. While they set out to explore Charles took the opportunity to refuel, but by some awful quirk of nature the petrol fumes attracted a swarm of wild bees. Charles was covered in them. He was so concerned for our friends that he shouted to them to jump into the river while he struggled to start the engine. Miraculously, he managed to get it started and to haul our friends on board despite the fact that he had been stung from head to toe. He had even been stung in the eyes, which made it almost impossible for him to see anything. One of our friends tried to assist Charles but she, too, had been badly stung. Fortunately a passing fishing boat realised they were in some distress and towed them back to the hotel.

I heard a boat coming in at high speed, which was forbidden because it upset the game. When I rushed out to reprimand those causing the racket I saw our boat being towed in with all the occupants lying down. I knew instinctively something awful had happened. At first I did not recognise Charles, his face was so hideously swollen.

We wasted no time in chartering a small aircraft and I accompanied Charles and our friends to the Livingstone Hospital. We were so overloaded I thought we would never be able to take off but thankfully we did because Charles had already begun to lose consciousness. One of our friends had been mildly stung but the other had also suffered numerous bee stings to her eyes. She was later flown to a specialist in Salisbury where she eventually made a full recovery. Charles, though, remained in a serious condition and for five days the doctors in Livingstone fought in vain to get his kidneys to respond to treatment. As his condition showed no signs of improving it was decided I would fly with him to Bulawayo, where he was immediately put into intensive care.

When all this was going on Simon was miles and miles away in the bush. Now it may sound strange to some but Simon and I always had an extraordinary form of telepathic communication between us and he had an uncanny habit of turning up when he was most needed. And so it was after Charles' accident. Simon heard over his radio that an accident had occurred and immediately got into his Landrover with nothing more than a packet of biltong, a packet of Marie biscuits and a waterbag. He drove solidly for about ten hours and arrived at the hospital to give me some much-needed support.

Charles was still gravely ill but we were sure he would pull through. Simon stayed for a while, which was of enormous comfort to me, and then had to return to his work in the bush. I guess that even Simon felt that it was just a matter of time before Charles would get over the worst and make a full recovery.

For six long weeks he waged a valiant battle against the bee poison that had invaded and damaged almost every organ in his body. But it was a hopeless battle. He died just days after he reminded me of the wonderful plans he had for our new house on the Chobe. We had been together for seven and a half very eventful years, five of which were spent shaping our Chobe dream.

After Charles' death that dream lost all its appeal. The magic had gone.

Chapter Nine

PARADISE LOST

After the accident the glamour of Chobe swiftly began to wane. It was not a place for a woman alone and, as much as I loved it I no longer felt the desire to proceed with all our grand plans on my own. If Robert had not been studying in Australia there may have been a way for him to take up the reins, but for once he seemed settled and intent on completing his law degree. It was all quite ironic, really. When he worked at Chobe he kept making veiled comments that we should allow him to take it over because, as he put it, he would 'make the place sing'. It was one takeover my son failed to pull off.

Simon, as always, had materialised by my side at the crucial moment. Again, his sixth sense had urged him to make the long and arduous trip back to Bulawayo and he arrived exhausted just forty-eight hours before Charles died. After that he helped make all the appropriate arrangements and in his sweet, gentle way gave me much-needed emotional support. So too did all my friends, one of whom agreed to step in as temporary manager at Chobe. Charles's daughter, Jo, flew to Bulawayo and was a great comfort. Soon after, I had a pleasant and unexpected phone call. Peter rang from Bulawayo to say that he was very sorry to read about Charles' terrible ordeal and death. He chatted for a long while and I felt, at that moment, that we had never been parted. It almost seemed as though he was saying sorry.

After the funeral Simon drove me back to Chobe where it was

decided that I would be far better off selling the hotel and starting a new life somewhere less stressful. Chobe was simply far too remote a place for me to operate on my own. Also, the workload itself was too punishing for me to tackle single-handed. It involved the hotel itself, the camping site, two stores, the pontoon operating across the Zambezi as well as the game-viewing trips and fishing expeditions. Initially, many people had expressed interest in coming in to business with me but without Charles Chobe would just never be the same again. We had achieved our dream, as short-lived as it had been, and it was time for me to move on.

I notified the government officials of my decision to sell Chobe as that was one of the conditions agreed upon from the outset. They were, thankfully, extremely cooperative and let it be known that they would 'vet' prospective buyers. However, I was confident we wouldn't have any problems finding a suitable buyer as it was the only hotel in the region and, more importantly, a very exciting tourist attraction. It made for a plum investment. Nevertheless, it was a sad time for all who had helped make Chobe a dream come true, including the government officials who had given us the green light and had helped us make it a twenty-four carat drawcard in the region.

I received a lovely letter from Mr M.O.H. Hawkins, permanent secretary to the Ministry of Commerce, Industry and Water Affairs in Gaborones in Bechuanaland. In it he wrote:

I can well imagine how much you miss the Chobe River and I hope you will return there. Development is slow because of the perpetual shortage of money for this purpose, but increasing interest is being taken in the area and it is possible to visualise marked expansion in the next year or two. You can feel proud that you pioneered the way there and laid the foundation of an important tourist centre.

After several attractive offers we settled on a buyer from South Africa known to all as Captain Excell. He had been a regular visitor to Chobe which served as a sort of fuelling stop when he flew people on to various neighbouring countries. He was quite a strange fellow and on one of his customary stopovers at our hotel he brought along a baby leopard which had flown with him. I remember him feeding the little leopard in the kitchen and thinking that he was a decent sort of chap. So I was quite thrilled that he was interested in taking over Chobe.

Later we had an agreeable discussion on the telephone regarding the sale and he said that he would be flying up from South Africa in a couple of days' time, accompanied by his solicitor and accountant so we could set about negotiating a deal. I, too, alerted my solicitor and close friend Eddie in Rhodesia, who thought it best that he also be present at the meeting. Eddie came well in advance of Captain Excell's party because he had decided to make some discreet inquiries with government officials about the pilot's background. He didn't like what he heard. In fact, he was warned not to enter into any form of business with Captain Excell as he was listed as *persona non grata*. Apparently he had been involved in a number of dubious operations and the government officials were none too pleased at the prospect of having him take over ownership of the prized Chobe development.

It left us in quite a quandary because Captain Excell was already on his way to Chobe. Predictably, he was beside himself with rage when, shortly after his arrival, we told him the deal was off. He resorted to the most ungentlemanly behaviour and hurled obscenities at me, accusing me of betrayal and double dealing as I had promised him over the phone that I would sell Chobe to him. He threatened to bring a case against me and to squeeze every penny out of me for failing to honour my side of the deal.

Moreover, he kept insisting that the government had no power to prohibit the sale. When he left Chobe, trailing a cloud of dust, I was not only enormously relieved but believed that it would be the last I'd see of the boorish, uncouth fellow. How wrong I was.

A businessman from Livingstone, Lolly Sussens, quickly made it known that he was quite keen to become Chobe's next proud owner. He knew the area very well and had a couple of boats operating on the Zambezi. So while Eddie was still at Chobe it was arranged for Lolly to come over and discuss the matter. He finally agreed to the sale and once the government gave us the nod we settled the deal. It was decided that while Lolly arranged the funds I should make all the final preparations.

It proved an awfully traumatic time for me because since Charles's death I had worked myself ragged, often the night through. One evening, though, feeling the need to get away and draw breath, I accepted a dinner invitation from friends on a neighbouring ranch. I took my dogs with me in the Landrover and drove through elephant and lion territory, feeling very much alone and vulnerable. After all, it was in that very area where Robert and I had a near-disastrous encounter with a charging elephant. Looking back now I'm quite staggered by my own foolhardiness for it was certainly asking for trouble driving through that part of the bush in the dark and unaccompanied.

Needless to say I survived and managed to get there and back without mishap, but the drive and the long day left me utterly exhausted and I looked forward to crawling into bed. However, on arrival back at the hotel I noticed an aircraft on the airstrip and instinctively felt something was amiss. No visitors were expected that night. As soon as I parked my car I was met by our local police officer, fondly known as Webbie, who seemed quite agitated. He told me that Captain Excell and several other men were waiting in the bar to see me. It was the kind of news that rang very loud alarm bells. Indeed, I sensed trouble, for Captain Excell's unannounced appearance meant that he was intent on having some sort of showdown with me. Even the dogs and Ching, my remaining Siamese cat, seemed strangely disturbed that night and refused to leave my side.

Webbie advised that I retreat to my suite where I was instructed to keep the door bolted until I was given the all-clear. I didn't sleep a wink that night and just lay on my bed rigid with fear. I knew then that Captain Excell would stop at nothing to have his own way. Excell was, I finally came to realise, not the sort of man to trifle with. As it turned out, the government had long suspected that he had been involved in flying jail-breakers and refugees from South Africa via Kasane and the Chobe River Hotel. As Bechuanaland was a neutral country we were obliged to allow aircraft to refuel, but we seldom saw any of the passengers who made the stopover.

The previous year, 1963, there was quite a sensational case involving two South African jail-breakers, Arthur Goldreich and Harold Wolpe. According to press reports, the men made a dramatic getaway by car and then plane and managed to elude one of the biggest manhunts ever launched in the Republic of South Africa. With £5000 on their heads the men were reportedly flown out of the country. When the plane called at Livingstone to refuel the men were said not to be on board. Later it was disclosed that they had been dropped at Kasane in Bechuanaland because they were afraid of travelling on to Livingstone. The pilot then returned to pick up Goldreich and Wolpe and flew them to Elizabethville in Zaire.

The pilot was none other than the notorious Captain Excell. Only, at the time, Charles and I were oblivious of all his devious shenanigans and of the massive manhunt under way across the border. It was not until Excell had taken off that we were alerted of the jailbreak. I'm sure had we known that Captain Excell was suspected of being an accomplice we would have devised a way of delaying his departure and maybe collected £5000 for our efforts.

It seemed unthinkable that I would have sold our beloved Chobe to that reprobate had it not been for Eddie, my solicitor, uncovering his unsavoury reputation. He was, undoubtedly, not the kind of man to cross and I thought of all that while I remained sequestered with my animals in my suite during that interminable night while he sat waiting for me in the bar. Suddenly it dawned on me why he was so extraordinarily keen to acquire our hotel – it would have made for an ideal base for all his sinister operations.

The next morning Webbie stealthily came to see me and informed me that Excell had returned to Chobe to serve me with a writ that would prevent me from leaving the country. However, as I was 'unavailable' this was technically impossible provided I remained out of sight. After a while Excell and his cohorts, tired of waiting for me, departed in high dudgeon.

However, I discovered that Excell had been in touch with Lolly Sussens and had let it be known that he intended taking me to court for breach of contract. Not only that, he took some delight in emphasising that he had never lost a legal battle, which I took to be a veiled threat. Lolly and I decided not to waste any time and hastily drew up a contract in case Excell initiated legal action against me. Everyone suspected he was only using standover tactics but I wasn't overly keen to call his bluff. He obviously kept company with some shady characters and I did not especially relish the prospect of them launching a vendetta against me. I felt an urgent need to put as much distance as possible between myself and the odious Captain Excell. Indeed, I packed up all my belongings in record-breaking time, with the help of some local friends, the Sussens family and Webbie's wife, Ruth.

Then came all the teary farewells and, as could be expected, my last evening at the Chobe River Hotel was as breathtakingly beautiful as it was heart-rending. I recall being enveloped by the balmy evening air while in the distance the calls of wild animals were gradually building up to a crescendo. I knew then I couldn't leave Chobe without performing one last ritual. I had to say goodbye to some of the animals that had so enraptured Charles and myself over almost five years.

The thought of leaving so awesome a place tore at my heart because I had no idea when I would next hear elephants taking their ritualistic mudbaths or catch a glimpse of the timid white-speckled Chobe bushbuck as they nervously picked their way to the riverbanks for a drink. As I drove one last time through the game park I remembered the many animals we had rescued over the years, all of them patiently nursed back to health and then carefully released back in the wild. I had so loved living cheek-by-jowl with African wildlife, big and small, and I couldn't envisage being some place else. Life at Chobe had never been dull since nature, in that part of Africa, simply knew not how to be subdued. She unleashed spectacular afternoon thunderstorms, inflicted crippling droughts and seduced us with staggeringly perfect days. And no matter what the conditions, I felt privileged to call Chobe home.

The mysteries of Africa never ceased to surprise me, as they did on the evening I took my farewell drive. About two years previously we had released a young leopard in the park. We had not been all that confident that Jasper, as we had named the leopard, would survive and as a precaution shot a baboon which was left as feed the day we released him. We often went back to look for the leopard but never caught sight of him. Then one day a game scout came to us with the good news that he had seen

Jasper with a mate and some young and that he appeared to be in excellent condition. Suddenly, to my delight on my final evening in Chobe, I came across Jasper sitting ever so serenely in the middle of the sand track. I like to think that he, too, came to bid me farewell.

Shortly before dawn on 4 August 1964 I took one last, lingering look at Chobe before clambering on board a truck that took me, my dogs and Ching as far as the Victoria Falls. It was decided that I make my escape under the cover of darkness and that we drive along a little-used route to avoid all the border posts. After several hours of enduring a bone-rattling trip and heaps of delays, again caused by herds of elephant who delighted in turning the tracks into obstacle courses, we made it to the falls undetected. There I was met by Lolly Sussens, the proud new owner of Chobe, who then kindly offered to drive me to Bulawayo where I had arranged to stay with friends, Dorothy and David Davies, who had spent many happy holidays with us at Chobe.

Meanwhile, Excell proved to be a man of his word and proceeded to file a case against me. The case was heard at Lobatse in Bechuanaland on 1 October 1964. I was advised by my solicitor not to appear in court for he feared Excell would serve me with a summons and sue me for damages. Instead, Eddie acted as my representative and it was not until 22 October that we finally won the case. All costs were met, bar the champagne. That I bought for us to celebrate.

I was now free to leave the country in safety and immediately set about arranging a trip to Australia. I needed to get away for a while and Robert was keen for me to spend some time with him and to become acquainted with his adopted country. I left my beloved menagerie with Jo and her husband Tony and then caught a train to Cape Town. There I stayed with Yvonne and Petey, the friends who had been involved in the ghastly boating accident that had claimed my husband's life. I had not been with them long when, one morning, I woke to find emblazoned across the *Cape Argus* newspaper the headline PILOT ARRESTED. It was none other than my *bête noire*, Captain Excell, who was reported to be facing criminal charges after shooting his attorney in the cheek. According to the report he was refused political asylum in Swaziland and was to appear in court in Mbabane. It seemed Captain Excell would no longer pose a threat to me. The law had finally caught up with him.

Before I set sail from Cape Town there were more reports in the newspapers, this time concerning our pontoon:

> **Captain Nelson's pontoon on the Zambezi . . . refugees pass through the lion's jaws on the freedom ferry . . . the pontoon plies across the Zambezi and is a stepping stone for hundreds of passportless political refugees who are taking the freedom trail from South Africa. They head for Cairo, Accra, Dar es Salaam and beyond. Here are opportunities for scholarships and training in the arts of subversion and sabotage.**

The Captain Nelson referred to in the reports was the boat boy who had helped us build the pontoon and I remembered him being inordinately proud of being its captain. The pontoon was an essential mode of transport for our hotel and the game park and it was a great money-spinner. It carried a minimum of a hundred trucks a month, road plant and tourist vehicles and Captain Nelson had also ferried across a prince, ambassadors, governors and millionaires. I had not been aware that his passenger list included fugitives from the law. How strange it all seemed that these very passengers would have disembarked at the rather unique sausage tree that marked one of the pontoon's landing sites. I was told that on its bark were carved the initials of the explorer David Livingstone.

On 23 December 1964, after a very pleasant stay with my friends, I set sail for Australia on board a Portuguese ship. The voyage took forever as the ship called in at numerous ports along the South African coast to load cargo. In addition to that the captain was forced to change course to avoid a cyclone which added even more days at sea. At one stage water had to be rationed, but as the captain's friends we were often invited to his suite. Here the captain, ever mindful to be a considerate host, had kept Veuve Cliquot packed in ice in his bath. The ship's water supply had run low but there was no risk of us getting thirsty.

I had managed to send word to Robert that the ship would not be docking in Melbourne as scheduled but in Albany. Apparently, ours was the first passenger ship to dock there since the war and subsequently our arrival caused quite a stir.

I was the only passenger to disembark in Albany and while standing at the top of the gangplank I scanned the crowd in search of Robert. I had not seen him for over two years and was beside myself with excitement at the prospect of being reunited with my son. Only there was no sign of him. Then, suddenly, I spotted a tall figure walking slowly through the crowd toward me. So much had happened since we had last seen each other. There had been Charles's accident and his resulting death, the uncertainty of what to do with Chobe and then the terrifying saga with the nefarious Captain Excell. Robert and I had a lot of catching up to do.

Fortunately Robert had organised for us to spend a couple of days in Albany, which allowed us time to ourselves. We swam at some lovely beaches, took a number of tours in and around Albany and, as usual, fell into our old habit of just talking and talking. He seemed so incredibly happy with his lot in life and I was under the impression that he was enjoying his studies as well as a very busy social life off campus.

We drove back to Perth in his little Volkswagen, crammed to the roof with all my luggage. As I was unsure of my future I thought it best to bring as much as I could. Robert had always insisted that I should sell up and move to Australia and kept saying, 'The writing's on the wall'. He was convinced that Africa would degenerate into political turmoil. Mindful of these warnings, I had arranged for the rest of my belongings and furniture to be placed in storage and to have them shipped to Australia if I decided to stay on.

And so it was, with Robert as my informative tour guide, that I began to explore his new country. We drove through beautiful karri forests where I caught my first sight of a kangaroo with her joey. Robert pointed out the unique blackboys, or grasstrees, that are native to Western Australia. The countryside was so similar to parts of Africa it was quite uncanny and I kept expecting to see an elephant or giraffe lope into view.

When we arrived in Perth, Robert booked me into a small hotel where we wined, dined and toasted our future. Over the next couple of days I met some of Robert's friends. The one I took an instant liking to was Chris Tangney, the delightful woman with whom he was boarding. It became quite evident that she absolutely doted on my son and, like so many other women in his life, she spoilt him rotten. At first, though, I was under the impression that she was afraid that with my move to Australia she stood to lose her much-loved boarder. I quickly assured her there was no risk of that as my son was well aware that on the domestic front I had little to commend myself. I was still an appalling cook and had never ironed a shirt in my life. No wonder Robert remained so comfortably ensconced at Chris's during the four years he was at university.

During that hectic week of meeting and greeting, Robert took me to a house in one of Perth's suburbs. As soon as we arrived a tall, good-looking and cheerful young girl came to meet us. With an expressionless face Robert turned to me and said, 'Meet my secretary.' There was a giggle and then she introduced herself as Janet Ranford. We were invited in for tea and it did not take me too long to discover that if Janet was being passed off as my son's secretary she was a highly efficient one at that. It was Janet who helped me to settle in Perth.

After a week in the hotel it was decided we should start looking for a flat and Janet volunteered to drive me around to inspect some of the flats advertised. We eventually found one in South Perth in a new building overlooking the Swan River. Admittedly it wasn't Chobe, but there was a pleasant enough esplanade that allowed for some wonderful strolls. Once we had signed the lease Janet took me shopping for 'essentials', things like brooms, dustpans, a small fridge and, horror of horrors, an ironing board. We had quite a giggle. She was so super-efficient and I think she was rather astonished that a woman could be so ill-prepared for a life without domestic help.

I made no apology for the way I was raised in Africa and for having had servants at my beck and call since childhood. That was just the way it was then and, not surprisingly, I was never expected to wash or iron a garment, let alone sweep the floor. Nevertheless, I soon came to realise you're never too old to learn new ways and Janet was a first-rate teacher. She taught me how to whip up a couple of easy dishes and how to iron. The ironing bit, though, proved the most daunting and in desperation I finally resorted to ever practical drip-dry clothing.

But having accomplished all those domestic feats another, much larger obstacle suddenly presented itself. For the first time in my life I began to wrestle with a terrible bout of loneliness. I remember the first night in that cold, stark flat on the seventh floor as if it were yesterday. It felt as if I had been cut off from the rest of the world and placed far beyond the comforting reach of Simon and all my beloved friends and animals.

The loneliness only evaporated, albeit briefly, when Robert dropped by. I used to live for the time he would come for a visit and took some pride in preparing him one of the simple dishes I had mastered. Usually it was a grilled steak with salad, accompanied by a bottle of wine. They were always such pleasant evenings and we would chat away late into the night. Often, after he left, my light would be the only one burning in the building. Looking out into the darkness always underscored my feelings of isolation. There I was in a poky little flat with no telephone, I had no car and at that stage all my money was still tied up in Bechuanaland and Rhodesia.

Robert and Janet did all they could to help me adjust to my new environment but, what with their studies there was only so much they could do. Janet's family was especially good to me and some Sundays I would catch a bus – another novel experience – and spend the day with them. Sometimes they would take me for a drive in the countryside to view the magnificent wildflowers the region is world-renowned for. Another person who helped keep my loneliness at bay was Betty Gibson, the secretary of the Simba Club, a support network for the many people who had left Kenya during the Mau Mau period of leadership (1952–1958) and had come to settle in Perth. The club also included a number of people from Rhodesia so I always looked forward to the social gatherings Betty organised. We all had so much in common and through the Simba Club were able to build lasting friendships.

One day Robert said someone called Nancy had been in touch with him and had invited us over for drinks. It turned out she had received a letter from a mutual friend of ours in Rhodesia who had alerted her to my arrival in Perth. They had befriended each other while studying at Oxford and had kept up correspondence over the years. Apparently my friend had asked Nancy to take me under her wing and to introduce me to some people. We ended up having a terrific evening and she asked me to come over and play tennis. It became a much-anticipated weekly routine after that, and through these social tennis gatherings I gradually began to meet more people.

But other than my game of social tennis there wasn't much else for me to do and I began to get terribly homesick. I missed Africa, Simon and all my friends and lived for the letters I'd receive from home. Perth was a nice enough place but try as I did I continued to feel like a stranger. Even at our tennis gatherings people had absolutely no idea of my background. No-one knew anything about Africa, let alone Bechuanaland.

On the days I was stuck without transport I'd walk to the zoo and spend time literally talking to all the animals. It was on one of those long, lonely walks that I decided the only way I would get out and meet people was if I took a job somewhere. I mentioned this to Robert who was somewhat taken aback but he promised to make some inquiries on my behalf.

It did not take him long to find something he thought would be ideal. A friend of his knew the owner of a stud farm south of Perth and she offered me a job helping out in the office. I was to do some typing, answer the telephone and take bookings for the three stallions standing at stud. It was not what I had done before but at least it was a job that involved working with horses again.

Robert drove me down the evening before I was to start my new job. I had no idea what I had let myself in for. For a start, I was woken up at five the following morning with a cup of tea by the head girl. She asked me to meet her at the stables and from there she would show me around the property and introduce me to all the staff.

I could not have picked a worse day to start a new job. It was a bitterly cold, wet and miserable June day and I tried to look enthused as I trudged disconsolately behind the head girl. She took me to where they were preparing the morning feed and I was utterly staggered to find a group of young girls make short work of the most physically demanding tasks. I stood in amazement as they lifted bales of hay, emptied heavy sacks of feed and pushed carts laden with feed bins to distant paddocks. I noticed one girl going off on a pushbike with a bucket of feed hanging from each handlebar and hay stacked on the carrier as she splashed her way through the puddles to one of the stallion boxes. Suitably impressed I followed these young Amazons to the main block for a breakfast of porridge and strong black tea that tasted as if it had been left to brew on the Aga all night long. Until then I had never had a meal in a kitchen and it marked my initiation to how differently things were done in Australia.

Later that morning I was shown to the office where I immediately busied myself typing and updating records. Lunch was a plate of stew with vegetables, followed by bottled fruit and custard and, again, washed down with strong brewed tea. Also, as with breakfast, it was served in the kitchen. The rest of the afternoon was spent taking telephone bookings for the three stallions. I was kept company in the office by two dogs and a cat who had made themselves very much at home. When I had completed all my clerical chores I took the dogs for a long walk around the paddocks to familiarise myself with my new surroundings.

The evening meal, known as tea, consisted of beans or corn on toast. Only this time we had the meal in front of the television on an enclosed verandah. I was told that when it became colder we would have tea in the kitchen. Conversation was somewhat strained and stilted as I had very little in common with all those strapping young girls, but they politely asked me questions about Africa and seemed quite interested in the different feeding programmes and the fact that most of the 'hard yakka' was done by African grooms. Certainly never by girls.

Within a matter of days my job description was drastically amended. One of the girls had taken a day off work and failed to return, leaving the farm short staffed. When I was asked to 'lend a hand' I was more than willing to oblige. Actually, I was quite excited at the prospect of working with the horses. Early the following morning I reported for duty at one of the feed sheds bright-eyed and enthusiastic. Here I was unceremoniously presented with a bicycle piled with hay on the back and buckets of feed on the handlebars. I was to feed one of the prized stallions but I was given strict instructions not to go into his stable. Instead, the feed had to be pushed through a hatch and into his bin.

It sounded simple enough. The hardest part was getting there because I couldn't reach the bicycle's pedals. Eventually I managed some form of mobility but the puddles got the better of me. I would have come a nasty cropper had I not thought it better to get off and push the bike to the stables. Once the stallion was fed I was dispatched to take care of a host of menial chores, the sort of things I had never done in my life. I had to muck out stables, renew bedding, move horses to various paddocks, clean out water troughs and liberate the mice swimming around in them, groom two yearlings, fill hay nets, drag bags of feed to an area where mixes were being made up, then fill buckets in readiness for the evening feed. An African groom in Rhodesia never worked as hard, let alone a woman forty-nine years of age.

It all reached flashpoint on a day marred by leaden skies and torrential downpours. Again it was back to the bicycle routine, only this time it had buckets of milk swinging from the handlebars. With these I was expected to negotiate all the puddles to a faraway paddock and feed some unruly yearlings. It was an extremely messy exercise and I was, to put it mildly, more than a little annoyed. But it was on the way back that I finally snapped. As I recall there was a big puddle, more like a pond, that suddenly materialised up ahead. I had no idea of how deep it was until I skidded through it and fell most inelegantly on my behind. That was the last straw. Covered in a very unsightly mix of mud and milk slop I got up, straightened my back and abandoned the bicycle. I had had enough of copping dirty and gruelling work that I had not been hired to do.

That evening Janet took me to an accountancy class I had begun in the hope that it would equip me with more knowledge on how to take stock of my financial affairs. Afterwards we went to Chris Tangney's house where she always treated us to coffee and sandwiches. I noticed Robert looking at me askance and before long he made some remark about my bruises and torn nails. I looked and felt awful and it did not take much persuasion on his part to get me to blurt out what had been happening on the farm. He became absolutely furious and insisted that I was not to stay there a day longer. I had lasted a week. So it was back to my bleak and lonely flat.

I could not keep imposing on Robert since he was extremely busy with his law studies. So too was Janet, who was teaching after having graduated with a science degree from the University of Western Australia. I believe she was the only woman to have majored in organic chemistry. So, I was back to square one and contemplating a future that seemed to be getting progressively bleaker. But I refused to give in and within a couple of days I began scouring newspaper advertisements for a job that did not require cycling with slop buckets. It did not make for an encouraging exercise as all jobs advertised were for women under twenty-one years old and I knew that even if I knocked a couple of years off my age I stood little chance of fooling prospective employers. Notwithstanding this blatant age bias I determined to do the rounds of the various employment agencies. I marched off optimistically, armed with a résumé I took some pride in and a conviction that somewhere in Perth there was an ideal job waiting for me. A job that would help turn my life around.

The first employment agency I walked into I was confronted by a rather disdainful woman who asked me to run through all my qualifications. I duly made mention of the hotel I had helped build and run, my riding school, my work in the airforce and the fact that I had a pilot's licence. None of it seemed to overly impress her and after a cursory look at my résumé she announced that she did not have anything 'suitable' for me. Her tone and manner erased the last scrap of my enthusiasm and, no longer able to face the prospect of more rejection, I disconsolately lugged my résumé home. I had all but given up hope of ever finding a job when someone in my tennis group mentioned that she knew of a doctor looking to employ a 'mature' receptionist. I had no idea what being a receptionist entailed but I certainly met the 'mature' requirement. I thought it worth a shot.

There were about forty applicants for the job but as luck would have it I was interviewed by a very nice doctor who was originally from Cape Town and had worked with my cousin Paul at the famous Groote Schuur Hospital. We fell into easy conversation and, without too many formalities or searching questions, I was hired. My elation at having triumphed after such a long, soul-destroying quest was somewhat short-lived, however, for no sooner had I bounded out the doctor's room than I came face to face with the dour sister in charge.

She was an intimidating, unsmiling woman about twice my height and with an unsettling habit of barking orders. And she wasted no time in giving me my first dose of directives. To look the part of a receptionist I was instructed to buy white drip-dry uniforms and white shoes and to report for duty no later than 7.50a.m. She was, I realised, not going to be the kind of colleague I would warm to but I was not going to let her overbearing manner sour my glorious taste of victory. At long last I had secured a job that did not require teetering precariously on a bicycle weighed down with feed buckets.

Early next morning I caught a bus full of rowdy schoolboys. As soon as I stepped on they fell strangely silent, which I found quite disconcerting. I put it down to the rather severe white uniform that would be my workday suit of armour. I then had to walk a fair distance to get to the clinic but fortunately I arrived just as the sister was unlocking the door to the surgery.

Then it was down to business. I was shown to a large, imposing desk on which stood the doctors' appointment book. Patients, I was told, were to be allotted no more than fifteen minutes for an appointment. It seemed straightforward enough until the phones began to ring as there were seven doctors in the clinic and it seemed as if all of Perth was desperate to consult with them. What I found especially difficult to cope with was the pronunciation of names. And I wasted no time in causing mayhem on that first day when I made an appointment for a Mr I. Rainbow. His real name was Mr A. Rambo and my error caused considerable confusion between doctor, sister and patient. Then there was the confounded switchboard, an instrument that caused me no end of grief. I began to detest the darn thing because I was forever putting calls through to the wrong doctors. It was one of those archaic switchboards where you had to stick the connections into the appropriate holes.

Of course, having applied for the job it was taken for granted that I was qualified as a receptionist. They were not to know that I didn't have a clue but I felt it best not to disabuse my new employers of that fact, especially the dictator in white plimsolls. She was terribly bossy and when I was not wrestling with the switchboard she made me perform chores such as tidying the rooms, emptying ashtrays and rearranging the magazines. For tea I was allowed only two digestive biscuits and a couple of minutes' respite from the dreaded telephone.

Minor surgical procedures were performed at the clinic and one day I was detailed to sit with a patient in the recovery room. She was an elderly lady and incredibly demanding and insisted that I get her a cup of tea. When I obliged all hell broke loose. Not only was the patient not allowed to have tea but I was not supposed to have left her unattended.

Not surprisingly, I did not make friends while working at the doctors' surgery. As a matter of fact, it was not a particularly friendly work environment and during my half-hour lunchbreak I'd walk to a nearby bus shelter where I would sit and have my sandwich and fruit. At least there I was spared yet another confrontation with the sister and it was infinitely better than having my lunch in the back room amid all the blood-stained bandages. That bus shelter became my favourite refuge and I remember sitting there one particularly cold and miserable day, watching people go by when suddenly I was hit by such a crushing wave of loneliness that it almost reduced me to tears. I knew then that I had sunk to my lowest ebb and that night I told Robert I wanted to return to Africa and my friends.

I don't think he was surprised for he had long known how

desperately unhappy I had become. My situation was not made any easier with all my money still tied up in Rhodesia. Robert, however, remained emphatic that I should look to beginning a future outside Africa. He also promised me he would return to Rhodesia after his final exams to help me finalise the sale of my house and farm. It was, he warned, not a particularly good time to be selling all my assets as the country was in the grip of political turmoil. As the struggle for independence swept through Africa, Prime Minister Ian Smith's government refused to allow black majority rule and illegally declared independence for white-ruled Rhodesia.

As a result, the international community decided to bring pressure to bear on the Smith Government by introducing a number of crippling trade sanctions. Subsequently many people, fearing a protracted and bloody civil war, sold their properties for next to nothing and joined the long queues outside foreign embassies for immigration visas.

Despite the pervading political climate I was so looking forward to returning home. I had tried to make the best of my short stay in Australia but for all my determined efforts it had not worked out. And once I had made the decision to go back I could hardly wait to quit my job at the surgery. I had lasted there a mere three months, but to me it had seemed like an eternity.

On 21 September 1965, after eight months in Western Australia, I boarded a cargo ship with ten other passengers in Fremantle and began my long journey home. Robert, Janet and a few of the friends I'd made came to see me off. As I stood on deck I could see Robert standing tall and composed on the quay and when we slipped anchor, prompting a chorus of goodbyes, I had this great lump in my throat. It seemed as if my life had been reduced to a succession of farewells, each more painful than the last.

I remained on deck until I could no longer see my son and for a fleeting moment I began to doubt my decision to return to Africa. Was I doing the right thing or should I have stuck it out in Australia? Time would eventually provide me with the answer.

Chapter Ten

RETURN TO AFRICA

When I stepped ashore in Durban everything seemed suffused with a welcoming light. Gone was the cloud of despondency that had overshadowed my stay in Australia. I was back on familiar territory, back in Africa, where I knew I belonged, despite Robert's dire predictions.

On my way to Salisbury I broke my journey for a few days in Francistown, Bechuanaland, where I stayed with my friends Patrick and Audrey Bromfield. Simon had managed to take a few days' leave to join me there and to help celebrate my fiftieth birthday. I had so missed Simon but, not surprisingly, found he had changed little, if at all, in the months I had been away. He still sported a deep tan, wore his customary khaki shorts and a pair of well-worn *veldskoene*, locally made desert boots that had become his stock in trade. Simon's meagre wardrobe, which extended to a few shirts and his 'Jesus sandals' that were made in Kenya, underscored his preference for an ascetic and uncluttered life. I think the only 'suit' he ever possessed was his school uniform and later his wetsuit.

It was during my stay with Simon and the Bromfields that I first became acquainted with Bodo Muche, my son's close friend. They shared an interest (more like a passion) in taxidermy and were both extraordinarily gifted sculptors. I was not to know that Bodo would later come to play such a pivotal part in my life. But then we were preoccupied with celebrating a major milestone in my life and my return home to the soul-stirring surrounds of the African bush. This joyous reunion made for an effective antidote to the months of uncertainty I had endured in Perth. I was, I realised then, simply not ready to bid Africa adieu. It still had too strong a magnetic hold on me.

When Simon had to return to his bush camp I continued my train journey to Salisbury where, once again, my stepdaughter Jo Alexander and her husband Tony gave me a warm welcome. In the time I had been away they had made extensive alterations to the cottage they had bought from me and had also added a swimming pool. But more importantly, they still had my old Siamese cat, Ching, who had no trouble in recognising me.

After months of having persevered with morale-crushing jobs in Australia I was anxious to find something a bit more rewarding and to sort out my affairs. My friend Diana, from our riding school days, had heard of a job going at a picturesque little country inn about twenty miles outside Umtali. I was keen to find a place of my own because I did not want to overstay my welcome with Jo and Tony, and I found the idea of living and working in a small country inn particularly appealing. I imagined it would involve the sort of work I had done in Chobe.

Diana kindly offered to drive me down and we spent the entire trip chatting away about all the things that had happened to us in the years since we had the riding school. We were so engrossed in our chitchat that we almost missed the turn-off to the Peplow Country House Inn which was almost on the border of Portuguese East Africa. Unlike my horror encounters in Perth the job interview went like a dream and my Chobe experience no doubt worked in my favour because I was told in no time that the job was mine.

I had been up against it for so long that getting the job in such a sublime setting represented a major shift in my luck. Indeed, I was in such a tearing hurry to settle in my new job that within a matter of days I packed Ching and some of my belongings into my new Volkswagen and headed for what I hoped would be balmier days.

At the Peplow Country House Inn it did not take me long to find that my job had no fixed routine. Rather, what I was required to do was about as vague as my new employer, a somewhat eccentric woman. However, she took some pride in making her establishment an attractive and restful retreat for her guests. And to help make it that way I was required to pick and arrange flowers from the garden and to paint the night's menu on a pretty china tile.

Guests were accommodated in bungalows overlooking a magnificent garden and a range of blue mountains in the distance. Breakfast was served on the verandah of each bungalow and there was no set time. Lunch was a casual, help-yourself kind of affair on the main building's verandah. But dinner, by comparison, was quite formal and served in the diningroom by waiters dressed in starched white uniforms and white gloves.

As jobs went mine was not an especially challenging one, which would account for my low wages. But fortunately I did not have a switchboard or a tyrannical nurse to contend with. Not that it did not come without its own set of peculiarities. When I was put in charge of preparing the menus I was expected to consult with the owner before deciding on the following day's meals. On my first day I called on her, as arranged, and was met at the door by her African maid and then shown into the bathroom. I was quite embarrassed to find my employer soaking in a huge bath where the maid then blithely proceeded to scrub her back. The only available seat was the loo, and it was there that I sat and conducted the most unusual of business meetings.

What I loved most about the job, though, was that I had the run of the place in my free time. During my lunchbreak I would take a swim in the pool with its captivating views of the mountains. Also, I was asked if I was interested in exercising some polo ponies. Needless to say I jumped at the chance.

Peplow was quite a popular haunt among the polo set and one of the three permanent residents kept his polo ponies in the stables and paddocks near the inn. They were the ponies I had agreed to exercise and the task was made a good deal easier by a groom who ensured that everything was ready for me before I set off and then took care of the ponies after the rides. It often made me think back to those strong, capable young women on the stud farm near Perth who seemed so nonplussed that in Africa we had grooms who took care of all the stabling and grooming.

At Peplow I soon began to revel in the quietude. To me it felt like being becalmed after a stormy passage. After Charles's death I had lurched from one catastrophe to the next until fortune finally brought me to the tranquil sanctum out in the Rhodesian countryside.

In February 1966 Robert kept his promise and flew out from Perth to help me settle all my financial affairs and to ensure that I fetched the best possible price for my properties given the volatile political climate. He came to stay at Peplow, where we spent our afternoons exercising the polo ponies and chatting endlessly about absolutely everything. When Robert and I got going there was never any risk of the conversation drying up. With his expert knowledge I was soon able to put the wheels in motion to dispose of all my assets. Even before he came to assist me in my affairs Robert had urged me to cut my losses and sell up. In his words, 'everything you've got in Rhodesia is a millstone around your neck. Sell the farm for whatever they can pay.'

The farm he referred to was Gardiner Farm, the one Charles and I had transformed into a dream place, with an old stone farmhouse and a river running through the property. But all I got from my tenants for the farm, the house and the stables was a miserly £3000. I could have wept. Also, the financial fiasco concerning Chobe still needed to be straightened out. But thankfully Robert made swift work of all that and arranged for my money to be sent to Australia, where he would invest it for me.

When he returned to Perth I truly did feel as if I had been relieved of a giant millstone, one that had weighed me down ever since I fled Chobe under cover of darkness. Although he didn't say much to the effect, I was under the impression that Robert also made use of his brief stay in Rhodesia to sort through some of his own personal affairs. In fact, not long after his return to Perth I received a cable – Robert was to announce his engagement to Janet. I was absolutely thrilled because from the moment I had met her I knew that she utterly adored my son.

Admittedly, when I was in Perth there was no indication that she would become the future Mrs Holmes à Court. I then felt they were so different in many ways. What they did have in common, however, was a love of driving around in Robert's car. I still have this image of her in my flat in South Perth, anxiously awaiting Robert's arrival. She kept going onto the balcony to see if she could spot his newly acquired red Porsche coming up the road. It so reminded me of the time I had kept watch for Peter's little red sports car when he came to stay at Christmas Gift Farm. When Janet sighted Robert's car she became so excited that within minutes she was gone. My flat was on the seventh floor and she didn't even wait for the lift. She flew down all seven flights of stairs in record time, just as Robert drove into the car park.

Later we all got into the Porsche with Janet at the wheel and went for a long, and not so leisurely, drive. Janet was an excellent driver and took some delight in passing most of the other cars on the road. We had great fun that day.

On another occasion we drove down to a lovely little cottage on the coast that Robert and Janet had rented for a long weekend. I remember being astonished at how efficient she was and how well she coped in the minute kitchen where she produced the most wonderful meals. Even then I got a glimpse of how she spoiled Robert because she would take him his breakfast in bed every morning. There was nothing she would not do for him, including washing his car. Now that, to me, was most unusual. For someone born and bred in Africa it was a novelty, but even in Australia I knew it was quite out of the ordinary for a girlfriend or wife to wash her man's car. But Janet did not seem to mind.

I don't know if Robert quite appreciated all the things Janet did for him then. Maybe he expected it because he too was raised in Africa where he had grown accustomed to having everything done for him. His adoring mother, however, drew the line at cooking for him – and she would certainly never have washed his car! Nevertheless, Janet seemed to delight in pleasing him and there was no mistaking that she loved him dearly. On occasions when I'd be visiting her parents she used to come home from work dead-beat and often she would head straight to bed. But if Robert phoned she would jump into the shower, change and be ready for a night out with him. One night they were going out to a ball and Janet had made a beautiful, long black frock for the occasion. She was still frantically sewing the hem when she heard Robert's car pull up. I don't know how she managed it but the hem was dealt with in a flash and then she was out the door before Robert could ring the bell. She was extraordinary.

Naturally I wasted no time in calling to congratulate both Robert and Janet on the news. Robert asked me to attend the wedding which they had planned to coincide with the May school holidays since Janet was teaching and also for Robert's graduation from the University of Western Australia on 4 May. I booked my flight so I would be in Perth for both those special events.

Meanwhile, back at Peplow both my work and the place had begun to lose their appeal. It all began to go flat after an incident involving a regular guest at the inn. He was a tall and nice-looking man who, at first, seemed pleasant enough. One evening he knocked on my door and asked me if I would like to accompany him for a walk in the garden. It seemed an innocent enough request and as he was a frequent visitor I graciously accepted the invitation. But we had not walked for more than a couple of minutes when he suddenly made very unwelcome advances toward me. I was quite taken aback because I did not fancy the chap at all. Somehow I managed to extricate myself from his unwanted embrace and bolted for my room. The next evening there was another knock on the door but this time I had taken the precaution of keeping my door locked. I was not in the mood for a repeat performance.

He obviously did not take kindly to being rebuffed by a woman and complained to my employer that I had snubbed him and been rude. Incredibly, she ticked me off like nothing on earth and said I had no business 'doing that to our guests'. I was dumbfounded. I had long suspected that Peplow was the sort of place many people used as a discreet weekend rendezvous, but I drew the line at being made to amuse lecherous male guests.

At about this time my friend Cath, who had been my bridesmaid back in 1936, and her husband had started a business in Salisbury called Copperwares. They had their own factory and were doing extremely well, exporting their products to a number of countries. Apparently one country was only able to barter so they offered Cath the most exquisite silks in exchange. Cath asked me if I would be interested in running their office and, what with my unpleasant garden encounter and my employer's curious code of duty, I needed no time to consider her kind offer. But I thought it best to delay my move back to Salisbury until after I had attended Robert and Janet's wedding.

I had hoped Simon would join me but he had taken leave from the Game Department to go diving off the coast of Portuguese East Africa and indulge his newfound passion for underwater photography. He sent me a cable informing me that he would be unable to take more leave to attend the wedding and, moreover, the only suit he possessed was a wetsuit.

My arrival back in Perth was in marked contrast from my previous visit. I felt infinitely more at ease than I did back in January 1965 and immediately fell into a busy social round. Also, as mother of the bridegroom, I thought the occasion warranted splurging out on a special new frock and matching hat but it became a toilsome task finding something I liked. In the end I found someone to make me something at short notice.

Robert did not seem nearly as fussed about keeping up appearances. On the wedding day I went to meet him at Chris Tangney's, where he was still comfortably installed as a boarder. I surprised him by taking him his early morning cup of tea, which was just as well because he then asked me to give his dinner suit the once-over. To my consternation I found that the bottom of his trousers were covered in mud. Fortunately Chris knew some cleaners and had them tended to posthaste.

The wedding was held in the early evening and Robert, who had developed a great passion for vintage cars, had hired a Rolls Royce from the vintage car museum. It was a lovely ceremony and Janet and Robert looked blissfully happy. Before they flew off for their honeymoon on Norfolk Island Robert asked me to reconsider my decision to stay in Africa. He said my investments in Australia were doing well and that I would be well taken care of once I settled back in Perth. Robert had little faith in southern Africa's political future and hoped that once I made the decision to emigrate Simon, too, would follow and we would be together. At that stage I was still not quite ready to make a permanent move and looked forward to returning to Salisbury and my new job with Copperwares.

I flew back to Rhodesia on 23 May and within a couple of weeks of my return I resigned from my job at Peplow and, once again, packed Ching and my chattels back in the Volkswagen. Luckily I was able to rent a small but delightful cottage in my friend Anne's garden in Borrowdale, near Salisbury. I made it quite homely with some of my furniture I had taken out of storage. The rest, including many treasured family heirlooms, was sent by container to Perth for Robert and Janet's new home.

At Copperwares I was kept frantically busy but it was rewarding work and, thankfully, a lot more challenging than some of the jobs I had landed in Perth and at the Peplow Inn. On the personal front I was kept equally on the go by a host of male escorts and one even offered to take me to the Canary Islands where he intended to settle. It was quite a romantic gesture and I was duly flattered but for once I was not tempted to make another move. Looking back, my time in Salisbury was wonderfully easeful – with some entertaining diversion. Anne, my landlady, was a devout Roman Catholic, although divorced, and on close terms with a group of monks who stayed at a neighbouring retreat. They were in the habit of popping over some nights to watch Anne's television and I soon grew accustomed to seeing cassock-shrouded monks about the place.

After work one day Anne asked me to join her and several of the monks for a drink. They were, contrary to all expectations, quite a lively, genial bunch. However, on that particular occasion there was a young and very bright young man who seemed to have caused Anne some concern. She drew me aside and said that he needed some advice and a sympathetic ear and would I be so kind as to give him some 'motherly attention'. Sensing her disquiet and wanting to be of some assistance I invited the very tense, furrow-browed young man to my cottage.

Realising that it would take some gentle coercion to get him to unburden himself, I slipped one of my more soothing records onto the radiogram and offered him a drink. Within minutes, and with hardly any prompting on my part, he began to pour out his troubled heart. It transpired that the dear boy was due to take his vows in Pretoria within a couple of months but had suddenly found himself haunted by episodes of self-doubt. He began to seriously question whether he was suited to a monastic life.

I tried my best to give him some of that motherly advice that Anne thought would help ease his anguish and in the process kept topping up his drink. As the night progressed the young man not only began to shed some of his anxiety but also much of his clerical attire. Off came the cassock and there he sat, in his white singlet, very much at home in my tiny cottage. At least he seemed a good deal more relaxed, and when a tango was playing on the radiogram he jumped to his feet, grabbed me around the waist and said, 'Let's tango'. And tango we did. By then we were up to our eyebrows in brandy and the young monk was quite animated.

At one stage I was struck by the absurdity of the situation and thought, Heavens, what am I doing dancing the tango with a man who was not only half my age but about to take his vows? But he seemed to be enjoying himself so much, that with me dipped low in his arms, he suddenly declared, 'I can't go on with it. I'm not going to take my vows.'

I was worried that he would become quite emotional and turned off the music, sat him down and then talked to him for what seemed a very long time. At one stage he came close to tears and was clearly cut up about it all. Yet for all his distress I think on that night it dawned on him what he would be renouncing once he became a priest. Personally, I thought it would be a waste of a very good-looking young man who was not only full of fun but a fabulous dancer. I don't know how helpful I was. After a very unholy diversion which involved dispensing maternal advice over many glasses of good brandy and to the lusty strains of the tango, that young man walked out into the night a changed man. Later I was told he never did take his vows.

In January 1967 Simon and his friend Julian, a fishery officer with the Game Department, had decided to take the golden handshake from the department. The Bechuanaland Protectorate had become independent the year before and, like so many young people, Simon and Julian were keen to move on and find new challenges. What I didn't expect to hear was that they intended using some of their money to buy a yacht.

Neither had ever sailed but Simon was confident they would have no difficulties in picking up the fundamentals once they acquired their yacht. Both were already reading every available book on sailing and Simon was studying a navigation course by correspondence. They had very ambitious plans, including forming a partnership to do charter work, running fishing trips, giving skin-diving instruction and doing underwater photography. I soon gathered this was no passing fancy and Simon even wrote to Robert asking him for advice on how to go about forming a partnership. The final paragraph read: 'I have retired from the game department, I have a pension and you are about to start working!'

But before their venture could get under way they had to find a thirty or forty-foot yacht. Living in a landlocked country they faced a difficult task finding one. I was keen to help because not only was their enthusiasm catching but I was convinced their plans had a good deal of merit and I desperately wanted their enterprise to succeed. We scanned all the newspapers and boating magazines and put the word out. Finally, they saw a yacht advertised for sale in Mauritius and decided to travel across to view it. Simon also made arrangements to stop over in the Seychelles on the way back as he had heard that it was relatively inexpensive to have a yacht built there.

No sooner had Simon left for Mauritius than I spotted an advertisement in a Rhodesian newspaper for a yacht that sounded exactly what the boys had been after. I immediately cabled Simon and he replied that Julian would fly back to inspect the yacht as he had already made arrangements to leave for the Seychelles on board a small Japanese boat.

As soon as Julian arrived we drove down to Beira where the yacht *Carina* was moored. Julian was most impressed with her but as a precaution sent a cable with all the relevant details to Simon before we made a decision. Apparently *Carina* had been beautifully built and had not sailed far, as the three young men who had owned her had struck bad weather on their maiden voyage and were forced to land at Madagascar. Later there were problems regarding their Rhodesian passports, which were not recognised by many of the countries they had planned to visit. In the end they returned to Beira and put *Carina* up for sale.

Simon promptly sent word that he thought *Carina* sounded exactly what they were after and asked me to put down a deposit on the yacht. As soon as he got back from the Seychelles and saw *Carina* for himself it was love at first sight. He bought her on the spot and arranged to commute part of his pension from the British Government.

Then it was down to learning how to sail. The yacht was moored in the lagoon at Savane. There they soon befriended other yachtsmen who warned Simon and Julian about the difficulties involved in getting out of the lagoon and stressed that it could only be negotiated when the tide was right. The first time Simon and Julian took *Carina* out to sea some of these helpful and more experienced yachtsmen escorted them out and then later brought them back in at high tide. They were gradually getting the hang of it but unfortunately Julian began to have grave doubts about their impending adventure. He finally lost his nerve one day when they hit a severe storm some miles out to sea. After they had made it safely back to land, Julian admitted that he had been scared stiff and realised that sailing was not for him. Simon, on the other hand, grew to love it and decided to proceed with the grand adventure on his own.

Even near-disasters failed to deter him in his quest to become an accomplished yachtsman. In a letter dated 13 August 1967 he wrote of an accident that would have cured most would-be sailors of any thoughts of tackling the high seas. Not Simon. It read as follows:

> *We tried to come into the lagoon. The mist suddenly came down, it was very thick. We were at the entrance and before we could turn back we found ourselves on the sand. We had to dig ourselves level at low tide and then wait for high tide.*
>
> *We took a hell of a pounding. We rolled right over with water on the top deck on one side, then the other. When we slipped off the sandbank the engine stopped. It was clogged with sand. We were wakened in the night by the boat falling on its side at low tide. Our bilge keel was buckled in. Luckily no damage to the hull. We've now taken the keel off to be fixed in Beira then we will refit it.*

I later discovered that when *Carina* was safely moored in the lagoon, Simon set off on foot carrying the heavy keel on his shoulder. At the time he had no car and had walked several miles when a car pulled up. It was his first meeting with Eve and Lloyd Barber, who owned the yacht *Rebel* that was tied up near *Carina*. They gave Simon a lift to Beira, which was about twenty miles away. That fortuitous meeting led to a lasting friendship and they taught Simon a great deal about sailing.

I met Eve and Lloyd when I went sailing with Simon at weekends and found them an absolutely delightful couple. Years later they took their yacht *Rebel*, which they had built, by road to South Africa and from there they set off on an adventurous voyage that finally took them to Australian shores. Eve later wrote a book *Twenty-four Feet of Adventure in Rebel*, based on their voyage and both she and Lloyd kept in regular touch with Simon.

My son, meanwhile, had met up with a man named Ron Wink who had expressed interest in undertaking the voyage with Simon. He was in South Africa visiting his family, but came up to Rhodesia for a few days and stayed with us in my cottage. I took an instant liking to him and he was marvellous company.

One evening both young men decided to treat me by cooking a special dinner. They had spent a good part of the day preparing it and although I cannot remember exactly what was served I do recall it was utterly sublime. I was quite humbled by the occasion as they far surpassed me in the cooking stakes. Also, it went some way in reassuring me that if Simon and Ron were to sail for distant shores they would not be surviving solely on tinned foods.

I enjoyed being swept along by all of Simon's grandiose plans but those happy times were marred by the sudden and shocking news of Peter's death. The first I knew of it was when I picked up the Sunday paper and saw a notice that Peter was being cremated.

He had died at the age of fifty-four. Friends rang me. They had obviously seen the notice as well but wouldn't mention it. All they said was would I like to join them for lunch. I knew no details until Simon told me how sick Peter had been and that he had suffered pneumonia every winter. Both Robert and Simon had kept in touch with their father but Peter and I had lost contact. He rang me only twice in all the years following our divorce.

Then, not much later, my beloved cat, Ching, died. He was fifteen years old and had been my most devoted companion. According to the vet his death had nothing to do with his vintage and he suspected Ching had eaten a poisoned mouse. Ching was given a very sad and moving funeral by Anne's children, who had come to love him very much. They buried him in the garden and covered his grave with flowers, just as I had done with my pets as a child. Amidst all this loss and sadness I received a cable dated 13 October 1967: 'Sailing ex Lourenço Marques to Durban. Love Simon.'

Both my sons were now headed in different directions while back in Rhodesia scores of my friends had also decided to leave the country following UDI (Unilateral Declaration of Independence). Diana, though, was staying put and so too were a few of my other friends. There was no denying, however, that the country was becoming increasingly unsettled. I also received letters from Robert and Janet impressing it upon me to move back to Australia where they offered to put me up until I found a place of my own.

Although my roots were in Rhodesia and I loved the lifestyle it offered, I knew deep within my heart that for all its attractions there was no getting away from the fact that the country was undergoing momentous changes. I did not particularly savour the thought of being left alone, without my family, during a time of political upheaval. I knew Robert was right. I had to look to the future.

I set about making plans and wrote to a couple of people I had befriended in Perth. One of them was Nancy, who kindly asked me to 'house sit' for her while she spent six months with her son in England. I booked my passage several months ahead, which gave me ample time to sell some of my furniture and to pack all my knick-knacks and my paintings, including the Tinus de Jonghs that both my sons coveted.

I was terribly sad to be leaving a job I had so enjoyed, all my wonderful friends and, above all, a country that was being rent apart by a bitter civil war. Because I knew that it was to be my final farewell. I was to bid Africa a last goodbye and when next I returned it would be as a visitor, but one who would never forget a unique inheritance. After all, I was born a child of Africa and would leave with precious memories of it carved forever on my nomadic soul.

Chapter Eleven

ROBERT AND SIMON: THE SUN AND THE MOON

'Ethnée, have you heard the news?' My late-night caller was my stepbrother Roualeyn who was on his Altyre Ranch, many miles away. 'I have just picked it up on my radio. Simon Holmes à Court, lone sailor, is overdue in reaching Durban,' he recounted, mindful to keep his voice steady and unruffled.

Although Roualeyn's news made my blood run ice-cold I resisted pushing the panic button. Simon had been in many perilous situations in his young life and somehow he managed to scrape through alive, if not always unscathed. I knew him to be resourceful and resilient under the most trying circumstances, and if he had run into trouble out at sea I was in no doubt that he would survive. I began phoning friends in Durban to find out if they had any more news. Details were quite sketchy but they promised to keep me informed during the night if there were any new developments. I also rang the port captain in Durban, who told me that at first light an aircraft would begin searching the Indian Ocean off Durban for Simon's thirty-one foot white ketch with its blue sail.

After a sleepless night came daybreak on 24 October 1967 with my son's plight splashed across the front pages of nearly all the daily papers in South Africa and Rhodesia. The headline of one such paper announced somewhat ominously, LONE SAILOR

OVERDUE. It did much to heighten the growing fear I felt for my son's safety. Somewhere off the east coast, Simon was waging a terrible and lonely battle against the elements and mountainous seas. The Mozambique Channel was an extremely busy shipping lane and notorious for its violent storms. Many ships and yachts had come to grief in the strait running along the east coast, which was why everyone held such grave fears for my son. Indeed, the first aircraft search failed to find any sign of *Carina* and my anxiety grew in direct proportion to the bleak bulletins being relayed on all the radio stations and on the front pages of the newspapers.

HOPES FOR CARINA FADING and STILL NO SIGN OF LONE YACHTSMAN OFF NATAL COAST the headlines screamed. I began to feel so utterly helpless being so far from the heart of the search operations that I decided, on impulse, to head for Durban. I needed to be close at hand if there were any major developments and, ultimately, to be there to welcome my son back on shore. A flight was hastily arranged and subsequently my plans to leave Rhodesia had to be brought forward by about three months. I got the packers in and my dear friend Diana kept vigil by the phone, which never seemed to stop ringing. But the news I was desperately awaiting never came.

I cabled Robert and Janet in Australia but they held little hope for Simon when told that he had gone missing in the Mozambique Channel. I refused to share their pessimism, however. Diana and Cath (my bridesmaid) drove me to the airport in Salisbury, where our parting was incredibly sad and tearful. As it turned out, it would be the last time I would ever see my two special friends. Cath succumbed to cancer within a year and Diana died suddenly a few years later.

Somehow I had managed to secure a priority seat on the aircraft to Johannesburg and was assured a seat on another plane to

Durban. As soon as I arrived in Johannesburg there were several cables pinned on a noticeboard for me, many of them from Simon's friends wishing for good news. Miraculously, that good news we had all been so anxiously awaiting came by way of the harbourmaster in Durban, who told me that the 'lone sailor' had been found and was safe. The *Sunday Times* newspaper in Johannesburg carried the triumphant news under the headline, LOST YACHT SAFE AFTER FOUR-DAY DRIFT. I learnt that Simon's stricken ketch, with its mast broken in two, was being towed back to Durban by the French oil tanker *Ville de Lyon*. The tanker had been en route from Dakar to the Persian Gulf when crewmen sighted *Carina*.

With that I caught the first plane to Durban where I was met with more, albeit alarming, news. According to a Durban newspaper report on 28 October, *Carina* was not only dismasted but badly battered. Fearing that Simon had been seriously injured, I boarded a yacht called *Snowgoose* with a doctor and several members of the press. *Snowgoose* was to tow *Carina* into Durban harbour, but no-one really knew what state Simon would be in. To our utter amazement, instead of appearing battered and bruised Simon skimmed effortlessly down a rope ladder on the side of the huge tanker and leapt onto his disabled ketch amid the tangled rigging and splintered woodwork.

After so many sleepless nights and an agonising wait for news of my son, seeing him so fit and well came as such an enormous and welcome relief. And I was not the only one overjoyed by my son's safe homecoming. As we neared the dock I could see several Michaelhouse boys, all wearing their school blazers, lined up to welcome their old schoolmate home after his ordeal at sea. They, like so many friends, had been following the news and felt moved enough to give him a personal and very touching welcome reception. Within hours the good news was carried on all the radio stations. We even had word from our former domestic worker Sarah Simmonds from our early Johannesburg days, who had been following the news closely and was elated to hear that Simon was found safe and well.

Even the salubrious Durban Yacht Club saw fit to make an exception to its normally rigid dress code by inviting Simon, sans the requisite tie and jacket, to lunch. It was there that Simon gave us and members of the press a detailed account of how he had struck torrential rains and heavy seas that drove *Carina* off course. But his troubles began the night he fell asleep at the tiller. The ketch jibed, tearing her main sails. He had to repair the sails six times while the ketch was being swept southwards by the strong current. Simon recounted rather nonchalantly:

> *I spent my twenty-eighth birthday on 26 October lost at sea. For seven hours I used the last of my motor fuel trying to get into what I thought was Durban. It was not. It was useless with my small engine. My sail slats were broken and this had ripped the sails. I tried to make new slats out of a water cask but it was useless. I heard over the radio that a plane was searching for me. There was too much fog. Every time a sail tore I settled down to sew it up again. It became a bit monotonous after a while.*

By all accounts he was extremely lucky to have made it back to shore alive, let alone uninjured, and we all felt his safe return warranted a major celebration. I can't remember champagne ever having tasted so good. Later, I decided to remain in Durban with friends until it was time to set sail for Australia. Simon, meanwhile, had put *Carina* on the slipway where he was already in the process of repairing her. I tried to help as best I could by cleaning up the yacht and it enabled me to spend some precious time with my son before I left for Australia.

Simon, it seemed, was intent on making *Carina* seaworthy again and was already making plans to sail to Lourenço Marques where he was sure he would be able to sell her and then buy another larger yacht. It became quite apparent to me that his near-disastrous voyage had done nothing to dissuade him from pursuing his dream of sailing around the world and making a wildlife documentary while doing so.

Then, all too quickly, the time for another farewell dawned. I was to set sail on the *Straat Banka* on 22 November 1967 and Simon, my friend Peggy Whittaker and others came on board for a farewell lunch. As it turned out the ship's departure was delayed until 10a.m. the following day and Simon, who had heard news of the ship's delay on the radio, surprised me by making a sudden appearance at breakfast. He had decided to come and stay with me for a couple of hours until the ship's departure. I knew I was going to miss him terribly and it seemed that, through the tyranny of distance, I would find myself in the unenviable position of being separated from one or other of my sons. When I was with Robert in Australia, I missed Simon terribly, and now that I was returning to Robert I knew I would long for the quiet, reassuring company of Simon. I hoped that it would not be too long before I saw him again.

When we docked at Singapore there was a cable waiting for me. It informed me that Robert had also embarked on an ambitious adventure of his own. He had set up a new legal practice where I was to be employed, together with Janet and his secretary Val Pitman (who was to remain with Robert for the next twenty-five years). I was very impressed and not a little excited. It also meant that I was to be spared the discouraging process of having to look for a job in Perth.

After my arrival in Perth I stayed with Janet and Robert for a while and then moved into Nancy's home, which I had agreed to house-sit for her. This time my stay in Australia was far removed from the miserable spell I had endured before. In fact, it was wonderfully exciting in Robert's new practice. Janet did all the conveyancing while I was busy trying to master an electronic typewriter and the trust accounts. Robert had a big office to himself whereas we three had to share another. I recall Robert once telling us that to help make a success of his practice we had to find a new client every day. Somehow, we managed to do precisely that and before long Robert was building himself a thriving practice.

We worked extremely hard in those early days but for all the long hours we put in it was a happy environment. Actually, too happy in Robert's view, and at one stage I was moved because he felt there was too much giggling and chatting going on. But for the occasional outbursts of hilarity and the chatter we were all, without exception, bent on helping Robert in his quest to expand his business. Janet, too, took instruction from him for Robert was The Boss. Indeed, that's what we all took to calling him – The Boss.

We did not get terrific salaries to begin with but there were numerous perks. To help me become more settled in Australia and to stop me hankering after my friends and Africa, Robert paid for a wonderful five-week trip around the country. I still remember his words when he told me to take some time off. 'I suppose you will never feel settled until we have horses.' And then he added, 'One day we will have a farm and we will have horses but in the meantime I think you need a holiday. Go and see the rest of Australia and get the feel of it. And meet Australians,' came the parting instruction.

Predictably, Robert's advice could not be faulted. The holiday turned out to be a wonderful tonic and I returned to Perth feeling a good deal more settled and with a far greater understanding of Australia. I needed that break to look around and to explore my new adopted country.

Shortly after my return I found a new flat and Robert insisted on paying the rent. His business was going from strength to strength and it reminded me of the time he made it known to me in no uncertain terms that he intended to become a millionaire before he turned thirty. His business acumen was such that he surpassed even that goal, however, for thanks to an uncanny ability in earmarking and staking companies and concerns ripe for takeover he became the most successful corporate genius of his time and one of Australia's few billionaires.

As his mother I was not unduly surprised by his galloping success. I always remembered him as a determined little boy and I knew that when my son set his heart on something he usually got it. That determined streak was in evidence from a very early age and even my mother used to get very irate with him when he became impossibly stubborn. But no matter what we did or said he would just put his head up high and keep going. Even as an adolescent he could be so persuasive that it was virtually impossible to challenge him. As his mother I found it especially difficult to say no to him when he turned on all eight cylinders of charm. I was not alone.

When Robert was studying for his exams at Michaelhouse he wrote to explain to me that it was imperative that he should have a motorbike if he passed his matriculation exams. So I am afraid that I replied that he could have a motorbike, provided he passed. And pass he did. So as promised we went to look at motorbikes during his school holidays and decided on a second-hand one which seemed fairly reasonable. Robert's friends also had bikes so the boys had great fun dashing over the hill country. Then disaster struck. I came home one day to find bloodstained clothing in the bathroom and then Robert appeared, looking ghostly pale. His arm was bandaged and his knees were grazed. He told me that he and another lad were racing a car driven by this lad's girlfriend when they both ended up in a ditch. The girl was very sympathetic and felt partly to blame for what happened so she drove the boys back to their respective homes and administered to their wounds. Robert decided, much to my relief, that he did not really enjoy the motorbike after all. So naturally the next best thing was a car.

When next Robert came home to Rhodesia during his holidays we started looking around for a car. I purchased a green MG which Robert had found and vetted. Then he persuaded me to let him take Simon and drive back to school, having in the process convinced me that this would save me the airfares. He and Simon duly set off very early one morning for the long journey to Michaelhouse via Johannesburg and I still have Robert's letter giving me a blow-by-blow account of their trip down to Balgowan. I quote:

> We had a terrific trip down. Junior [Simon] didn't moan a hell of a lot. We drove non-stop to Beit Bridge, arrived 5.10a.m. Junior drove 100 miles in two stretches of two hours each. We had a sleep in the car. I woke at 7a.m. to see a donkey inspecting my feet (which were sticking out the window). No trouble with customs. They asked for six pounds deposit on the car but I said that I didn't have it. So he gave me a temporary import permit free. The man next to me had to deposit three hundred pounds on his Buick. The next day I drove non-stop 'til 1a.m. Junior wouldn't drive again . . . we arrived at 4p.m. Clem's [headmaster] jaw dropped when we arrived and hasn't yet been able to say much. He is completely baffled. He said, 'You can't do this, you can't turn up in a car.' Brooks [housemaster] said 'And what possessed you to do a thing like this?' Your letter quietened them down a bit.
>
> There isn't a spare garage here for the car but Mr Carey [master] had lent me his garage for ten days and there are thousands of other

offers. Now about a horse. I went to see a Mr Chapman about the Anglo-Arab and I've offered him twenty pounds. I've told him I'm not going any higher, and I won't, altho' the filly is worth more. Chisholm [master] is prepared to keep her for me and will most certainly buy her when I leave. I should get forty pounds out of him. I hope to start a riding club and give lessons. I don't think I'll have any trouble paying for the car. Everyone is so jealous about it, even Brooks. I can use it as a taxi on Sundays!

If you come across the Readers' Digest *July number read 'Don't raise your son without a Cadillac!' It's quite a sensible article!!! It will give you all the proof you want that you were right in getting the MG. Thanks a lot for everything Mum, it was terrific coming down by car. You can borrow my car next hols and I needn't borrow yours — won't that be a change. Dazzle, the filly, is still the best horse here and sends you her love and reckons she wants to meet you when you come down in July. Lots of love, Rob.*

Later, when he decided to read law at the University of Cape Town, rather than fly down Robert suggested that he might have my Citroen car. It was a smart black Light 15 which sported a rather fetching silver fox mascot that I had acquired while on my equitation course in England. Robert did not have a trouble-free journey that time, and I gathered the engine had packed up for some reason which necessitated railing the car to Cape Town. The expense, of course, was covered by me.

What I found most frustrating about Robert was that no matter how hard I tried I could not get him to change his mind or point of view. Sure, he would go through the motions of hearing you out and at times he would appear quite sympathetic to your views, but he was quite inflexible. And the most maddening thing was that he was almost always right. I think that's why a lot of people were quite content to just follow Robert's advice and instructions. They didn't dare argue with him or to take issue with some of the things he recommended. Then again, he was, from a very early age, quite accustomed to being the leader. He took over.

Naturally, he measured success in terms of takeovers and dollars and had begun to amass some wealth. But by the same token, I know a lot of people invested in companies like the Albany Woollen Mills precisely because they admired Robert for what he had managed to achieve in such a staggeringly short time. The woollen mills was his first acquisition in the early 1970s and it helped set him on a trajectory to success. It was the first company to be controlled by Robert, who said at the time he was attracted to it because it was the smallest listed company in the country. And his investors even then made it known that they had an unshakeable faith in Robert and he, in turn, did very well for a lot of people.

I went along to all the annual general meetings and was always surprised at the large number of people who attended them. They all clearly adored Robert. I can still call to mind how he used to walk into the hall with that unhurried gait of his and how everyone would fall silent. You could hear a pin drop. And then he would flash us a captivating smile as he stepped up to the microphone. All of it seemed to be conducted in slow motion, but it was very effective for he emitted nothing but supreme confidence and self-assurance.

As his mother I could be excused for being biased but Robert was, without doubt, one of the most impressive and eloquent speakers of his time and it was an observation shared by many of his former teachers and university lecturers who all knew him to be a superlative debater. As a businessman he parlayed those talents into his takeover forays, where his powers of persuasion seldom seemed to fail.

When he told me that he was going to be a millionaire before he turned thirty and that he would be driving a Rolls Royce, I all but scoffed at the idea. 'Besides, only old men drive around in Rolls Royces,' I added dismissively. But, blow me down, within a matter of years of pooh-poohing the mere notion of this, Robert was behind the wheel of a Rolls Royce. He was certainly the youngest person I had ever encountered who drove such a luxury car. Later he had one customised and fitted out with the carpets and leather of his choice.

I guess, looking back, there were always signs that Robert was possessed of an enterprising streak. In fact both my sons, back in their Michaelhouse days, had been involved in a number of money-making ventures. The most financially rewarding of these was the magic circle they had formed. Simon was particularly good at his tricks and they would entertain the other schoolboys and charge them a thruppence for a magic session. I gathered that was one of the many lucrative ways they earned some extra pocket money.

Indeed, my sons had much in common. For instance, they both had this thing for snakes and used to write and tell me of how they had caught this or that type of snake to sell to the snake park. Those they were unable to sell they would then smuggle home in their luggage and I had little alternative but to become accustomed to having them around the house. In Simon's final year at Michaelhouse in 1957 he caught a huge, very poisonous snake which I believe was a ringhals and he kept this in his laundry bag in his locker at the foot of his bed. He had every intention of selling this to the snake park for a vast sum of money. That was not to be. The Housemaster, Mr Brooks heard that Simon was keeping a snake in the dormitory and all hell was let loose! Mr Brooks wrote to me and apologised for having to cane Simon and appealed to me to ask him not to keep snakes in the future. Simon wrote: 'Mr

Brooks thought fit to cane me when he found out about my snake
. . . of course the trouble is he is scared stiff of snakes.'

When the boys went back to school I was left in charge of
several snakes in a cage with strict instructions on how to feed
them. However, there was a bit of a disaster one day when the
white mice, which were the snakes' customary feed, turned out to
be rats and had begun eating one of my sons' prized snakes from
the tail up.

One holiday Simon was bitten by his 'tame' red-lipped herald
snake. He treated himself, as he often did, with our Fitzsimons
snakebite kit. A couple of days later Robert announced that the
same snake had bitten him. At first I thought he was pulling my leg
and did not pay him much attention, but when he held up his
finger I noticed a distinct red mark. Then Robert grew deathly pale.

We rushed off to the bathroom where I kept the snakebite kit
but before I administered the injection I made a call to our doctor,
whose surgery was about twelve miles away. He gave me
instructions on what to do and said that he would come out
immediately. No sooner had I given Robert the injection he
collapsed on the floor. Fortunately Simon was home and helped me
carry Robert to his bed. Time seemed to drag on and I became
extremely concerned about Robert's condition. When the doctor
eventually arrived he discovered that Robert was allergic to the
snakebite serum and rushed him to hospital.

He made a speedy recovery but after that I became exceedingly
concerned that Robert would not be able to take anti-serum
injections in the future. Robert, however, seemed remarkably
unperturbed by the near-fatal consequences that could result from
another snakebite and like Simon remained fearlessly keen on
snakes.

One day I had a letter from the sister in charge of the school sanatorium who said that Robert was the bravest boy she had met. He had been working in the school's photographic studio, printing films to sell to his schoolmates, when he met with a horrid accident. He fell through a glass window and slashed his arm very badly. The sister saw him walking towards her holding his arm up, which was bleeding quite profusely, and immediately realised he was in shock. She rushed him into the sanatorium and then called for a doctor to stitch up the wound.

Years later, after she had retired and returned to England, Robert was working on a takeover bid concerning Lord Lew Grade's theatres which made the news in London's newspapers. She composed a very funny little poem recalling his accident and his early days at Michaelhouse and sent it to him. Robert was rather touched by the poem so I wrote it out in Indian ink while doing a course in calligraphy and then made a leather frame for it as a birthday present. I was always looking for something different because it wasn't easy finding presents that would appeal to him.

Sometimes Simon would say, 'Give me an idea of what you want for your birthday, something other than bath salts.' Apart from a lion skin and a table lamp made from the leg of a zebra, the gift I treasured most was a small lioness he moulded in dass (a type of plasticine). Later I had this cast in bronze, one for myself and one as a present for Robert.

Simon was very artistic and while he was still at Cordwalles prep school he showed himself to be exceptionally gifted at modelling. He did a head of a Zulu girl which won a prize at the Pietermaritzburg Show. He was about nine years old at the time and the headmaster predicted then that he would be a famous sculptor one day. Simon all but turned up his nose at the idea because he felt modelling was 'very sissy' and didn't model again for many years. At Michaelhouse, though, he turned his artistic talents to photography, a passion he shared with his older brother. However, Simon continued to pursue it long after leaving school and when he worked as a game ranger he took the most extraordinary shots of wildlife. Later he mastered underwater photography and thought nothing of swimming among crocodiles and sharks without the security of a cage to get the best shots. A big American film company called Wild Kingdom saw some of Simon's photographs, including a spectacular one of a charging elephant, and began to commission quite a lot of work.

In many respects, though, Robert and Simon were remarkably different. In fact, they were the sun and the moon – in temperament, in physical appearance and in their aspirations. Simon had my colouring with his sandy hair and grey-green eyes and was rather compactly built. He loved to dress down, eschewed the trappings of wealth and was quite solitary by nature. Robert, on the other hand, was six foot three inches, lean, always immaculately turned out and most comfortable in the frenetic, highly charged world of stocks and shares.

I don't think Simon would have survived in Robert's world but having said that he wasn't especially overawed by the glamour that came with his brother's leatherbound lifestyle. During one of his visits to Perth he came with us to the races dressed in a pair of shorts that had seen better days, whereas his brother looked as suave as ever in an elegantly tailored suit. But that was Simon. He was as happy as a sandboy tracking elephants in his shorts and *veldskoene* or sporting nothing more than a pair of swimming trunks while out on his yacht.

But I was inordinately proud of them both because they were extraordinary achievers in their own right. Robert was the audacious tycoon-in-the-making who proved himself a tough negotiator and a corporate genius, and Simon was more contemplative with a soul as deep as his beloved Africa and was, above all, a man of simple means. Where his brother acquired the sumptuous accoutrements befitting a powerhouse businessman, Simon possessed not so much as a credit card. But what he had in abundance was an appetite for adventure. Robert could never have sailed single-handedly from Lourenço Marques or around the world filming wildlife documentaries, or have tracked wounded elephants in Africa's brutal heat for days on end. It wasn't his scene. Yet my sons shared a mutual respect and admired each other's accomplishments.

Admittedly, at one stage, when they were at Michaelhouse I felt that Robert was perhaps overshadowing Simon. Even Robert once said that Simon was a very good swimmer and would have been captain of one of the swimming teams but he didn't want to be. Instead, Robert was made captain. That happened a lot. I seriously considered moving Simon from Michaelhouse and sending him to another school but came to realise it wouldn't have made much difference. Simon was just not competitive.

When they were little boys, though, Robert had a tendency to bully Simon a bit. I would often hear Simon cry out, 'Obbie, Obbie, No!' Later, during their playroom skirmishes, Simon's protests had graduated to 'R-o-b-e-r-t S-t-o-p-e-r-t!' which then required me to investigate what they were up to.

What I loved about both my sons was that they were always keen for me to join them in their respective pursuits. Through them I learned so much and was exposed to all kinds of new experiences. With Simon it was sailing and exploring all the marvels of African wildlife and with Robert it was learning to fly. When he was learning to fly in New Zealand I decided to compete and acquired my flying licence while at Chobe.

Then, after I had worked for Robert for over four years he catapulted me into an exciting new orbit when, as promised, he bought the much-promised farm, on 3 May 1971. Those first 400 acres of land in the Keysbrook area, about an hour's drive south of Perth, boasted nothing more than an old, dilapidated farmhouse and a shed but it marked the genesis of Heytesbury Stud. Robert took me down to see the property and I was absolutely thrilled. So was he, for he turned to me with a beaming smile and said, 'Didn't I tell you we'd get a farm and horses some day?'

After Janet had done all the conveyancing and the sale was finalised we immediately set to work. First came the loo that we built outside the old farm shed and which consisted of little more than sacks and a tarpaulin strung together. It was all rather rough-going to begin with. But I thought the farm was the next best thing to paradise and would spend most weekends there exercising Robert's polo pony. Eventually, when they fixed up the old farmhouse, I'd sleep some nights on a bed I had made out of logs, bricks and the frame of an old bed. Discomfort was but a minor price to pay for a dose of bucolic bliss and an opportunity to ride to my heart's content.

Later I hired a caravan from a friend and put it among the trees, so I was able to spend all my free time at Heytesbury. Robert and I had gone to the yearling sales, where he bought two yearlings that we hoped would become future racehorses. They were to be the forerunners of what Robert intended to transform into the finest stud in the country.

While Robert embarked on this new enterprise, Simon sold *Carina* and flew to England where he soon found a sea dog (ketch) up for sale. She was exactly what he needed for his round-the-world voyage and once he officially laid claim to *Maggie May II* he then took on board two young crewmen and set sail on his dream adventure. His 27,000 mile sea voyage began on October 1969 in the United Kingdom and from there he planned to sail to the

Canary Islands, Barbados, the Panama Canal, the Galapagos Islands, the Marquesas, Tahiti, Fiji, the New Hebrides, Santa Cruz, over the top end of Australia, Komodo, Bali, the Seychelles, Aldabra and then, finally, on to Durban.

Not long after Robert had bought the farm I took a month's holiday and met up with Simon in Fiji where we spent all four glorious weeks just sailing around palm-fringed islands. I so treasured that time I spent with my son for it gave me first-hand insight into the immense task he had set himself. Not only was he intent on covering vast distances but he had begun accumulating the most extraordinary footage for his documentary, *A True Life Adventure Film on Board Maggie May II*.

It included the vine jumpers on Pentecost where the villagers jumped only once a year in the belief that a good jump would ensure them a plentiful crop of yams. The men cut and secured their own vines and the jumps were done from different levels. When Simon filmed them jumping, the highest jump recorded was 70 feet and the lowest, done by a ten-year-old, was about 50 feet.

The most fascinating segment, however, was the one done on 'feather money', the rarest form of currency found on Ndeni Island, a small island in the Santa Cruz group. The money was made by only a few men singled out by villagers to spend their entire lives dedicated to the craft. Feather belts were used mainly for bridal payments and a good wife was said to cost as much as five belts. The feathers of some 1000 sunbirds went into the making of each of these colourful belts, which gives some indication of the comparative value of a clutch of these belts. The brilliant red male sunbirds were caught and stripped of their exquisite plumage before being released to grow new feathers. These belts were displayed only on special festive occasions at which time a wife will carry all the belts that were paid for her neatly rolled up on her head. I desisted from doing the same when Simon presented me with a beautiful belt of feather money he had somehow managed to acquire for me as a special gift. Unfortunately some years later it became host to an invading army of weevils and moths which reduced an exotic souvenir into a dismal, bald-patched rag.

Also on Simon's documentary was some rather gruesome footage of a pig-killing ceremony in the Solomons which did not make for especially comfortable viewing. Surprisingly, Simon made no apologies for having filmed the ceremony. Indeed, before his documentary was released he gave a detailed account of how he had come to film it:

> It was part of a genuine and incredible ceremony which was authentically filmed as it happened. There was a remarkable incident connected with this ceremony. For four consecutive days I had to ask the people to postpone the ceremony as the continuous rains, caused by a cyclone in the near vicinity, would spoil the photography.
>
> Eventually someone suggested that I ask the priest to bring good weather. This I did. The priest demanded 10 cents and then went into his house and discussed the matter with the skulls of prominent ancestors. He then announced that the following day would be fine. Next morning the low barometer predicted gloom, the radio forecast predicted torrential rain and an unabated cyclone. Outside the sky was blue and clear for the first time in a week. When we finished filming, down came the rain which continued for another week.

Ron Wink, the charming fellow who had come to stay with us in Rhodesia, joined Simon in Curaçao and sailed with him for two years. He was with Simon when I was reunited with my son in Fiji during my sun-soaked, sailing holiday. They were such magical days, sailing to uninhabited islands, swimming and snorkelling in the azure waters of the Pacific and living off fish and local produce.

How different it all was from the bush life Simon had once enjoyed with the Game Department. But he was just as happy sailing, diving and filming as he had once been tracking and monitoring the whereabouts of his beloved elephants.

When he wasn't sailing or filming, Simon would dive down with his aqualung and spear a huge fish while Ron went ashore to find a sheltered spot where he could prepare our dinner. This would normally be on a beach under some coconut palms where he would then proceed to dig a hole in the sand for a fire. Later he would place the prepared fish in the 'oven', where it was left to cook slowly. When ready this mouth-watering meal was usually served with some gin that Simon had acquired when going through the Panama Canal and mixed with fresh coconut milk. It was not a drink I would recommend.

Afterwards, on those balmy evenings, we would lie around the fire like three well-fed and contented cats and talk of times past. Ron would entertain us with anecdotes of their eventful voyage. He recounted a particularly frightening night when he was on watch and heard a rumbling noise in the distance which seemed to grow louder by the second. He shouted to Simon, who scrambled on deck just in time to witness the most incredible sight. The sea seemed to be boiling and the noise became ear-shattering. Suddenly the angry sea threw up enormous sheets of water and the loud rumbling noises continued. *Maggie May* had sailed across the top of an underwater volcano.

Later, nearing the Cook Islands all seemed calm until, without warning, there was a large tail of a whale as close to the yacht as it was possible to be. Luckily for Simon and Ron, the owner of the tail flapped outwards to the ocean. 'If it had flapped onto the yacht I leave it to your imagination as to the result,' added Ron somewhat gravely.

The two intrepid sailors had another, equally harrowing encounter one very dark night when Simon spotted a freighter bearing down on *Maggie May* at frightening speed. The freighter was well lit and Simon made sure that all the yacht's lights were also on. Yet the freighter kept on what would have been a collision course had Simon not managed to inch *Maggie May* away at the crucial moment. The freighter, however, was so close that Simon was able to see its name. He never reported the matter to the authorities for in that typical insouciant manner of his he felt there was no need given that they had managed to avert disaster.

In a lighter vein, Ron made fun of Simon's obsession with having everything in good trim on board *Maggie May*. He described with great relish an incident shortly after he joined Simon in Curaçao. Simon was busy checking absolutely everything on the yacht before they were deemed ready to set sail for the Panama Canal. When he checked the cutlery he found, to his dismay, a teaspoon missing. Normally this would hardly give cause for alarm to your average yachtsman but it was enough to send Simon overboard in search of the missing object. After diving for what seemed like ages he eventually found the teaspoon. On another occasion the winch handle fell overboard and Simon immediately dived down to retrieve it. He hated to lose anything, and everything was kept immaculate on *Maggie May*.

But for all his fastidiousness and dedication to his mission Simon, like Robert, had a wicked sense of humour. His friend Bodo Muche, the sculptor, once recounted an incident which betrayed my son's mischievous streak – one that made world headline news. It occurred in 1966 when Simon was a game ranger based in Francistown, Botswana, then the spy capital of the world. These so-called spies came from all corners of the globe to monitor developments in Rhodesia after UDI.

According to Bodo, the British Government had sent the largest contingent with linguists, communication experts, listeners, broadcasters, a German shepherd squad and a company of soldiers. The soldiers, thought to be the 'Glorious Gloucesters', had set up their compound just north of Francistown next to a small kopje or hill. It was not too far from the Game Department where Simon, Bodo and another comrade-in-arms decided to put some thunder flashes to the test. These had originally been entrusted to them for the sole purpose of scaring charging rhinos and elephants. But it wasn't large game they frightened when, around midnight, they lobbed them over the security fences and into three corners of the soldiers' camp. The next day the BBC World News led with a bulletin claiming Rhodesian Security Forces had attacked the British Army Base at Francistown. The true culprits, of course, knew otherwise and thought it all a huge joke.

That holiday I spent sailing on board *Maggie May* with Simon and Ron remains one of my most treasured memories. We leisurely cruised through the most beautiful, turquoise waters and when we dropped anchor Simon would dive down for more underwater photography while I swam and snorkelled on the coral reefs. Ron busied himself on deck, preparing some of his delicious meals.

One evening we were invited to visit a nearby island to dine with the chief. We arrived by dinghy and Simon had to carry me through the surf, desperately trying to hold onto several packets of sugar which were to be presented as gifts. We entered a low-ceilinged bamboo room and sat in a circle on mats. There were dishes of odd-looking food in the centre but all I recognised were some tiny dried fish. We helped ourselves and I did my utmost to look as if I were enjoying every mouthful. Then the national drink, kava, was passed around in a half coconut shell which was shared by all. Simon sensed my reluctance to sample this traditional concoction and whispered to me that I had to take a sip or our host would be deeply offended. He assured me that it was not alcoholic but I was of the view it would have tasted infinitely better had it been. When we sailed away the next morning to explore other waters, all the young girls gathered along the shore and waved and sang as we passed their lovely island one last time. Simon often said that he was sorely tempted to settle in that part of the world but, alas, never made it back.

We visited one more island in the archipelago which was as picturesque and tranquil as our previous island destination. Only this island was much more sparsely populated and the women wore traditional dress, hibiscus in their hair and fragrant garlands of frangipani. Again, Simon and Ron busied themselves fishing and photographing while I was given a paintbrush and a pot of blue paint with which to retouch parts of *Maggie May*. I quite enjoyed the task as it made me feel like a member of the team. After his dive Simon photographed some of the local women and taped their joyous songs which he then, to their utter delight, played back to them.

Sadly, those sun-drenched, palmy days in the Pacific slipped by all too swiftly. My blissful holiday finally drew to an end and it was time to head back to Heytesbury and our horses. I would not see Simon for some time, not until his extraordinary odyssey was over and he came to Australia to do post-production work on his documentary. But that magical time I spent with him on so unique a journey would remain carved in my memory.

Before heading home Robert asked me to fly via New Zealand to look for suitable brood mares for the stud. Mutual friends and an agent had arranged for me to visit several studs. Also, as Robert had spent two years studying forestry and agriculture in New Zealand, I met up with a number of his old college friends and they mentioned *en passant* some stories I had not been privy to before. I gathered Robert had enjoyed quite a social spell while at university.

Unfortunately all the brood mares I really liked were not for sale and when I mentioned this to Robert he asked me to fly on to Sydney and Adelaide, where he hoped I would have better luck. Again an agent took me on a tour of all the stud farms in search of brood mares that were deemed suitable for our burgeoning stud. I found it all enormously informative and began to learn about some of the methods involved in running a stud. I knew a lot about horses but nothing much about studs, so I made a point of picking up all the knowledge I could along the way. After a couple of days on this fact-finding mission I flew back to Perth armed with a bundle of photographs and scores of detailed notes I had made of some of the suitable mares I had found.

That very night Robert, the manager and I sat down in the old farmhouse to study my notes. Robert seemed quite impressed and he turned to the farm manager, and said, 'Okay, we will go and see what Ethnée's found.' Within a matter of days Robert purchased six of the mares I had recommended, including Brenta, as well as six weanlings which we were then going to prepare for the Perth yearling sales.

The mares and weanlings arrived at Heytesbury late one night in July 1971 in the middle of a bitterly cold night. I made sure I was there to give them a welcome reception and just as well for standing there, flashlight in hand, I detected a grey mare I knew we had not bought. We discovered one of our mares had been mistakenly delivered to a neighbouring farm and I managed to get the error hastily rectified before Robert got to hear of it.

All the mares were in foal and when the birth of our firstborn was near I took guard at the paddock to make sure nothing went wrong. All night long I sat huddled and shivering in my car with my hot water bottle and my Rhodesian Ridgeback. When I saw that the time was approaching I alerted the farm manager and had everything ready for the delivery of Heytesbury Stud's first foal. It was one night I didn't mind not getting any sleep since it was such a momentous occasion. Even Robert and Janet were excited and helped to celebrate the event. After that we began channelling all our energies and a lot of Robert's resources into improving Heytesbury's bloodstock. Later Robert started to import mares with impressive performance records from various countries.

Not long after, Robert turned to me one day and declared, in that earnest way of his, 'We must buy a stallion'. And it was not to be any old stallion. The stallion Robert Holmes à Court was after had to be a Melbourne Cup winner. I duly contacted an agent and he then set all the wheels in motion. He phoned Sir Walter Norwood in New Zealand who was the owner of Silver Knight (NZ), winner of the Melbourne Cup in 1971.

What followed was one of the quickest and most hassle-free deals ever clinched. Apparently when the agent called he simply stated that he had a potential buyer for the horse. When asked how much he would want for it the reply was $65,000. Robert was contacted and he did not even need a second to think about it. 'Buy him,' came the rapid-fire response.

And so it was that Heytesbury became the new owner of Silver Knight, who had won the cup in the second fastest time. In only three seasons the horse proved to be one of the best young stayers in the world. He was a winner at two, three and four years old from six furlongs to two miles. When Silver Knight left for Australia his strapper travelled across the Tasman Sea with him because the horse so hated flying. When they docked in Melbourne she grew quite distressed and very tearful before parting from 'her horse'.

It did not take us long before we began to enjoy much success with some of the horses we bred. They went on to win some very good races and they later produced outstanding youngsters for which we fetched good prices at the sales. We never took any short cuts and great emphasis was placed on introducing and following the very latest in breeding procedures, as well as ensuring that Heytesbury offered nothing but the best environment for these most precious thoroughbreds.

From the outset Heytesbury was Robert's dream come true and he was very hands-on in just about every aspect of the stud. He demanded that we consult him on everything only because he so loved being part of Heytesbury's growing success. I can remember so many occasions sitting down late at night with Robert and a list of all the brood mares. He would always decide which stallion they would go to, and just as well, since he had a keen eye which never failed him. Indeed, it was his decision to have Brenta covered by Silver Knight.

Actually, one newspaper reported that the purchase of Silver Knight was a coup for stud-breeding purposes in Western Australia. The article pointed out that as a three-year-old he had set an Australasian record for fourteen furlongs. His time of 2.54 was only 1.4 seconds outside the world record set by Buen Ojo at Montevideo, Uruguay, in 1922.

However, we were not quite certain how successful we would be trying to pair the champion with Brenta. He had a penchant for chestnuts and she was a striking brunette. The union, however, proved successful and I was present when Brenta foaled a black colt on 27 August 1979. We named him Black Knight. Three years later, on 4 August 1982, Black Knight gave us a tantalising foretaste of greater things to come when he won at Geelong in Victoria. Soon there were headlines in the papers heralding the appearance of a promising new star on the racetrack. WA BRED HORSE BURSTS ON CUP SCENE read one to our great delight.

After trialing in Perth, Black Knight was transferred to Melbourne, where he was placed in the care of George Hanlon, the eccentric Victorian trainer. Not long after his move to Melbourne Black Knight won the Lord Mayor's Plate at Flemington and all the punters were quite excited. Commentators in the press began to hint that he stood a good chance of becoming the first WA-owned stayer to win the Melbourne Cup.

Robert, of course, kept an eagle eye on Black Knight's progress every step of the way. In fact, George Hanlon took some delight in recounting an occasion when Robert arrived at the race track in a taxi to watch his prized racehorse being worked: 'The boy riding Black Knight was having a bit of trouble so Robert gave the cab driver his coat, tucked his trousers into his socks, changed the stirrup irons and rode him on the track.'

The trainer was absolutely dumbstruck because no owner had ever ridden his own horse around the track or shown that much interest. But Robert knew and loved horses, which is not at all surprising given that I was still riding when I was seven months pregnant with him. He was practically born on a horse. Indeed, it was not that long after his birth that I'd go for rides with Robert perched in the saddle in front of me. He absolutely loved it and would grin from ear to ear. I still have photographs of him riding when he was twenty-three months old, with me leading the horse of course. He cleared his first jump when he was about six years old and by the time he was ten he was riding and competing in the show ring.

Robert was absolutely fearless in the saddle and whenever he was home during the school holidays he would compete in all the shows. Simon also rode and enjoyed it as a little boy, until he had a very nasty accident. A horse bolted with him and not only did he fall off but one of his feet stuck in a stirrup iron and he was dragged along. I was riding behind him when it happened. All I could see was my son bumping along on the ground. It was absolutely ghastly. When I finally managed to gain control of the horse and free Simon there was blood everywhere. He was quite badly cut and bruised but that night, while he lay tucked in bed he looked up at me and said plaintively, 'Mum, I think I need more practice'.

After that incident I don't think Simon enjoyed riding as much as he used to. He continued to ride and still won prizes and cups at the show and years later, when he was a game warden, he'd occasionally go for a ride, but he stopped competing. Robert, on the other hand, continued to excel in the show ring. Once, during the school holidays, Robert failed to turn up at the airport with Simon. When I asked Simon where his brother was he replied somewhat enigmatically, 'Robert says to tell you he has drowned himself'.

No doubt Simon had been instructed by his brother to cover for him but I soon found out that Robert had stopped off in Johannesburg where he stayed with a school friend. The friend's family apparently had a number of fine horses, one of which was lent to Robert to go hunting at the Rand Hunt Club. Later I was told that he became quite popular with the family and the hostess thought nothing of allowing my son the use of her car. They lent him a horse and they lent him a car. But that was Robert, he could charm the spots off a leopard. I should have been furious with him when he failed to accompany his brother home for the holidays, but I wasn't. Especially after he admitted, straight-faced, that he simply found the invitation to hunt with the club too enticing to resist.

For someone so mad keen on horses, particularly the first champion to be produced by Heytesbury, it seemed almost inconceivable that Robert was fast asleep on 6 November 1984 when his dream of breeding a Melbourne Cup winner was fulfilled. The first he heard of Black Knight's big win was when Janet phoned him at 4a.m. in London, where he was on business, with the news. It made him the only West Australian to have bred a Melbourne Cup winner in 134 years.

Robert continued to have a lot of winners over the years, including Speed Check, who finished second in the Golden Slipper Stakes, the greatest two-year-old event run in Australia or New Zealand. I keep umpteen files and records on all the stallions who have stood at stud at Heytesbury and I am still in the habit of keeping all their scrapbooks up to date because I know that is what Robert would have wanted. He also asked me to photograph all the foals and I have now filled well over ten albums with all my photographs.

The stud means a lot to me for I have been involved with it from its very inception. After a fairly short period of two unsatisfactory managers Robert asked me to take over and to run the stud for him. Initially I was a little reluctant to take on such a huge responsibility because I enjoyed working for him in the practice and my work there enabled me to pursue my other interests. I instructed at pony clubs, judged at some of the shows and enjoyed sailing with ex-Rhodesian friends Ron and Lesley Deuchar in their boat, *Penga*, at the weekends. But, not surprisingly, my love of horses won in the end.

I moved into the cottage which Robert had originally built as a weekender for his family, which had rapidly expanded to four bright children – Peter, Catherine, Simon and Paul. Later he built a more spacious and handsome house complete with a large swimming pool, a squash court, a gymnasium and an all-weather tennis court which I make used of quite regularly. He also had a guest complex built where businessmen and celebrities were invited to stay. These celebrities included the late Paul Eddington, star of the popular *Yes Minister* television series, and Prince Andrew and Fergie who came to stay to avoid the press. They loved the privacy that Heytesbury offered and Fergie was anxious to see a mare served. They were duly invited to the serving barn one afternoon. The mare was not interested and wouldn't stand and next minute Fergie yells out: 'Oh come on, girl. You don't bloody well know what you're missing.'

Shortly after I settled in at the cottage I determined to meet my new neighbours. I was quite lonely some nights on the farm and craved company, especially after a long, hard day of working with the stud's horses. But in the process of making new acquaintances I had to grow accustomed to some 'cultural differences'.

On one particular occasion my neighbours kindly invited me over for dinner. However, it soon dawned on me that things were done somewhat differently in rural Australia. Within seconds of my arrival I was whisked indoors and seated at the table, where I was expected to watch television until my hostess had finished preparing the evening meal. A cup of sweet tea was placed before me, followed shortly thereafter by a large plate piled high with homegrown vegetables. Nestled beside the potatoes was a small roasted bird which I mistook for a quail. Unbeknownst to me, my host was a pigeon fancier and was held in high regard by the racing fraternity. Our dinner, I later discovered to my horror, was comprised of pigeons that had not quite made the grade.

Another eventful evening was when other neighbours kindly invited me to a Christmas Eve party. They had lived on their farm for about thirty years and knew just about everyone in the district. I arrived wearing a long, smart frock, which was the required dress at soirées in Africa, only to find all the other guests very casually dressed. Despite my faux pas it turned out to be a most enjoyable party. Beth, the hostess, and I became close friends over the years. We joined a book club together and later attended a memory course at the university which was quite hilarious really, given that we were much older than any of the other students. Sadly Beth, like so many of my friends, died of cancer last year.

My neighbours have, over the years, not only extended friendship to me but on many occasions also come to my rescue. I had not been living in the cottage long when I was woken late one night by the pounding of hooves that did not sound as if they belonged to a horse. They also seemed far too close for comfort. I grabbed the flashlight, called my Rhodesian Ridgeback and went out into the night to investigate. There, giving me the most baleful look, was Barney the bull. Now Barney was not the kind of animal to take on single-handedly and I thought it wiser to call my neighbour Joy for help. She arrived with her three teenaged children and together we tried to chase Barney back into his paddock. What a production! First we had to make sure we kept him well clear of some young eucalypts which Robert and Janet had just planted. I remembered someone passing the remark, 'You can do most things here but don't bloody well destroy a tree'. So naturally I was most anxious that Barney didn't bulldoze his way through Robert's cherished saplings.

Through our frantic efforts to steer Barney away from the trees the poor beast got confused and galloped off in the wrong direction until he landed, with a huge splash, in the swimming pool. Joy's kids thought it was such a hoot but I was utterly dismayed. Fortunately, after much shouting and clapping of hands we managed to direct Barney to the steps where he clambered out most indignantly. The unexpected midnight dip had done much to calm him down, however, and he no longer put up any resistance when we guided him back to his paddock.

Heytesbury, meanwhile, continued on its winning streak. The second stallion to stand at the stud was Haulpak, a name that will be remembered by many breeders and racegoers. He was a remarkable horse and one of the most courageous that Western Australia has known. Robert bought him as a yearling at the Sydney sales and paid $17,000 for him. He had seven starts at Ascot race course in Perth for four wins, two seconds, a third and the stakes of $13,080. Then Haulpak broke down in the near side knee in an accident and we never saw the best of the horse. But Haulpak became an instant success at stud and one trainer made the comment, 'The Haulpak progeny are turning into smart performers. I would like to have a few of them in my stable.'

Such was the admiration and respect that Robert commanded as a breeder that he was later voted by his peers in the industry as breeder of the year in 1987. By then Heytesbury Stud had bred the winners of 115 races. Almost simultaneously, Robert's outrageous daring in the corporate sphere had made him a cause célèbre and he was constantly in the news with his audacious takeover bids.

It seemed then that the Holmes à Courts were locked into a golden and auspicious phase. I had finally found my place in the sun and loved my work at Heytesbury. I also saw a lot of Robert, for he, Janet and my grandchildren spent most weekends on the farm. During these weekend stays I would go for long rides with my son which allowed us time to discuss at length what was happening on the stud. But most importantly, those short spells on his dream farm provided Robert with a much-needed release from his work.

Although it was at times stressful work and he was constantly making headlines with his takeover bids, Robert assured me he never became overly concerned when he failed in some of his more ambitious ventures. He used to say, 'If it doesn't work out I'll get second prize which is just as gratifying.' There was a rather controversial bid he made for a mammoth Australian company which I knew he was very keen to pull off yet when it failed Robert, instead of fuming, was somewhat amused when his opponent likened his takeover bid to 'an elephant being raped by a flea'. Robert thought it was hilarious.

For all his winning ways Robert, the consummate corporate grandee, had a marvellous capacity for putting everything into perspective. The only thing he ever allowed himself to get sentimental about, however, was Heytesbury. It was his passion and his great love. Oddly enough, his sentimentality never extended to the point where he would put a wager on his racehorses. He never placed a bet and always quipped he was more interested in collecting the prize money.

Money held little, if no appeal, for Simon, though. When he first came to Australia in 1972 to do some post-production work on his documentary, Robert was keen to help him market and distribute it. His very words were, 'Give me the film and I will make you a million.' Simon, in that characteristic laid-back style of his, turned to his brother and replied, 'Robert, what do I want a million for?' Instead, Simon returned to Durban where he produced a booklet about the voyage, bought a VW van and then travelled around South Africa, screening his documentary in countless community halls along the way.

So many of my friends saw the documentary and were all, without exception, enormously impressed by it. A number of them had invited Simon to stay with them but my fiercely independent son graciously declined. It seemed he preferred to stay in his cramped van.

After travelling the length and breadth of the country with his film we tried to encourage Simon to move to Australia but he had begun to express an interest in producing wildlife sculptures. He spent several months working in a factory in Pretoria and studying bronze casting under a rather rude but very talented man. Then, having mastered bronze casting, Simon returned to the wilds of Botswana where he intended to base himself as a sculptor. It allowed him to live, once again, among the animals he so loved and never tired of observing. Moreover, he was intent on capturing their beauty and mystique in the most exacting of art forms.

Needless to say, I was very sad that we would continue to live so far apart as I had long harboured a secret wish that he would find something to do here in Australia. Unfortunately it was not to be and I had to console myself with the knowledge that my son had at last settled down and had found a vocation that not only engaged his passion for Africa's magnificent creatures but tapped into his outstanding creative talents.

He was, it seemed, poised for artistic and commercial success and in his letters to me he excitedly made mention of a steady stream of commissions starting to pour in. He sculpted mostly elephants and sold his work to a gallery in Johannesburg as well as to a growing number of tourists. One popular piece was his bronze sculpture of a charging elephant, and apparently a bronze casting of it had been bought for US President Ford by his secretary, who then had it shipped to the United States.

With both my sons pursuing their stellar ambitions I allowed myself to be lulled into a wondrous sense of security. I had also begun to carve a new and challenging life for myself in Australia and no longer suffered from bouts of nostalgia for Africa. Indeed, the traumas and travails of the preceding years had begun to recede behind a veil of time. However, having allowed myself to luxuriate in the embrace of such good fortune I was blind to the lengthening shadows, shadows that would, before long, cast me into terrifying darkness.

Chapter Twelve

SIMON GOES MISSING

The cryptic telegram awaiting my collection at the local post office gave no hint of anything untoward. 'Big Tube and I missing you. Where are you? Frog.' I did not have an inkling what it was about. Who on earth was Frog?

All day my mind was taunted and teased by this peculiar and rather disconcerting telegram. At first I thought it may have been sent as some sort of joke. But the tenor of it seemed to suggest that it had been sent by someone who was very worried. But who? If only there had been some clue as to the identity of Frog, the mysterious sender, it would doubtlessly have helped me unravel the puzzle.

When I mentioned the curious cable to Robert he quickly dismissed it and advised me to do likewise. He was convinced it was unimportant and that the true purpose of it would eventually be revealed. Indeed, within a matter of days I received a late-night call – but of the kind that always seems to presage bad news – from Tim Liversedge, a friend of Simon's. He told me he was concerned about Simon, who had, it seemed, failed to return from a business trip to South Africa. Apparently Simon had driven to Johannesburg on 5 May 1977 on a seven-day permit to purchase numerous supplies for his bronze sculptures and his new foundry.

When he failed to return after several weeks, Tim at first thought that Simon may have decided, on impulse, to extend his stay in South Africa. But as the weeks turned into months all

Simon's friends in Botswana became increasingly alarmed. Those friends included Daphne, aka Frog, who as a last resort had sent me that enigmatic cable, apparently in the hope that Simon may have decided to visit me in Australia.

The cable was sent two months after Simon had set off from his home, a nondescript little 'grass hut' on the banks of a river overlooking the famous Okavango delta. It was later revealed to me that Daphne's brother had made the hut available to Simon and that it was in close proximity to her own house. And it was with Daphne, or Frog as she was affectionately known, that Simon would often go floating down the river on a big, inflatable tube to observe more closely all the animals that converged on one of the most unique waterways in the world.

To Simon it was a wellspring of inspiration. Here he photographed and then painstakingly sculpted the creatures that never ceased to fascinate him. He had turned his hand to several small sculptures, including one of a lion cub, another of a lion stalking prey, a cheetah chasing an impala and a pair of sable bulls locked in mortal combat. But Simon remained tirelessly transfixed by his elephants and was apparently in the process of putting the finishing touches to a massive elephant that was promising to be the most ambitious project he had yet attempted. It was for this remarkable masterpiece-in-the-making that Simon needed to travel to Johannesburg to buy various supplies.

When Tim discovered I knew nothing of my son's whereabouts and that in fact I had not heard from him for some time, he decided to leave for South Africa immediately to try and find out what had happened. Everyone, of course, was well aware that Simon had a long history of going walkabout and that he often did so without feeling the need to notify his nearest and dearest. But given all that I couldn't shrug off a terrible sense of foreboding.

Robert, however, tried to reassure me as best he could and made a point of reminding me of all the times Simon had 'disappeared' in the past only to make it home safe and well after we had worked ourselves into a frenzy of concern. 'Please don't worry,' he said. 'Remember when Simon went off to Sumatra for three months to photograph near-extinct rhino and we never heard a word? And then there was the time he was lost at sea. And he survived that, not to mention the times he'd go tracking elephants for days before anyone sighted him.'

Robert was right. Simon was notorious for wandering off without telling anyone where he was headed or for how long he would be away. He was very much a free spirit in that sense and had an incurable habit of heading off into the bush whenever the fancy took him. But somehow the telegram and then the call from his friend seemed to suggest that even for those well acquainted with Simon's idiosyncrasies this prolonged absence was out of the ordinary. Something was not right.

I began re-reading some of Simon's letters in the hope that in one of them he may have alluded to a trip or project he intended following through at some later date. All they contained, however, was bright, detailed news of his work and his delight at being back in Botswana. In one of them he seemed so happy with his lot in life and told me about how he had set up a workshop in an old bus which he had purchased for next to nothing and that he had built his own foundry. The last letter he wrote to me was posted in Maun only days before he apparently set off on his business trip to Johannesburg. In it he wrote:

> I now live in Maun and lease some grass huts. It is very peaceful by the river and a good place to do my sculptures. I will also do casting here in somewhat primitive conditions. I have a commission which I must do sometime in the next few months. It is for that horsewoman in the UK,

Pat Smythe. She and her husband did a trip in the swamps on a houseboat belonging to some friends of mine. They saw one of my bronzes on the boat and he wrote to me asking me to do a sitatunga as a surprise gift for his wife. A sitatunga is a swamp antelope. I had a terrible Christmas because I went down with malaria for a week but I recovered in time for New Year and am fine now . . . I got a letter from Rob and a very nice Xmas cheque both a great surprise and very nice.

It contained nothing more that would have explained why Simon had not returned to the work he had become so passionate about and that had held such promise. Everything seemed to be going extremely well and he had a lot of work lined up. Simon may have loved to go roaming but it was certainly not like him to leave things unfinished.

Meanwhile, I had managed to confirm by sighting his signature that Simon had indeed crossed the Botswana border on 5 May 1977 but after that no-one knew anything of my son's whereabouts. What was especially strange was that Simon had left Maun via Francistown without dropping in to see his friend Bodo Muche. This, I gathered, was completely out of character for Simon who never drove through the town without at least stopping for a cup of coffee with his long-time friend. When no new leads were forthcoming everyone became increasingly concerned, even the normally imperturbable Robert.

Simon was reported missing to the police and the press soon followed with reports on his mysterious disappearance with one newspaper running a front page story under the headline BOTSWANA SCULPTOR VANISHES ON SEVEN-DAY TRIP TO SA. But I still clung to the belief that Simon was somewhere out in the bush, totally oblivious of the widespread alarm he had set off. I imagined him to be somewhere off the beaten track, beyond the reach of civilisation and the desperate search that had been set in train. I kept thinking of the time he had taken off on one of his typical bush odysseys and stayed away for what seemed like ages. On that occasion, just as suddenly, I received a telegram out of the blue with no explanation given, only a request to meet his train at the specified time. And there were several similar incidents when Simon would just materialise on my doorstep after long absences.

But my feelings of unease grew more acute after I received the chilling news on 10 June 1977 that Simon's Datsun pick-up was found abandoned by forest workers in the Tsitsikamma National Forest, which stretches along the coast of the Cape Province in South Africa. It was thought that the vehicle had been left there for some time as it was almost buried in leaves. Even more worrying came the news that the numberplates had been removed and that the engine number had been scratched off, leaving almost no means of identification. Yet, amazingly, the police were able to trace the Datsun back to Simon. According to the police, Simon's pick-up was found on a lonely forest path at the top of the Bloukrans Pass near Storms River. Added to my son's mysterious disappearance was the fact that none of his possessions were in the vehicle. The police found not so much as a scrap of evidence that would have enabled them to at least speculate about what may have happened to Simon.

The thought that Simon, a man so preternaturally good-natured, could have been harmed in some way did not bear thinking about. Although finding the pick-up was a major breakthrough, we came no closer to making sense of it all. No-one could understand what Simon's Datsun was doing so far from Johannesburg. And what we found especially strange was that no-one had sighted Simon after he crossed the Botswana border.

The police at Storms River took possession of the vehicle and I was kept informed of the investigation by Simon's friends. The phone rang incessantly during those long, stressful weeks and because of the time difference I went for days without sleep. But by September the investigation all but limped along and had failed to deliver any new clues. My son, it seemed, had literally vanished without a trace. However, I found it impossible to even entertain the thought that a man who had encountered and survived so many physical hardships in the African bush and on the high seas could have met with some mishap while on a short business trip. There had to be an answer somewhere, a vital clue that would lead me to my son and I was not going to find it by waiting for the telephone to ring. I needed to go back to South Africa and Botswana to start looking for Simon myself.

Robert at that stage was chairman of Bell Bros and chairman of the Albany Woollen Mills and had too many pressing business commitments to accompany me to South Africa. But he was desperate for me to go and do all I could and insisted that he pay all the costs during my twelve-day search for Simon.

I left on 19 September and was met by Tim, who took me to a Johannesburg hotel where we immediately set to work plotting our course of action. The first thing we did early the following morning was meet with the police in Johannesburg and then we flew down to Port Elizabeth where we were met by a detective and two other police officers. They drove us to Storms River where Simon's pick-up was found. I had, up until then, willed myself into believing that the police would provide me with some slim shred of hope. But they had nothing new for us to go on. Instead, they took us to the spot where a group of foresters had stumbled upon Simon's pick-up and to me, standing there amid gigantic yellowwood and stinkwood trees, it seemed as if the forest was shrouded in a conspiratorial silence. And I felt certain that somewhere in its thick undergrowth it held a secret, the key that would help us unlock the tormenting riddle. But whatever happened to my son in that remote, eerie forest remained concealed to us on that agonisingly sad day.

We returned to the small police station at Storms River and took possession of Simon's Datsun and then drove back to our hotel in Port Elizabeth. There were a number of newspaper reporters waiting to interview me. My son's disappearance had been given some prominence over the months since he was reported missing and it was thought my arrival would help establish a new lead. Sadly, it proved not to be the case.

The following morning Tim returned to Johannesburg but I decided to break my journey in Durban and spend the night with my friend Peggy Whittaker, who was such a great comfort to me. Once back in Johannesburg I went to the hotel where my son had evidently planned on staying. The manager at the Johannesburger Hotel kindly allowed me to go through the hotel's register to see if I could find an entry in Simon's handwriting. Again, nothing.

I felt myself rapidly losing my grip on the tiny bit of hope that had kept me buoyed throughout the interminable ordeal. In desperation I had even consulted a clairvoyant, but to no avail. She could throw no new light on what may have happened to my son. Instead, the mystery deepened at almost every turn we took. We thought of all sorts of things that may have befallen Simon, including the possibility that perhaps he had suffered a loss of memory and wandered off somewhere. We contacted scores of hospitals but no-one had seen anyone matching Simon's description.

After we had exhausted all avenues of inquiry in Johannesburg, Tim and I flew in his single-engine aircraft to Botswana. There, at the small airport in Maun, we were met by Daphne who had invited us to stay with her. She was a cheerful, outgoing woman who was still distressed about Simon's disappearance. We had a very long chat about everything that had happened and it ended with both of us in floods of tears. Daphne, too, wouldn't let go of her conviction that Simon was still alive. Apparently she was the last person who saw Simon on the day he left for Johannesburg. He had borrowed an overnight grip from her and then had a cup of coffee with her the morning he drove off in his brand-new Datsun. I gathered from Daphne they were very sad to part but Simon made it quite clear to her that he would be coming back within a matter of days. She told me they were very close friends and had known each other for a couple of years.

That night we went to Simon's to pack his belongings and to sort out all his moulds, which he had left neatly labelled in his usual methodical manner. The large elephant he had been working on was still on the work bench in 'plasticine' form. I managed to pack his moulds and the few belongings Simon had accumulated over the years into five black, tin trunks I had bought from a local African store. I had decided to have everything sent to Australia where I would take care of them.

The large elephant, though, proved somewhat more cumbersome and we drove to a friend of Simon's with it perched on my lap. I was terrified it would crack during the rough ride over Botswana's rutted tracks but miraculously it survived unscathed. Simon's friend offered to do the next stage of casting it in plaster of Paris and to have it packed for the flight to Australia where I then hoped to have it cast in bronze. It was an exquisite sculpture, my son's finest, and I knew he would have wanted it well taken care of.

Daphne came to see us off the next day and it made for a very tearful farewell. She was quite distraught and although a lot was left unspoken between the two of us our concern and love for Simon had forged a very strong bond between us. Before we took off on that final day in Botswana she promised to always keep in touch. In a letter she later wrote to me she summed my Simon up: 'Simon truly had a wonderful inner feeling that far surpassed the sixth sense, of the ways of nature, a feeling that cannot be explained to a layman, for it is surely a sense that was instilled over the years of living on unspoiled earth.'

We reached Gaborone, which is near the border of Botswana, just before dusk, making it too late for us to refuel. As we were unable to continue our flight to Johannesburg we all but hightailed it to the only hotel in town where we were told there was no accommodation available and that the best they could offer us was some room in the coffee shop. Fortunately, just before having to bed down in such insalubrious quarters I was given the room of a guest who had failed to arrive. Tim, however, wasn't quite so lucky.

When we flew out of Botswana early the following morning I felt so sick at heart. I had come back to Africa determined to find my son, or to at least make some sense of his strange disappearance, only to end up leaving with scores of unanswered questions. For weeks I had pursued every possible line of inquiry but each one, without exception, had led me to a hope-crushing dead end. If only I had something to go on, no matter how peripheral, it would have kept those embers of hope alive. I was so desperate for something, anything, of hopeful significance that would release us all from that waking nightmare. But most of all I wanted confirmation that my son was alive and well. But as Tim's plane headed south, away from the country that had exerted such a magnetic pull on my son and had featured so prominently in my own life, I grew more and more despondent.

We had uncovered so many inconsistencies in the search for my son, none of which brought us any closer to solving the mystery. Why, I thought, had there been no mail for him since the day he left Botswana? I found that most odd, for surely there must have been a letter for him. Then there were the police records which stated that Simon's briefcase was missing. How did they ascertain this? As far as I knew Simon never made use of a briefcase. Furthermore, they found a set of prospecting tools in the pick-up but when I questioned Simon's friends they said he possessed no such tools. Also there were jerry cans of petrol in the vehicle, which was most unusual because South Africa at the time had introduced strict petrol rationing.

There were so many things that just failed to add up. For instance, Simon's Datsun was found abandoned near Storms River, about 700 miles south of Johannesburg where he was supposedly going to buy all his art supplies. Curiously, the location was within striking distance of the Addo Elephant National Park, which lies about forty miles north of Port Elizabeth. The park had been partitioned off from the surrounding Addo forest to protect the few survivors of the great herds of elephant that had once roamed the forests. Maybe Simon, the elephant-lover that he was, had decided on the spur of the moment to head south to visit the park.

Stranger still, a friend of Simon's in Botswana had, for some extraordinary reason, once remarked that if Simon ever wanted to drop out of sight he could make use of his cottage near the Tsitsikamma National Forest where he would be assured privacy. Patrick Bromfield had come to hear of this offer and was to question the chap about it but shortly before they were to meet the man was killed in a plane crash. We will never know if he had some vital information regarding Simon's disappearance.

There were so many theories, some more fantastic than others. But what everyone knows for sure was that Simon was a very brave and competent man in the bush. All the game scouts who had worked with him in Botswana would attest to that. When it came to civilisation, however, he was a lost soul. All his life he preferred the serenity of the bush and his animals to the frenetic pace of cities.

In many ways Simon did not belong to the fast-paced, commercially driven world. He was too gentle, too sensitive to have survived the brashness and chaos that comes with living and working in the city. I guess it was that sensitive, caring streak of his that allowed him to work his miracles with animals. I remember once he took a baby cheetah away from its mother and then he felt so guilt-stricken about it that he returned the cheetah within a matter of hours. Even more surprisingly, the mother did not reject the baby. But then Simon had a special way with animals.

Even before he went to prep school, when he was about six years old, he showed signs of this extraordinary empathy with animals. We had this wonderful Siamese cat who, I think, had a liaison with a most unsuitable alley cat. Well, the upshot of all this was that she took longer than usual to produce her litter of kittens. The birth, in fact, was horrendous and she was in a terrible amount of pain but Simon stayed with her and lovingly and gently helped deliver all five kittens.

When he was a game ranger he had to put down a pregnant elephant that had been wounded by poachers. The poor creature was so lame and sick and had developed gangrene in one of her legs – Simon had no alternative but to put her out of her misery. However, he managed to perform a Caesarean on the elephant to help rescue her calf. And having done so he immediately put a call through to the Pretoria Zoo to find out what he needed to feed the calf. He was told not to give it milk. Milk, they stressed, was death. Simon tried his utmost to handfeed the little calf with powdered formula, but it was so weak that it survived but a few days.

Everyone knew him to be a very, very sensitive young man and a man who was easily wounded. Patrick Bromfield related an incident that involved a young girl in Francistown whom Simon was said to be very much in love with. Being the shy and retiring person that he was, however, he somehow failed to convey the depth of his feelings to this young woman. She no doubt tired of waiting for Simon to make some kind of commitment and unexpectedly announced her engagement to someone else. Simon was apparently so shattered by this that he went off on one of his bush camps for three solid weeks. Patrick and one of the game scouts eventually managed to track him down but he told them he needed the time in the bush to think about things. Did he feel the need to do the same when he headed for the remote Tsitsikamma Forest? It was one of the more credible theories that were energetically pursued by the investigating officers.

What I found most upsetting, though, was the suggestion by some that Simon could have committed suicide. As a mother I just knew, deep within my heart, that it was highly unlikely and in this I was supported by all Simon's closest friends, including Bodo, Ron Wink and Patrick Bromfield. Even all the clairvoyants I have been to have made no mention of suicide. Of everyone, Bodo was the most adamant in ruling out suicide. He shared a rather uncanny experience with me regarding Simon. Apparently just days before a friend called with the news that Simon's Datsun had been found he had a vivid and unsettling dream about Simon:

> In it Simon had an accident at the Tlaponeng Bridge in Maun and got killed. He was in his Landrover, which fell into the deep hole on the Maun side of the bridge. Water was gushing in and I tried to dive down but failed. We used to swim in that hole, socialising with fellow pale faces, swinging from the branches of the fig tree and dropping into it.
>
> The dream was so vivid and I immediately feared the worst. It turned out that Simon had driven via Francistown and Gaborone, leaving

Botswana at the Tlhokweng border post. According to my recollection it is more than likely that we passed each other on the Gaborone road and I would have had this dream a day or so after he arrived in South Africa.

According to Bodo, he had discussed all aspects of Simon's disappearance with their mutual friends but no-one was able to throw new light on the case. The head of the Botswana CID, Kevin Calinan, told him he thought that Simon had met with foul play by the African underworld.

Bodo, together with some of Simon's friends, went to visit the place where the Datsun pick-up had been found. It was, he noted, within sight of a well-known picnic area on a track situated on the south side of the Storms River Bridge. 'I had strong vibes that Simon and the secret of his disappearance were in that forest,' remarked Bodo. 'The Tsitsikamma Forest was reasonably thick but one could walk through without having to use a *panga* [machete]. I raised some questions why that forest had not been searched.'

It remained one of the many imponderables that dogged our exhaustive investigations. I called Robert, who had been footing all the bills and expenses during our unsuccessful search, and it was decided that I should leave the case in the hands of the police and return to Australia. As a mother I had done all I could in what had amounted to a frustrating and futile search for my missing son. I left South Africa with a myriad unanswered questions and a deep-seated fear that something terrible had happened to Simon. But what I found most unbearable was the not knowing, the absence of any information that would have helped us put the whole heartbreaking episode to rest.

From the day my son had been reported missing I lived in a state of limbo. We all did, including Robert, who, I suspect, tried to cope with it by losing himself in his work. I tried to do likewise shortly after I returned to Australia but it wasn't easy. Some days were worse than others but thankfully Heytesbury and the horses were my salvation. During quiet spells, though, my mind would always stray to that dark, dank forest where I knew the truth lay concealed. It would take years before the dark forces finally allowed it to be unearthed.

Chapter Thirteen

THE FULL CIRCLE

Sadness followed me at heel like a predator stalking its prey. I might well have faltered and succumbed during that harrowing year after Simon's disappearance had the hand of destiny not delivered me Lieutenant-Colonel Ronald Critchley. Ronnie, I might add, was no stranger to me. Our acquaintance dated back to the postwar years in Northern Rhodesia where he ran a splendid ranch before he married Erica, one of my closest friends. It was Erica who, as one of my most devoted correspondents, used to unintentionally rekindle my nostalgia for Africa with her long, always amusing, letters from their farm Blue Lagoon.

In the year following Simon's disappearance, though, I received a very sad letter from Ronnie to tell me that Erica had lost her battle against cancer. It came as a terrible blow and I immediately wrote back to Ronnie to sympathise and to let him know of Simon's disappearance in South Africa. We corresponded for several months, reminiscing about happier times and how we had first met in 1948. Erica had invited Peter, myself and the boys up to her farm for the duration of the Lusaka Show, in which we were to compete. At that time she was Erica Lafone and married to her second husband, Michael. They were a rather socially prominent couple and prided themselves on hosting sumptuous soirées on their farm Chikupi, which means 'cry of the fish eagle'. Hardly a weekend went by without Erica treating a house full of guests to her inimitable brand of hospitality. And it was during one of these very popular weekend gatherings that I first met Ronnie. I remember the day so vividly for he was sitting with Erica on the verandah awaiting our arrival that afternoon.

Erica, the quintessential hostess, knew we had endured a long and uncomfortably hot drive up from Salisbury and immediately slipped into the role of gracious hostess by calling out, 'Gin or tea?' I think it was Ronnie who said he thought it would be wiser to have tea first. This was then served by domestic servants dressed in exquisitely embroidered waistcoats over white *kanzus*, the long traditional robes. Ronnie, we soon found out, was a neighbouring farmer and a regular fixture at Erica's weekend parties. I distinctly remember thinking him strikingly handsome and, admittedly, he made quite an impression. But at the time I was happily married to Peter.

Our horses were stabled at the racecourse in readiness for the show but we were concerned about Simon's pony because it had not travelled well and needed a good deal of exercise. Robert took it for a ride early the next day but ended up having to hold on for dear life when the pony suddenly took fright and bolted with him. It was terrifying to watch and all I could do was yell out to Robert to not let go. Miraculously he managed to stay on but the pony streaked through an archway leading into the stable yard and suddenly put on the brakes, sending Robert flying through the air. He suffered a very nasty gash on the jaw, but being the fearless rider that he was, he immediately mounted again. The pony's behaviour, however, did not improve and we thought it prudent not to let Simon ride it in the show.

When Ronnie, an accomplished polo player, got to hear of the incident he kindly offered to exercise the pony until he got all the 'nonsense' out of it. He must have spent hours lunging the pony in the round yard until he felt satisfied it would no longer misbehave.

Indeed, when Simon rode him in the show ring later that day he behaved so impeccably that they won first prize.

After that weekend I saw Ronnie again when he stopped over in Salisbury on his way to South Africa where he was about to buy some polo ponies. I found him to be a most fascinating man and knew of his reputation as a distinguished and decorated soldier who had fought in both the Ethiopian and Burma campaigns. After the war he spent two years as military attaché in Argentina and then returned to the United Kingdom. However, he had not been there long before deciding to sell his ancestral home in Scotland and to explore prospects in Africa.

Ronnie, who was married and divorced twice, bought Makeni, a cattle ranch of 19,000 acres, not far from Erica's Chikupi. Evidently he fell into the social whirl of Chikupi quite happily and shared Michael's passion for polo. However, it was general knowledge at the time that Erica and Michael's marriage was in serious trouble. I gathered that initially they had lived together for a while and, by all reports, quite happily but shortly after they were married their relationship had soured. Erica was a great raconteur and entertained her guests at dinner with the most outrageous stories. Predictably, much alcohol was consumed but Erica somehow always managed to keep a good head. Not so Michael, who fell asleep with his head in the soup at one of Erica's grand parties. Although it must have caused her some degree of embarrassment, Erica wouldn't so much as bat an eyelid but would, instead, coolly instruct the servants to carry the Bwana (boss) to bed. It seemed they too had grown accustomed to their employer's unseemly behaviour.

Erica, for all her infectious vivacity, was not the type of woman to cross. Indeed, her fierce temper and feisty antics had become legendary in the neighbourhood. There was one marvellous tale that rapidly did the rounds of how Erica had found an Afrikaans farmer poaching one of her eland and became so incensed that she shot him in the leg. On another occasion, she had gone to a nightclub in Nairobi, Kenya, with a friend who had asked the band conductor to stop playing a certain tune as it upset her. When the conductor refused, Erica's friend drew her revolver and shot him in the leg as well.

The first I knew that Ronnie and Erica had become close friends was when I accidentally bumped into them in Salisbury. They were on their way to the club and invited me to come along. At the time my personal circumstances had changed dramatically. Peter had left me and I was extremely busy running the riding school with Diana and Charles. I was struck by how blissfully happy Ronnie and Erica appeared to be on that day, so it came as no surprise to me that not long afterwards Erica left Michael for Ronnie. As a couple they were ideally suited to each other because they shared a deep and abiding passion for the conservation of wildlife and had founded the Wildlife Conservation Society. When they were married they sold Makeni ranch and made Blue Lagoon their home, a farm they had bought and then transformed into a wildlife sanctuary.

Over the years, with both Erica and myself remarried, we became a friendly foursome. Erica and Ronnie were enormously supportive during the years that Charles and I worked so hard to make our Chobe dream become a reality. In fact, they were elated we were doing something that involved wildlife and often came to stay with us at Chobe. They loved it there, especially Ronnie, who would spend hours fishing in the Chobe River. At night the four of us would play bridge, something Charles and Ronnie excelled at and I dreaded. I was never good at it.

Actually, it was Erica and Ronnie who came to inherit Jeremy, the recalcitrant vervet monkey that had terrorised so many of our guests. Erica, who had heard of our travails with Jeremy, offered to release him on Blue Lagoon among a large colony of resident monkeys. Jeremy, to our relief, quickly made himself at home and never gave Erica and Ronnie a spot of trouble.

When Charles was rushed to hospital after the horrendous bee attack, Erica was one of the first people I called. She kept in close touch throughout the ordeal. When Charles was transferred to the intensive care unit at Bulawayo Hospital and it was thought he would pull through, she invited us to come and stay at Blue Lagoon so he could recuperate. We never got there. After Charles's funeral Erica again asked me to come and stay with her and Ronnie but I had too much to sort out. I had to try and sell the hotel and then there was the ghastly business with Captain Excell.

I'm sorry I never managed to go because Erica made Blue Lagoon sound so entrancing in her letters to me when I moved to Australia. She was inordinately proud of the wildlife sanctuary they had established and it had become renowned for its herds of lechwe antelope. She kept me up to date with all the conservation work she and Ronnie had become involved in, including organising game-viewing camps and the building of a special educational camp in Kafue National Park. When the massive Kariba Dam was being constructed they raised £15,000 from the Fauna Preservation Society in London in order to organise rescue operations on the lake. Her letters filled me with such nostalgia, especially when she wrote of waking in the early mornings to find lechwe calves asleep on their verandah and bateleur eagles and tawny eagles circling in the skies above.

There is a belief in Africa that the eagle owl can sense the impending death of a member of the human race and, eerily, on their last night together at Blue Lagoon the eagle owl came and sang his traditional song of farewell. Erica passed away in June 1976. Ronnie had nursed her to the very end. Afterwards he arranged the most moving farewell for a woman who had such a deep love for the continent and its wildlife. A helicopter carrying her ashes flew first over Chikupi, where some of them were scattered and then over Blue Lagoon, where the remaining ashes were released over the causeway from where she and Ronnie had spent so many glorious hours watching the thousands of lechwe antelope and all the birds.

Zambia's President Kenneth Kaunda authorised the use of the army helicopter. He had long been an admirer of Erica's unwavering commitment to conservation as well as her charitable works within the community. She was also much loved by all their employees and they were all there on that causeway to pay their respects, singing in those rich harmonising tones of Africa a heart-rending and final tribute to her. I was so touched when I read all this in Ronnie's letter and thought it the most wonderful thing to do for a wife.

After Erica's death Ronnie found that living alone at Blue Lagoon had lost its appeal. He had had twenty years of such great happiness with Erica that without her the farm would simply never be the same. He felt as overwhelmed by his sadness over losing Erica as I did over Simon's disappearance, and through our letters we were able to share our grief. Ronnie wrote and told me of his decision to return to Scotland where he had managed to rent a farmhouse. Before leaving Africa he had Blue Lagoon placed under President Kaunda's personal jurisdiction, thereby ensuring it was kept as a shrine for Erica. The furniture and pictures remained in the house and Langston, the old faithful 'house boy', remained behind to care for it.

Unfortunately, the move back to Scotland unsettled Ronnie even more and did little to dispel his loneliness. He knew that I was planning to take a trip to Ireland where Robert had wanted me to visit the Irish National Stud, and he invited me to spend a week at his farmhouse. Then we intended to visit several studs in England. The trip and my stay with Ronnie fell through, however, due to two quite unrelated accidents. The first happened when I was knocked to the ground and kicked by one of the horses that had been released up in the hills. I suffered quite a few nasty bruises and cuts and had to delay my trip. Then, no sooner had I recovered from this mishap than I was involved in a car accident on the way into Perth. My doctor thought I had been knocked around enough by two serious accidents in succession and warned me off travelling abroad. I had to cancel my trip but the correspondence and telephone calls continued unabated.

Not long after my car accident Ronnie mentioned taking a holiday in Australia. I thought it was a wonderful idea but before I could make the appropriate arrangements his holiday plans were unexpectedly revised. He was considering immigrating and asked if I would like a companion. I had been widowed and on my own for fifteen years and I wasn't quite sure if I wanted a companion. Robert, who remembered Ronnie from the Lusaka Horse Show days, was even more doubtful. When I told him that Ronnie was coming out to see me and that he was contemplating staying on, I was met with a long silence so typical of Robert. Then he turned to me and said, 'Do you know what you are doing?'

In all honesty I don't think I did at the time. It all seemed to have happened so quickly. Ronnie wrote asking me if he should bring his silver and his paintings and I replied with questions of my own such as could he cook and had he stopped smoking? He arrived on 6 October 1978.

Some friends of mine had arranged a party for my birthday a

week later and Ronnie was an instant hit. It was a marvellous celebration, during the course of which Ronnie announced he did not see much point in returning to Scotland and had decided to stay on in Australia. Within a month of his arrival we were married – the fourth time around for both of us.

Strangely, with Ronnie I had finally come full circle. He had known Peter and Charles and my sons and he had been there when Chobe evolved. He knew of the struggles, the setbacks and the tragedies. Indeed, it was through pain that we had become reunited. He was the best thing that happened to me in that year after Simon's disappearance. And, not surprisingly, he fell in love with Heytesbury from the outset. Although I had retired from active work on the stud I ran the office and maintained an active interest in it. I also considered it my duty to continue keeping photographic records of every foal born at Heytesbury as well as of all the visiting mares and foals.

The most exciting aspect of my new life with Ronnie was that we began to travel the world together. In 1979, the year after we were married, we flew to New Zealand and fished in the South Island and visited several studs then explored the North Island and stayed with some ex-Army friends. The following year he took me to all his old haunts in India. We also went to Agra to see the Taj Mahal, and in Kashmir we stayed at the magnificent hotel which had been the palace of the Maharajah of Kashmir. Ronnie had played polo with him in the 1930s.

And so it was that we eased ourselves, ever so effortlessly, into a contented and harmonious marriage. It was a marriage built on a sturdy foundation of mutual respect, great companionship and an empathy for what we each had endured before fate brought us back together. I am in fact deeply indebted to those karmic forces for orchestrating our union because had it not been for Ronnie I don't think I could have withstood the most savage blow that hit me just as I had begun to sample such sublime happiness.

It came by way of a telephone call at precisely 6p.m. on 13 February 1980. The voice on the other end was unfamiliar. 'Ja! Hullo, hullo . . . Is that Mevrou Holmes. This is polisie . . . Storms River . . . Suid Afrika.' My heart skipped a beat for I instantly knew he was the bearer of news of Simon. I hoped it was a new lead that would help them in their search for him. He went on: 'Some skeleton remains have been found by the Vark Rivier, near here. We think they are Mr Holmes's.'

I was incapable of coherent thought, let alone able to grasp the devastating finality in which this news was conveyed. Somewhere deep inside, where maternal instinct resides, hope still thrashed about. 'How can you be sure, Inspector?' I cried out.

I was mute with shock and ran to Ronnie, who was out walking and enjoying what had up until then been a lovely clear evening. I sobbed out all the details of the phone call and when he managed to calm me down we decided to call my cousin Dr Paul Oates in Cape Town and to ask him to find out more information for us. According to a local forester, a Mr Pierre Theron, the remains were found in a part of the Tsitsikamma National Forest where people rarely ventured. 'There are lots of bushbuck and bush pigs and a few leopards. The bush is very thick between the plantation and the forest and difficult to get through,' he was reported as saying.

The forensic tests were conducted within weeks and from the remains experts were able to ascertain the height and weight of the deceased. The measurements matched Simon's. Paul arranged for the remains to be cremated and then, three years after he had gone missing, what remained of my son was sent to me.

Simon would no doubt have loved to be put to rest near his beloved elephants in Africa, but that was too difficult for me to organise. Instead, we decided to scatter his ashes at sea, which was his other great love. On 17 August 1980 I mixed some of his ashes with wildflower petals and proteas and then Milton Skinner, one of Simon's sailing friends, kindly took us out in his boat and we scattered them at sea. Afterwards Ronnie, myself and Milton – Robert did not want to go – opened a bottle of champagne and wished Simon well. It was a simple but deeply moving send-off on a day that was so insistently lovely, so full of promise that as a mother I couldn't help but dwell on what might have been. But I took solace from the fact that my thirty-eight-year-old son had led the life of his choice.

Later I had one more important task to fulfil – on my own. I had kept some of Simon's ashes and these I scattered around a tree I had planted in remembrance beside the dam he used to fish in when he was at Heytesbury. Having done that I felt I had kept a part of my son close by.

Back in South Africa the police assured me Simon's case would remain open but I doubt whether that was true. All the policemen involved in the investigation have long since retired and somewhere, in the bowels of the Hillbrow Police Station in Johannesburg under layers of dust my son's file lies abandoned. I have now come to accept – or have I? – that we may never know what had happened to Simon in that coastal forest. His death, like so much of his wayfaring life, will remain an enigma.

Ronnie, bless him, was my Rock of Gibraltar. The support he gave me when I was trying so desperately to come to terms with Simon's death was of such a quiet, gentle kind. I don't know what I would have done without him. For a while we tried to lose ourselves in the comforting, everyday distractions of Heytesbury. There were umpteen things to do and gradually, with time, came a calm acceptance of life without Simon.

I think some people expected me to sit in a corner, curled up in grief. But I didn't. Ronnie was the only person I allowed to see my tears. And it helped so much being with someone who understood both how I felt and my way of coping with it all.

And, of course, even then riding Robert's old polo pony was a great consolation. I would ride for hours at a time, talking to my horse and to my Rhodesian Ridgeback dog and I would always feel that much better for it.

Later in 1981 Ronnie and I resumed our travelling. We flew to Vancouver, where we visited one of Robert's factories and were wined and dined by the manager and his wife. We travelled by train to San Francisco and flew on to Kentucky, where we were taken to see several studs. After that it was New York, where one of Ronnie's nieces gave us a quick tour of Manhattan, and then it was on to London.

On our way back home to Australia we stopped over in Kenya and stayed with friends who were kind enough to let us use their Landrover for tours of the game parks. After Kenya we flew over to the Seychelles and made a point of spending some time at the yacht club where Simon had called in during his sea voyage on *Maggie May II*. I would have loved to have gone to the island of Aldabra, which had been so special to Simon and where he and Gregg Lott completed his film. But unfortunately there was no way of getting there.

Hardly a year seemed to go by without us exploring some exotic and fascinating part of the world. We visited Sri Lanka, where I rode an elephant, London where we met the Queen Mother at a Special Forces Club Dinner at the Imperial War Museum and to Scotland where Ronnie celebrated his eightieth birthday and arranged a pheasant shoot (it snowed and was bitterly cold but the men managed to bag about 300 pheasants in two days).

We went fishing in Alaska where we stayed at Talaheim Lodge which could only be reached by float plane and was very much in the wilds. We had a delightful cabin, although the loo was some distance away and if nature called during the night we had to be escorted by the owner, Mark, who was armed with a rifle in case we met with a grizzly along the way. We fished in various stretches of the river and I caught a sixty-pound salmon. I wrestled with it for some time before I gave up the struggle and called for assistance. It took three of us to land my catch. Mark smoked it for us and, naturally, I thought it the best smoked salmon I had ever sampled.

On the way to Alaska we stopped in to Hong Kong for a few days' shopping (I was horrified to find that horses were kept in high-rise flats there – I am told that this is no longer the case) and from there we went to Japan to see some studs.

Another highlight was our trip to South America in 1989 where we travelled as far south as Puerto Williams in Tierra del Fuego. The place held some special significance for Ronnie as he had fished there during his time as military attaché in Argentina. There we boarded the *World Discoverer* to Antarctica via Cape Horn and through the Drake Passage.

At Cape Horn we climbed to the top and I was amazed at how well Ronnie coped, considering he had a bad ankle and the going was quite tough and slippery. We also made many landings by Zodiac to view the fascinating wildlife – sea lions, all sorts of birds and all eleven different types of penguins. One calm evening as we stood on the deck, having protected ourselves against the cold by wearing thermal underwear and anoraks, a spectacular iceberg came into view and passed by so close on the starboard side that we sat mesmerised. I will never forget that awesome sight and how the iceberg caught the full reflection of the sun in brilliant orange and pink hues.

Another holiday in 1990 took us to Double Island in Far North Queensland. Robert had bought the island as a getaway destination for his family as well as for friends and staff members. It was at Robert's suggestion that we visit the island and within minutes of our arrival he was on the phone wanting to know what we thought of it. He loved the island and had hoped to build a house there, but it was one of Robert's dreams that would never come to fruition.

Chapter Fourteen

THE FUTURE BECKONS

Monday 19 October 1987 went down as one of the blackest days in stockmarket history with more than $1000 billion wiped from the world's share markets. In Australia Robert was hardest hit of all the country's entrepreneurs and it was reported that just twelve months after the crash his wealth fell from $1.4 billion to $550 million.

Unlike so many of the corporate high-fliers who went down, however, Robert, the survivor and cunning strategist that he was, set about single-mindedly clawing his way back to the top. Some financial observers would never have thought such a resurrection possible yet Robert, in that quiet, understated way of his, began disposing of many of his assets and achieved the unthinkable – he made his second fortune within years of the crash. In April 1990 the Australian financial journal, *Business Review Weekly*, listed Robert's wealth at $800 million, second only to media owner Kerry Packer. But this miraculous feat came at some personal cost. Robert had put in excruciatingly long hours, leaving him precious little time or energy to go riding as much as he used to when he came down to Heytesbury.

I worried about that a lot because Robert was always fastidious about his exercise. He used to love going for long walks around the farm, and visitors who came and stayed did so knowing they would invariably be walked off their feet. He also swam a great deal when he came to the stud at weekends and made a point of getting a ride in before he returned to the city.

Work, however, gradually began to consume nearly all his time. He was always on the phone and began to keep peculiar hours so he could call London and New York during their trading hours. By then, I guess, we had all grown accustomed to Robert's relentless drive and his capacity for work. When I worked for him in his legal practice we would sometimes be in the office until eleven o'clock at night and Val, his secretary, would go out and buy us a carton of milk and some sandwiches.

Yet for all his preoccupation with rebuilding his business empire, hardly a weekend went by without Robert making his customary pilgrimage to Heytesbury. Fortunately it was a ritual he maintained and I so looked forward to seeing him and the family when they came to stay at the main house. Although in those stressful times our rides had become less frequent, I was at least able to touch base with him when he dropped by for a chat at the cottage.

The first weekend in September 1990 began as usual but then came Janet's call in the early hours of Sunday morning to tell me that Robert had suffered a massive heart attack. We were all – Janet, my grandchildren, Ronnie and myself – pulverised by shock and it took us a long time to come to grips with Robert's sudden death. It seemed so absurd in a way, that someone who had been so vital and so in charge of his life would no longer be in our midst. And, chillingly, it made me recall my former husband Peter's prophetic warning that the Holmes à Courts 'don't make old bones'. It seemed to have come to pass with his own death at fifty-four, followed by the untimely deaths of his sons before they, too, had reached their mid-fifties.

Predictably, news of Robert's death spread in no time and people began calling from all over the world to pass on their condolences. No-one, I think, could quite grasp the fact that the master corporate tactician who had once come within a whisker of acquiring BHP, Australia's biggest company, and who had been such a dominant financial player would never again enter a boardroom. Politicians, community leaders, friends and former business adversaries all paid tribute to my son and spoke warmly of a man they had come to respect for both his business acumen and his compassion. Paul Keating, who was then Federal Treasurer, described him as 'a prince of the corporate play' and a visionary.

To me he remained that fun-loving son who rode his horses fearlessly and superbly and dreamt of making his fortune. He turned that into a reality sooner than I thought possible with an innate drive that set him apart and which, ultimately, brought people from all walks of life to Perth on 5 September 1990 to pay their respects to a man they had come to revere as 'the master of the deal'. Nearly 1000 people attended his memorial service in the University of Western Australia's Winthrop Hall where Robert, some twenty-four years before, had received his law degree. There were no hymns and no public prayers during the brief service, only praise and moving dedications from the people who had come to know and love him over the years.

Jon Elbery, a long-term business associate and general manager of Heytesbury Holdings said in his moving tribute:

> Robert made you feel as if there were no barriers to your own potential.
> He had an unblinkered view of what was possible. He used to tell his
> employees, 'I'll expect you to work like one of my jockeys — to be given
> some guidelines but if conditions change mid-race, you'll be expected to
> act accordingly'. He loved the challenges that an ever-changing business
> situation could set.
>
> To those who did not know him he may have seemed cold and aloof.
> To those who knew him, he was warm and compassionate with a

compelling loyalty to those who were loyal to him. He was a family man. He loved the company of his family. He took every opportunity to spend time with them and they were very much a part of his business life. In a very practical way that he probably never realised, he managed to maintain a lifestyle where there was no conflict between work and family life. The two were for him intimately entwined.

Then Jon provoked a ripple of laughter among the mourners when he recalled Robert's wicked sense of humour. He recounted an incident involving a journalist who he knew was in the process of writing an article on one of Robert's businesses: 'Robert believed the journalist was not getting his sums right or drawing the right conclusions. Robert sent him a calculator. The journalist apparently persisted with the inaccuracies and Robert sent him the calculator's instruction booklet.'

Then came more laughter when he recounted Robert's dealings with the then chairman of the Herald and Weekly Times who warned Robert, 'You will only take this company over my dead body'. Robert's reply was something along the lines of, 'Thank goodness, I was afraid you were going to say it was not for sale at any price'. But my son had his weaknesses and Jon let it be known that Robert, for all his intellectual brilliance, was unable to come to grips with modern technology:

He is the only person I have ever met who once tried to turn on a television by using a calculator. He spent half his life on a telephone but I doubt he ever knew what his phone number was. He once locked himself out of his flat in London where Janet was waiting for him to return from work. His only way of contacting Janet was to phone the housekeeper in Perth and ask her to ask Janet to let him in. He was unwilling to learn how to get in and out of the office by using a security key. He never carried keys or money, for that matter. His vision leapt beyond the boundaries that confine ordinary minds. His time horizons were longer, his focus sharper, his vision clearer. One of Robert's associates once said of his style that he yells with a whisper.

It was a very moving tribute but as a mother and grandmother I found it nowhere near as heartrending as when my twenty-three-year-old grandson Peter, looking so vulnerable and alone, stepped up to the podium and in a tremulous voice vented his loss and grief.

Last Saturday was one of the happiest days in my memory. On the property that he carved from treeless acres of mediocre land into one of the finest in the country he spent a peaceful day in the manner he most enjoyed, surrounded by as many of his family as possible, relaxing, reading, watching and talking with the family.

It was a wonderful day that defies description in this short time. He retired early that night with a broad smile on his face. He was unparalleled in his role as a husband, a son, a friend, a business acquaintance, an adversary, a leader and as a father to the four of us. Dad, how we all loved you.

Ronnie once said to me that when he thinks of Robert and his achievements he is reminded of these lines of Rudyard Kipling about Cecil Rhodes . . .
'The immense and brooding spirit
Still shall quicken and control
Living he was the land
And dead his soul shall be her soul.'

We were not surprised when we read a newly discovered planet had been named Holmes à Court. Robert was a shooting star – he surely reached for the stars.

Robert's death shook us all to the core but no-one more so than

Janet who, as Robert's principal beneficiary faced the daunting prospect of having to assume the responsibilities of an $800 million corporate empire, which included twenty-three cattle stations up north, the Vasse Felix winery, Key Transport which operated a large fleet of trucks, and a vast art collection. But Janet, who had always been intimately involved in the running of Robert's privately held company, bravely set to work. As could be expected there were some changes and she publicly quipped that while Robert was called 'the great acquirer' she would be 'the great disposer'.

She shed many of the company's pastoral holdings and sold the Georgian-style mansion that she and Robert had bought in Perth's exclusive suburb of Peppermint Grove a few years before his death, as well as much of what was said to have been the world's biggest collections of indigenous art. Certainly she did it tough in the years following Robert's death, but there's no doubt that my son would have been proud of the way in which she has controlled and organised the many business ventures that he originated.

Janet has over the years achieved some stupendous results and in 1996 she won the Veuve Cliquot award as Britain's most successful businesswoman. This was awarded her in recognition of her efforts in turning around the fortunes of the Stoll Moss theatre group. The company, a subsidiary of Heytesbury Holdings Ltd, owns and operates ten West End theatres, including Her Majesty's, The Theatre Royal, Drury Lane and The Palladium. Her success made Janet the first Australian to be named British businesswoman of the year.

Closer to home, it was found necessary to reduce the vast number of brood mares at Heytesbury to about forty-five and to stand only three stallions. Then the company Heytesbury Thoroughbreds added a professional race track on the property to facilitate pre-training on the stud. Given all that, Heytesbury remains the leading stud in Western Australia. Moreover, despite all the tumult and the uncertain times in the wake of Robert's death, Heytesbury continues to be home to Ronnie and myself. It has been our oasis of tranquillity and security.

But that's not to say we have not had our setbacks. A year after Robert's death, Ronnie suffered a bad fall on Wallhallow Station in 1991, where Janet had flown us and our friends, the Millers of Zambia, in her King Air aircraft for a short holiday. He slipped down some steps onto a concrete floor and was in agony. No amount of painkillers helped so at first light we were flown to Cairns where Ronnie was rushed to hospital. There doctors confirmed our worst fears: Ronnie had a badly smashed hip. The result was a hip replacement but this failed to heal properly and after five weeks we flew to Perth where followed more operations. The replacement hip was removed, which in turn necessitated a long period in traction before they could do another replacement. To add to all his woes there were no less than three dislocations.

Remarkably, it did not take Ronnie long before he regained all his strength and was declared fit and well for us to take more of our wonderful trips together.

In 1993 I had a short break on my own. I was invited to Bullo River Station by the owner, Sara Henderson. Sara and I knew each other through her former housekeeper, Jacque, who used to do the night foaling at Heytesbury during the stud season. I had a great time with Sara and saw station life at its busiest as it was mustering season. I even spent a day on a stock horse mustering with the boys! Sara had just launched her first book, *From Strength to Strength*, which was already showing signs of being the bestseller it now is. She laughed and said to me that she would now be able to afford a ceiling in their large open living area!

However it was our return trip to Africa in 1994 that held

special significance for both of us. We had been invited by Ronnie's friends Peter and Annette Miller to stay at the Lilayi Lodge that they had built on their farm in Zambia. It was such a splendid setting and from our rondavel we could see various antelope grazing and vervet monkeys scampering about. And when riding out on horseback I spotted giraffe, waterbuck, kudu and flocks of magnificent birds. The Millers kept everything but the 'big five' (elephant, buffalo, lion, leopard and rhino) on their farm. During our stay the Millers drove us down to Ronnie's old ranch, Blue Lagoon. The road had deteriorated so much that our vehicle threw up clouds of dust whenever it hit deep potholes. Annette and I were in the back seat and had to literally hang on for dear life. It was not a comfortable journey but we persevered as Ronnie was keen to retrieve some of the paintings he had left on the ranch.

We were met by Langston, Ronnie's old houseboy, who was so delighted to see his old Bwano (boss) again. Ronnie had given Langston huts and some land before he sold Blue Lagoon to the government with the proviso that the ranch be maintained as a national park for wildlife. But sadly, things had changed, and none for the better. There was little wildlife to speak of because the flood regime on the Kafue riverflats had been permanently damaged after a dam was constructed further upstream. We saw only one bateleur eagle soaring in the sky when we walked out onto the causeway to view the memorial plaques Ronnie had placed there for Erica. These, thankfully, had been beautifully cared for by the ever-loyal Langston.

A few days later we flew to the Victoria Falls and from there Ronnie and I drove to Botswana and then on to Chobe National Park to see my old home. Thirty years had elapsed since Charles and I had created the Game Reserve Camp and built the Chobe River Hotel (now the Chobe Safari Lodge) and so much had changed in the intervening years. The once rutted road to Chobe had been sealed and it made for a much more civilised drive to Kasane, which I found to be a very different place.

It had become a thriving village with sealed roads, shops, a bank and three hotels. There were tented camps and more camping sites and several hotels in the district near Kazangula. Also, a new aerodrome had been built to accommodate larger aircraft and our old airstrip had to make way for the newest property, Cresta Mowana Safari Lodge.

Miraculously the pontoon was still operating but the *Chobe Belle* paddle-steamer had sunk some years previously after it had apparently been overloaded. I was told by the manager at the Chobe Safari Lodge that they had managed to salvage only the paddlewheel and the ship's loo from the depths of the river. But by and large everything had progressed since the game park was proclaimed Chobe National Park in 1968. And the wildlife in the region remained its most popular drawcard. It was what brought me to the Chobe River in 1959 and again in 1994.

It was a bit disappointing to find that the dense bush and the large trees were no more and for this the estimated 3500 elephants in the park were held responsible. Strangely enough, it made it a lot easier to spot the game but at the expense of the excitement we felt in those days when an elephant would suddenly appear from behind the bushes. These close encounters often required quick action, usually a lot of reversing, for in most cases you could count on more elephants being not too far behind.

I remembered Kasane as both remote and enchanting. It was no longer remote but thankfully it had lost none of its charm. One or two locals remembered me. One was the chef at our old hotel, whose father had been our gardener. Several people were interested in meeting me and learning more about our pioneering days at Chobe.

I could have spent several weeks exploring the old areas where we had cut the first tracks but time ran out. No doubt thousands of visitors to Chobe will have lasting impressions of one of the world's most unspoiled and exciting wildlife habitats, but to me it will always be a storehouse of many cherished and special memories . . . the kind that stay with you forever.

The following year, 1995, was very significant for both of us. We celebrated Ronnie's ninetieth birthday in grand style at the Cavalry Club in London with many old friends Ronnie had not seen for almost fifty years. Ronnie also took delivery of a special birthday message:

> 'Many congratulations. I send warm wishes on your ninetieth birthday and hope that all assembled at the Cavalry and Guards Club make sure that this special occasion is celebrated in traditional style.'
>
> Diana, Colonel in Chief The Light Dragoons
> (the late Princess of Wales, Diana Spencer).

I also achieved one of my greatest wishes; we were able to see the Lipizzaners performance at the Spanish Riding School in Vienna. Squired by Ronnie's nephew, Benedict, we were treated to an evening performance which thrilled me. The stallions were so near, I could almost touch them. We had excellent seats, so close to the manège and the setting was breathtaking. Magnificent chandeliers radiated a peace which is essential for work with these horses. One hears only the dull thud of hooves and the heavy breathing of the white stallions.

EPILOGUE

There is much truth in the old saying: 'When one door shuts another opens'. One should look for that and not dwell on the door which is shut.

It is almost impossible in reviewing one's life to do so without revisiting past tragedies and catastrophes. I have outlived my two much adored sons, three husbands and so many of my close friends. However, by the same token it has been a blessed life which saw me come of age in Africa, where I experienced great love, developed a love of adventure which brought me to Australia, attained much success and overcame obstacles which seemed at first insurmountable.

Flashbacks have a habit of sneaking up on me. When taking my Rhodesian Ridgeback dog for a walk on the stud, I frequently visualise Robert slowly walking along one of the avenues of silver barked eucalypts or see Simon placidly fishing beside the dam.

We are surrounded by our mementoes of treasured times. When I glance at the Tinus de Jongh paintings which Peter and I bought just before the war, I am reminded of how Robert and Simon used to argue as to who would inherit them! Then there are the bronze sculptures Simon cast shortly before he disappeared, and the crested glasses with the Chobe bushbuck we drink from on special occasions – to our winning fillies! Ronnie has his wildlife paintings and a wonderful time-worn carpet from Chikupi that no doubt could tell us many tales. These are some of our sentimental markers to an extraordinary bygone era.

There are other more ethereal reminders of my long, distant past. Heytesbury lies beneath the Darling Ranges and one of my favourite hour long walks is up in the hills which overlook the stud. The magnificent view reminds me of World's View from Rhodes' grave in the Matopos Hills near Bulawayo in Rhodesia. It also offers restorative quietude. Robert loved this spot and it seemed fitting that Janet selected it for his memorial which was constructed from huge old timbers from the Bunbury jetty, south of Perth. The inscription reads: 'Michael Robert Hamilton Holmes à Court 1937–1990: I stood among them but not of them. In a shroud of thought which were not their thoughts.'

Looking down from that hill I can imagine the two red flowering Moort eucalypts I planted on the bank of the dam in memory of my beloved sons, whose exploits during their brief lives filled my heart with pride. In spring these trees will be emblazoned with red flowers which will attract many beautiful birds. They will shade my memorial to the two young men cut down in their prime.

I derive great joy from following the careers of my four grandchildren who have done splendidly in their own spheres – how proud their father would have been. All have graduated from various universities and are doing 'their own thing'.

Now we will continue to do 'our own thing'. We are already planning our next overseas trip – perhaps the beginning of my next book!

Ethnée Holmes à Court, Heytesbury Stud, Western Australia

INDEX